ANALYZING REAL ESTATE DECISIONS

Using Lotus 1-2-3®

Austin J. Jaffe

College of Business Administration
The Pennsylvania State University

Reston Publishing Company, Inc.
A Prentice-Hall Company
Reston, Virginia

Library of Congress Cataloging in Publication Data

Jaffe, Austin J.
  Analyzing real estate decisions using Lotus 1-2-3.

  Includes index.
  1. Real estate business—Data processing. 2. Real
estate investment—Decision making—Data processing.
3. LOTUS 1-2-3 (Computer Program) I. Title.
HD1380.J33 1985   333.33′028′5425   85-2177
ISBN 0-8359-9192-X

Apple is a registered trademark of Apple Computer, Inc., Sunnyvale,
California. Lotus and 1-2-3 are registered trademarks of Lotus Development
Corporation. Symphony is a trademark of Lotus Development Corporation. IBM,
IBM PC, and IBM PC*jr* are registered trademarks of the IBM Corporation.
Hewlett-Packard is a registered trademark of the Hewlett-Packard Company.
Macintosh is a trademark licensed to Apple Computer, Inc. MS-DOS and
Microsoft are registered trademarks of Microsoft Corporation. VisiCalc is a
registered trademark of VisiCorp. REALTORS is a registered trademark
of the National Association of Realtors.

© 1985 by Reston Publishing Company, Inc.
    A Prentice-Hall Company
    Reston, Virginia 22090

10   9   8   7   6   5   4   3   2   1

PRINTED IN THE UNITED STATES OF AMERICA

To Lynn,
who continues to be a computer widow
for countless hours, days, and weeks

Mail this coupon to:

Stephen Landis
Prentice-Hall, Inc.
Book Distribution Center
Route 59 at Brook Hill Dr.
West Nyack, NY 10995

Please send me＿＿＿＿ Lotus 1-2-3 real estate software package(s).
Package includes five diskettes for $99.95 (ISBN 0-8359-9193-8).

Name: ＿＿＿＿＿＿＿＿＿＿＿＿＿＿ Phone: ＿＿＿＿＿＿＿＿＿＿

Address: ＿＿＿＿＿＿＿＿＿＿＿＿＿＿＿＿＿＿＿＿＿＿＿＿

＿＿＿＿＿＿＿＿＿＿＿＿＿＿＿＿＿＿＿＿＿＿＿＿＿＿＿＿

City: ＿＿＿＿＿＿＿＿ State: ＿＿＿＿＿＿ Zip: ＿＿＿＿＿

☐ Enclosed is my check, plus my state's sales tax

☐ Bill me

Charge my:

    ☐ VISA   ☐ MASTERCARD

    No: ＿＿＿＿＿＿＿＿＿＿＿＿ Exp: ＿＿＿＿＿＿＿＿

    Signature: ＿＿＿＿＿＿＿＿＿＿＿＿＿＿＿＿＿＿＿

Prices subject to change without notice. Please allow 4 to 6 weeks for delivery.

D-RELD-QZ-(7)

Contents

PART II
REAL ESTATE APPLICATIONS 37

6   Lending/Borrowing Decisions   121

Preface

This book features a complete set of real estate Lotus 1-2-3 models or so-called *templates* which have been designed for both beginning and experienced Lotus 1-2-3 microcomputer users and real estate analysts. The templates cover a wide range of real estate topics from basic decisions such as buyer qualification statements to sophisticated statistical analyses such as linear regression. Some of the templates are simple and narrow in scope; others are complex and broad based. All have been linked together by index system and are designed to build upon one another. The system is completely menu-driven and as a result is "user-friendly" and convenient. In this manner, the user can proceed through the series and develop expertise using Lotus 1-2-3 as well as make increasingly complex real estate decisions.

The book is intended to be used by active real estate practitioners who are faced with a variety of financial decisions and requisite calculations each day. These may include REALTORS® and other salespersons and brokers, builders and developers, property owners and investors, managers and counselors, real estate assessors and appraisers, mortgage lenders and bankers, and other real estate professionals. In addition, real estate students at colleges and universities may find this book helpful. Computers have a long history in business education, and microcomputer applications of real estate decision making is another area where these templates are likely to be useful.

The book is designed to enable an inexperienced Lotus 1-2-3 user to become acquainted with the Lotus 1-2-3 program in Part I and try out some of the real estate applications in Part II. The applications in Part II are relatively simple in the first few chapters and are intended for such users as households, real estate salespersons and brokers, and homeowners. For example, the HUD Settlement Statement is included in its entirety.

In the later chapters, the templates become more complex as the analysis becomes more technical. Models in these chapters are intended to help lenders, investors, accountants, real estate appraisers, and others. Templates include complete amortization schedules, income statements, tax and depreciation calculations, financial ratios, discounted cash flow models, appraisal methods, and statistical applications. By the end of the book, an integrated system of templates has been created for a wide variety of real estate applications and decisions.

To the best of my knowledge, no other book provides such an extensive collection of Lotus 1-2-3 templates for real estate decisions. Furthermore, the complete set of diskettes with the index system is also available to accompany the user's guide. All of the diskettes contain custom designed menus for this system. The set of diskettes may be purchased by sending the coupon in the front of this book to the publisher.

The author wishes to thank three reviewers of the manuscript who offered a variety of comments during the project's production: Joe Coyne of Prosource, Minneapolis, MN; William Hout, Consultant, Houston, TX; and Bill Weaver, North Texas State University, Denton, TX. Several of their suggestions have improved this book. The author also wishes to thank Catherine Rossbach and Monica Finnigan at Reston Publishing for their interest, support, and patience. Finally, thanks go to my wife, Lynn, who put up with more "hacking" during the creation of the templates and the writing of the book than she should have had to. Thanks very much to all of you.

Austin J. Jaffe

PART

I

A BRIEF GUIDE
TO LOTUS 1-2-3

This part provides an introduction to the microcomputer software employed in this book. Lotus 1-2-3 has become the most popular microcomputer financial software and serves as one of the major developments in business and financial analysis, including real estate decision making. Part I is devoted to providing an introduction to Lotus 1-2-3 since some users may not be familiar with its operation or only mildly familiar with its usage.

Chapter 1 is a general introduction to the world of Lotus 1-2-3. It is general in nature and attempts to familiarize an inexperienced reader with this important and exciting tool. Chapter 2 provides a brief overview of the major functions of Lotus 1-2-3 and highlights the special functions of the software. After a review of these two chapters, a reader should be ready to begin to examine, understand, and most importantly, use Lotus 1-2-3 in solving real estate problems in a variety of areas.

1 Welcome to LOTUS 1-2-3

Introduction to the World of Lotus 1-2-3

It is generally acknowledged that VisiCalc started a revolution in 1978 with the development of "electronic spreadsheets." But the success of Lotus Development Corporation's first product (called "Lotus 1-2-3" or simply "1-2-3") exceeded even the rosiest dreams of its president, Mitch Kapor. Consider the following sample of opinions:

> If 1-2-3 were just a spreadsheet, it would be a very useful tool. But it is much, much more.[1]

> . . . it is fair to state that 1-2-3 has set the new standard against which users will be judged.[2]

---

[1]Advertising Brochure, *Lotus 1-2-3*. (Cambridge, MA: Lotus Development Corporation, 1983).
[2]Edouard J. Desautels, *Lotus 1-2-3 for the IBM Personal Computer and XT*. (Dubuque, IA: Wm. C. Brown Publishers, 1984), p. 1.

Each one of the three major functions in 1-2-3—spreadsheet, database manager, and graphics—has the quality of an individual software package that could sell for close to 1-2-3's total . . . retail price tag.[3]

. . . it's a real pleasure working with Lotus 1-2-3. Its user-friendly operation is unmatched by any product.[4]

If VisiCalc is the grandfather of electronic spreadsheets, then 1-2-3 is the wonder child.[5]

These, of course, are only a few of the positive commentaries about the most successful microcomputer product in the history of this young industry. Without question, the performance of the product has been spectacular.

Since its introduction to the general public in January, 1983, it has risen quickly to the top of the sales charts. Within only three months of introduction, it replaced VisiCalc as the top selling spreadsheet of nearly five years.[6] Subsequent to the week of January 31, 1983, *for every consecutive week as this book goes to press*, 1-2-3 has been the number one best selling microcomputer software of any type.[7] An April, 1984 survey on software usage, which reported that "1983 was the year that 1-2-3 demolished all opposition" included several products with head starts and sizable advertising and developmental budgets.[8] It was called the 1983 Product of the Year by *Fortune* Magazine and *InfoWorld*. The *New York Times* heralded it as "the wave of the future in business software."[9]

OK! OK! So it is popular in many circles, including business applications! For most readers, however, this acclaim, no matter how pervasive or exhortative, will never be enough. The true tests are: will *you* be able to harness the power of Lotus 1-2-3 to solve your problems? Can it work for a wide variety of sophisticated users with specialized problems? Can you use it even if you are not a computer expert? Can it be used even if you are unfamiliar with computers and computer software?

Fortunately, the answer to all of these questions is YES! (What else did

---

[3]Frank J. Derfler, Jr., "1-2-3: A Program You Can Count On," *PC Magazine*, 1 (March 1983), p. 188.

[4]Barry Crawford, "1-2-3: The Jewel in the Lotus," *Personal Computer Age*, 2 (July 1983), p. 48.

[5]Geoffrey T. LeBlond and Douglas Ford Cobb, *Using 1-2-3*. (Indianapolis, IN: Que Corporation, 1983), p. 11.

[6]*Ibid.*, p. 1.

[7]Advertisement, *Wall Street Journal*, April 4, 1984, p. 23.

[8]"The Most Popular Software Poll Results!" *Softalk* (April 1984), 132–39. The survey reported 271 "first-place" votes for Lotus 1-2-3. The next highest number of such votes was 46 for any software and only 13 for the second favorite spreadsheet, VisiCalc. Taking into account votes besides first-place votes, Lotus scored 4,274. The next highest software was 1,810 and VisiCalc's total was 684.

[9]Advertisement, *Wall Street Journal*, *op. cit.*

you expect?!) Much of the charm of Lotus 1-2-3 is its "user-friendliness" or the ability of novice users to interact with the program with a minimal amount of difficulty. One report cites this attribute as the key to its success.[10]

While initially introduced for the IBM PC market, the success of the product has permitted Lotus to provide versions for a variety of computers. Hewlett-Packard introduced a "lap-sized" computer with 1-2-3 built into its permanent memory. Apple's recent hardware, including Macintosh, can run special versions of the product. A new version has also appeared for IBM's PC*jr*. In addition, there are several "IBM compatible" computers, nearly all of which can support 1-2-3.

It has also been said that VisiCalc helped to sell hardware and expanded the market for computers; a first at the time when the hardware typically sold the supporting software rather than the other way around. The entry of Lotus 1-2-3 into the market established the importance of software across all types of hardware. Now, Lotus 1-2-3 is the test of hardware compatibility and a continuing nightmare for competing software firms.

At this point, the end is not in sight. A recent article reported that up to 23,000 new Lotus 1-2-3 users were sitting at their terminals *each month* as of the beginning of 1984.[11] Huge supporting markets for tutorial books and diskettes (despite the extensive tutorials and large manual that accompanies the Lotus software) have appeared throughout the country. Cassettes offer detailed instruction; videocassettes permit further detail. Several keyboard templates are available as overlays. Seminars are presented daily throughout the country. The Lotus revolution is underway.

Do not be discouraged by all of the clamor! It is not too late for you! In fact, you are right on time! Lotus 1-2-3 and compatible spreadsheets are going to be fundamental tools for several years to come.

Real Estate Decisions and Lotus 1-2-3

Real estate professionals are well suited to 1-2-3 and its power. This book is designed as a user's guide to a set of "templates" or models which have been designed to facilitate careful and critical analysis of small as well as large real estate decisions. Each template can be used independently if the user so desires or several can be used in conjunction with each other to perform various analyses. Later, they may be incorporated into a major set of recommendations. Thus, the templates in this book are developed as a system of real estate decisions. The templates may be used "as is" or by implementing some of the suggested modifications throughout the book to fit the user's needs.

The book is divided into two parts. Part I contains this introductory chapter

---

[10]"Lotus 1-2-3," *Business Computer Systems*, 3 (November 1984), p. 150.
[11]William K. Howard, "Armed For Learning 1-2-3," *PC Magazine*, 2 (April 17, 1984), p. 133.

and an overview of the special functions and features of Lotus 1-2-3. Part II provides 41 fully integrated Lotus 1-2-3 real estate templates. Examples are provided for each template and the results are shown in each chapter. A discussion is included which permits real estate beginners as well as seasoned professionals the opportunity to utilize Lotus 1-2-3 when making real estate decisions.

These templates are available in conjunction with this book so that users do not have to enter the keystrokes by hand. Since these templates are often complex and because entering cell formulas and labels is a tedious task, it is highly recommended that the reader obtain a copy of the diskettes for this system. They are available from the publisher by using the coupon in the front of the book. Some computer stores may have the software in stock. The programs are available on 5¼″ double-sided diskettes. All of the programs have been checked and double-checked for errors and mistakes.

A special feature of Lotus 1-2-3 is the ability to link a series of templates together into a system. The real estate templates make use of this facility so that the user can move quickly through a wide range of applications and analyses. In addition, custom-designed menus have been developed so that even inexperienced Lotus users can perform the analyses with a minimum amount of confusion. There are virtually no excuses for not using this powerful financial tool to assist in making real estate decisions! *Purchasers of the diskettes will be working on actual real estate problems within ten minutes of turning on the computer!*

However, before you begin to examine the real estate applications in this book, you may wish to read about some background information on spreadsheets, some of the basic features of Lotus 1-2-3, and a look toward the future. If you are anxious to skip ahead, feel free to do so; you can always return back here later.

What is a Spreadsheet?

Spreadsheets take their names from the accounting columnar pads that have been one of the main tools of accountants for years. However, electronic spreadsheets such as 1-2-3 have far more power and flexibility than a simple pad of paper with columns and a calculator. Spreadsheets are actually sophisticated tools to assist in financial modeling, business and household planning, extensive recordkeeping, and perhaps most importantly, to ask "What if . . . ?" questions. The user will receive almost instantaneous results. As such, the popularity of electronic spreadsheets extends far beyond professional accountants and financial planners. Real estate investors, lenders, counselors, property managers, appraisers, and others will find much of value with spreadsheets such as Lotus 1-2-3.

A recent book which deals with professional managers and microcomputing, lists five ways that spreadsheets can improve managerial performance over the old-fashioned methods of paper, pencil, and calculators:

1. They're faster.

2. They're more accurate.

3. You can handle more complexity and detail.

4. You can keep planning longer.

5. You can do more "what if" analysis.[12]

It is also important to note that technological developments have resulted in cost reductions so that some spreadsheet software is now relatively inexpensive, often as low as $200. There is no question about it: spreadsheets are here to stay and have begun to change the ways in which financial decisions are analyzed.

For the real estate professional, these developments could not have come at a better time. Mortgage amortizations are tedious using calculators and tables of amortization factors are of little help to the busy professional. Calculating cash flows is difficult for many investors, especially those who are infrequent investors or those who do not have time to keep current with the latest changes in the federal tax laws. Real estate appraisers will increasingly look to spreadsheets to assist with data maintenance and appraisal analysis. Even homeowners are faced with a myriad of financial decisions and accounts. Spreadsheets help to remove the mystique of "computerese" and permit the non-technical user to get results, quickly, accurately, and with a minimum amount of frustration.

Spreadsheets are powerful without any previously designed templates. However, a system of templates such as those provided later in this book further decreases the time between when the user sits down at the computer and when the information has been evaluated to assist in the financial decision. One of the major advantages of using a well-designed system of templates such as those included in this book is that someone who is totally unfamiliar with computers, real estate modeling, and to a large extent, 1-2-3 can "load" the template into Lotus, enter the appropriate set of inputs (such as rents, mortgage amounts, interest rates, tax rates, etc.) and get results. How quickly and easily? *Almost instantly!!*

I promise that with a basic introduction to the features of Lotus 1-2-3 (such as is provided below), a willingness to follow a very few simple directions as provided with each template, and a little patience when working with your computer (remember, the computer is your friend and truly wants to please

---

[12]Dick Heiser, *Real Managers Use Personal Computers*. (Indianapolis, IN: Que Corporation, 1983), pp. 19–20.

you), you can get results within ten minutes! With practice, you will be very comfortable with 1-2-3 and even more so, with the system of real estate templates designed for the book. Soon you will find your computer a constant friend.

One thing is certain: spreadsheets in general, and Lotus 1-2-3 in particular, remain the most important type of software available for microcomputers. As recently as 1983, four of the top ten best-selling programs for the IBM PC were spreadsheets.[13] By using the menu capabilities and the system of real estate templates, there is no reason to approximate or guess at numerical calculations again; the computer will easily serve your most detailed real estate needs!

Basic Features of Lotus 1-2-3

By "booting" 1-2-3 by itself, the user sees a matrix of cells. The dimensions of the cells are 256 columns and 2048 rows of variably sized cells. The user may either "load" a previously designed template or "create" a new one. Of course, Lotus permits users to "save" original templates by asking the user for a "name" when the user is ready to stop inputting data or designing the model.

If the user wishes to design a new template, the complete matrix is at the user's disposal; it is totally blank. If the user wishes to use an existing template such as those included in this book, the user should choose one of two options: 1. automatically load 1-2-3 by accessing the "index" file which links all of the templates, or 2. manually load the index file ("auto123"). (See the instructions below for either choice.) In either case, the user is off and running!

It is important to note that if the user wants to save some or all of the analysis, additional, blank diskettes are needed to serve as "data diskettes" for the user. There are several, high-quality brands available at most computer stores and even some bookstores. If you plan to work with 1-2-3, you will use several of these diskettes. They are frequently sold ten to a box.

If 1-2-3 is loaded without the real estate system and the blank matrix of cells appears, it is important to note that the program itself requires 117K of Random Access Memory (RAM) for its operations and over 200 help screens. Thus, in order to be able to use Lotus 1-2-3, at least 192K of RAM is required for MS DOS 1.1, the MicroSoft Disk Operating System (Version 1.1). If MS DOS 2.0 or 2.1 is used, the memory requirement is higher.

It is recommended that at least 256K of RAM be available for MS DOS 1.1 users and 320K of RAM for users with MS DOS 2.0 or 2.1. If this is a bit confusing, do not worry; it is relatively easy to identify how much RAM your system has (run the Diagnostics diskette). If you have recently bought your

---

[13]Thomas B. Henderson, Douglas Ford Cobb, and Gena Berg Cobb, *Spreadsheet Software From VisiCalc to 1-2-3.* (Indianapolis, IN: Que Corporation, 1983), p. 1.

computer, it probably has at least 256K of RAM. This is true for IBM as well as many other computers using MS DOS operating systems. Several of the real estate diskettes take up a lot of RAM in order to perform their functions. However, if your computer has 256K of RAM, you should not have any difficulty using the templates.

The command structure begins with the "slash" (/) key. This has become the standard for most spreadsheets when a command is requested. The slash key results in the following well-known, generic menu:

Worksheet Range Copy Move File Print Graph Data Quit

Each of these represents a different menu. These menus may be accessed by "pointing" to them with the cursor keys or by typing the first letters of any of the commands for any menu. (Detailed discussions of each command may be found in the Lotus manual.) In a short period of time, new users will become so familiar with the keys that they will rarely have to look at the them for verification.

There are 51 preprogrammed functions in 1-2-3. Some of the more useful functions for real estate users are discussed in Chapter 2. Several of these have been built into the templates used in this book. These functions are classified as mathematical, financial, statistical, and logical (or Boolean) functions. Some of these functions help to distinguish Lotus 1-2-3 as a so-called "third generation" spreadsheet from earlier generations of spreadsheet software. (Appendix A provides a complete listing of all of the Lotus 1-2-3 conventions, special keys, functions, and commands. These tables should serve as useful guides as users begin to work with 1-2-3.)

For users of the real estate diskettes, the menus have been custom-designed. The general form of the real estate menus which automatically appears when a template is selected is as follows:

Title Input(s) Output(s) Solutions Summary User Options Quit

In general, the user provides inputs in the first part of the spreadsheet, as the cursor automatically moves from cell to cell and awaits your data. When completed, the user may examine the output(s) and/or the solutions. In many cases, a summary has been included to help synthesize and display the results. In the event the user suspects an input error has been made, it is a simple matter to return to the input page and reenter any or all of the data. If the user wishes to review the results for the seventh or the twenty-seventh time, the computer is at the user's command. Note also that the user may "quit" at any time. Remember, though, if the quit command is elected before the results of the most recent analysis are saved, the results will be lost.

The only other command is the so-called "User Options." This choice has a separate submenu for the real estate templates:

Print Graph(s) Save Retrieve Menu Index Quit

It is this menu where the analyst can print the results of the analysis, generate beautiful color graphs with the touch of a button (if your hardware will support graphics), save the results in a file for future study, retrieve other files, the previous menu, or the index of all templates in the system. In addition, the user may quit and do something else. Thus, the "User Options" menu is shown only when the user needs it.

How to Use Lotus 1-2-3 and the Real Estate Templates in Ten Easy Steps

Even if you are not very familiar with Lotus, the custom-designed menus make it easy to work with the real estate templates right away. For an IBM PC, follow these easy directions:

1. "Boot" Lotus 1-2-3. (Insert the program into the diskdrive and turn the computer on. If your computer has two diskdrives, place the Lotus diskette in Drive A (the one on the left). If the computer is already on, press "Ctrl", "Alt", and "Del" together. This will cause the computer to read the Lotus diskette.)

2. After a few whirls and the user pressing the "Enter" key at least twice, either the blank matrix will appear if one of the preprogrammed real estate diskettes has not been placed in Drive B (the one on the right), or the logo page of the system of diskettes will appear as an introduction to the real estate diskettes in Drive B. (If you are interested in the real estate templates which accompany this book, place one of the diskettes in Drive B. If you have a single diskdrive system, change the diskettes at the appropriate times so as to replicate a two-diskdrive system.)

3. Note that every time you turn the computer on, Lotus must be booted once again. Whether you wish to examine the real estate diskettes in this book or design your own with the "generic" Lotus menus, 1-2-3 will determine which diskette should be placed in Drive B. The Lotus System Diskette is always placed in Drive A. (Note that for Version 1A, the current and most popular version of 1-2-3, the Lotus software package contains five floppy diskettes: two Lotus System diskettes, the Lotus Utilities diskette, the Lotus Tutorial diskette, and the Lotus PrintGraph diskette.)

4. Notice that the real estate system of templates consists of five different diskettes. The first four contain real estate templates. They are located sequentially on the diskettes by topic. The fifth diskette contains the PrintGraph files of all of the examples in the book. Note that Appendix B contains camera-ready reproductions of each of the graphs. Also, each of the diskettes contains the index file which links the five diskettes.

5. Assuming you are interested in the real estate diskettes, when you indicate that you would like to "retrieve" a file using the "index" file, the complete set of available templates is displayed at the top of the screen. Using the cursors, "point" to the template you are interested in examining. (If you do not see the one you desire to view, you have inserted the wrong real estate diskette. Don't worry; press "Esc" (Escape), remove the diskette and replace it with one of the other real estate diskettes. Now "retrieve" once again and see the available templates on the new real estate diskette. For example, if you wanted to load Template "lot501," you would "point" to it on the menu, and press "Enter." If it is not on the menu, the template must first be located on one of the other diskettes.)

6. When the template is loaded, Lotus displays the "title page" of the template and the custom-designed menu. The menu is unique for each template in several ways. First, each menu is structured for the particular template and the specific locations of its cells. Second, some templates are more elaborate than others so that the menus reflect the necessary detail. Finally, each menu takes the user to only those cells where inputs are required, automatically, so the user does not have to worry about "getting around" the spreadsheet. Spanning outputs and summaries are similarly accomplished.

7. Note that Lotus 1-2-3 automatically performs the necessary calculations. This is done either initially before the template appears on the screen or at selected times within the operation of the template. (You can tell when this is taking place. When the "WAIT" display is shown in the upper right-hand corner of the screen, Lotus is busy at work!)

8. All of the templates in this book are self-explanatory and "user-friendly." This means you should enter data as inputs where asked and you may never have any trouble using the templates. After each entry, the user must press "Enter." The cursor will then move to the next input cell. At the end of the inputs, the user will be automatically returned to the menu. If no input change is desired, pressing "Enter" twice proceeds to the next cell.

9. If you accidentally press "Enter" but you wish to return to the previous cell, or if you are finished with data entry but there are several blank cells ahead, you may return to the menu without pressing "Enter" 27 more times. This is done by these two simple rules:

   a. To stop inputting (or outputting), press "Ctrl" and "Break" together. (This will break the command string and permit you to return to the menu.)

   b. To invoke the real estate menu, press "Alt" and "M" together. (This employs a "macro" string, M for "menu" and the menu appears.)

These two rules are repeated as reminders throughout the templates. With use, they will become automatic. Also, they are the only rules you have to memorize to use the entire system. They may be invoked at any time during usage.

10. You need to create a new file on your empty data diskette to save your results. IMPORTANT: DO NOT save your file using the name of the empty template (e.g., "lot501"). Give your specific analysis a different name (e.g., "ajj501"). Notice that the examples in the book have been named with the letter "x" as in "lot501x".

    To save your results, point to "Save" on the "User Options" menu. For example, if you wanted to save your results as "ajj501", you would enter "ajj501" in response to the inquiry under the "Save" option. When completed, it will be stored for future usage and accessed over and over again.

That's all that there is to it! You are now a Lotus Real Estate Analyst!! Congratulations!!!

The Future of Lotus 1-2-3 and Spreadsheet Usage

Most observers predict the continued use of spreadsheets for the next several years. Lotus has begun to play a major role in this development. Spreadsheet applications are likely to become increasingly widespread and commonplace in many work environments. In addition, templates are likely to become more sophisticated and more refined. More complex functions are likely to be added to future enhancements and upgrades. Greater flexibility and power await users as software developers explore new approaches to problem solving.

For the experienced user, these are exciting predictions. For the beginner, it is far from too late. One thing is certain: the future will be one where computerization of financial calculations will be the standard method of operation. In the area of real estate, the best is yet to come. This system of templates may be the only real estate software you need. Best of all, you should have a minimum amount of difficulty getting solutions to your real estate problems right away. Good luck and happy computing!

Partial Listing of Lotus 1-2-3 Books and Articles

Cain, Thomas and Nancy Woodard Cain. *Lotus 1-2-3 at Work.* Reston, VA: Reston Publishing Co., Inc., 1984.

Crawford, Barry. "1-2-3: The Jewel in the Lotus." *Personal Computer Age,* (July 1983).

Derfler, Frank J., Jr. "1-2-3: A Program You Can Count On." *PC Magazine,* (March 1983).

Desautels, Edouard J. *Lotus 1-2-3 for the IBM Personal Computer and XT*. Dubuque, IA: Wm C. Brown Publishers, 1984.

Dickinson, John. "1-2-3's Printer Driver." *Softalk for the IBM Personal Computer*, (August 1984).

Heck, Mike. "Lotus 1-2-3: A New Generation of Integrated Software." *Interface Age*, (July 1983).

Howard, William K. "Armed For Learning 1-2-3." *PC Magazine*, (April 17, 1984).

Kohler, Pat. "Unleashing the Power of Lotus." *PC Week*, (July 10, 1984).

LeBlond, Geoffrey T. and Douglas Ford Cobb. *Using 1-2-3*. Indianapolis: Que Corp., 1983.

[Several articles], *PC Magazine*, (April 17, 1984).

Shaffer, Daniel N. *1-2-3 Revealed*. Reston, VA: Reston Publishing Co., Inc., 1984.

"Software Firms Beef Up Marketing As Power of Word of Mouth Wanes," *Wall Street Journal*, March 26, 1984.

Weiss, Eric. "/X Marks the Macro." *PC World*, (March 1984).

2 Functions and Special Features of LOTUS 1-2-3

It has been said that in the very near future there will be two types of individuals: those who can use the computer to assist them in various ways and those who cannot. If you seek membership in the first club, this chapter may be very useful to you. Lotus 1-2-3, as the leading integrative and best-selling microcomputer software, is an excellent choice, especially if this is your first experience with computers. Even if you are an experienced user, this short chapter provides an overview of some of the built-in Lotus commands, functions, and special features. In addition, the chapter includes an overview of the custom-designed real estate menus for use with this system of templates. A discussion of some of the few limitations of Lotus 1-2-3 is also presented. By the time you finish this chapter, you should be ready for the real estate applications found in Part II.

A Brief Overview of the Lotus 1-2-3 Commands

As indicated in the last chapter, the slash (/) key informs Lotus 1-2-3 that you wish to call one of several commands if custom-designed menus are not used. This convention was created by the inventors of VisiCalc, an earlier spreadsheet upon which the creators of Lotus 1-2-3 built. In response to the "/" key, the "basic command menu" is presented. The user either "points" to the option desired through the use of the cursor keys or types the first letter of the selected option such as "W" (or "w") for "Worksheet."

The "basic command menu" is shown as follows:

Worksheet Range Copy Move File Print Graph Data Quit

Each of these options leads to a series of other choices in an elaborate command structure. The "Command Paths" are listed in Appendix A. Experienced Lotus users become quite familiar with many of the options and their locations within the program. Novices using Lotus 1-2-3 in conjunction with the real estate templates need not worry; special menus are employed to assist you as much as possible.

The basic command paths are outlined and discussed below. The menus are logically designed; each set of options under the basic command menu option is related to specific types of activities. With practice, it will become second nature to look for certain options in specific menus.

Worksheet Options

/W (The Worksheet Menu).   This is the most extensive and fundamental menu in the Lotus 1-2-3 program. It contains features which determine the basic shape and nature of the spreadsheet.

/WG (The Global Command).   This command provides the user with the capability of changing the environment for the entire spreadsheet. All of these selections are reversible at any time.

/WGF (The Global Format Option).   This option provides the facility for altering the format (i.e., the manner in which data is shown on the screen) for the entire spreadsheet. The choices are "F" (Fixed number of decimal places), "S" (Scientific notation with a specified number of decimal places), "C" (Currency notation or the "$" sign and commas with a specified number of decimal places), "," (Comma option with a specified number of decimal places), "G" (General option with a specified number of decimal places), "+" (Plus and minus option showing negative values in parentheses), "P" (Percent option with a specified number of decimal places), "D" (Date option in three formats), and "T" (Text option to display formulas).

/WGL (The Global Label-Prefix Option).   This choice permits altering the label justification from left to right or center for each cell.

/WGC (The Global Column-Width Option).   This option permits the user to modify the column-width of the entire spreadsheet from the default value of 9 to any number from 1 to 72.

/WGR (The Global Recalculation Option).   This is a very useful option for large spreadsheets. It is often faster to enter data without automatically recalculating the results after each entry and then recalculating the results, manually, with the F9 function key. (With the real estate templates and where useful, this feature is automatically built into the template.) The options are "**N**" (Natural order), "**C**" (Columnwise), "**R**" (Rowwise), "**A**" (Automatic), "**M**" (Manual), or "**I**" (Iteration). The problem of "forward referencing" may sometimes be avoided using these options.

/WGP (The Global Protection Option).   This option permits the designer of the spreadsheet to "protect" the spreadsheet from being accidentally changed. If the option is invoked, the user is unable to change any cells in the entire spreadsheet. Note, however, that under the Range Command, it is possible to "unprotect" cells. Thus, the user can employ both of these options in conjunction with each other to free certain cells but protect the remainder of the spreadsheet. (This has been used in every spreadsheet in the real estate templates series.) There are two options here: "**E**" (Enable the global protection) and "**D**" (Disable the global protection, the default).

/WGD (The Global Default Option).   This choice provides the user with the opportunity to alter the various default values of Lotus 1-2-3. These include "**P**" (Printer defaults such as interface options, margins, page-lengths, setup strings and others), "**D**" (Directory default for reading diskdrives), "**S**" (Status option for viewing currently set parameter values), "**U**" (Update option to alter defaults), and "**Q**" (Quit option to leave Lotus 1-2-3).

/WI (The Insert Command).   This feature permits the user to insert one or more rows or columns into the spreadsheet. As such, it is an indispensable command.

/WIC (The Insert Column Option).   When invoked, one or more columns are inserted to the right of the cursor.

/WIR (The Insert Row Option).   When invoked, one or more rows are inserted below the cursor.

/WD (The Delete Command). This feature permits the deletion of one or more rows or columns. As such, it is very powerful and must be used with care.

/WDC (The Delete Column Option). When invoked, one or more columns are deleted according to the pointing of the cursor.

/WDR (The Delete Row Option). When invoked, one or more rows are deleted according to the pointing of the cursor.

/WC (The Column-Width Command). This option enables the column-width to be changed for any column in the spreadsheet.

/WCS (The Set Column-Width Option). Any column may be set as small as one character to as many as 72 characters.

/WCR (The Column-Width Reset Option). This election resets the column-width of any column to the default value of nine characters.

/WE (The Erase Command). This choice erases the spreadsheet in current memory.

/WEN (The No Erase Option). This provides the user with a safety valve in the event he really does not want to erase the spreadsheet.

/WEY (The Yes Erase Option). This option is chosen when a clear spreadsheet is desired.

/WT (The Titles Command). The titles facility permits the user to develop spreadsheets which scroll under a displayed portion of the screen. This may be useful, for example, in applications where a long list of data is to be entered or reviewed. (At least one real estate template makes use of this feature. Can you find the one with this option?)

/WTB (The Both Titles Option). This feature enables both horizontal and vertical titles.

/WTH (The Horizontal Titles Option). This choice enables the horizontal, and probably the most useful, title.

/WTV (The Vertical Titles Option). This choice enables the vertical title option.

/WTC (The Titles Clear Option). This election clears the spreadsheet of titles. (Note that the spreadsheet is limited to only one title location at any point in time.)

/WW (The Window Command). Like titles, windows are very useful for examining data and results of analysis using spreadsheets. Windows provide the user with the opportunity to examine two parts of the spreadsheet at the same time.

/WWH (The Horizontal Window Option). This provides two "windows" into the spreadsheet, one at the top of the screen; the other at the bottom. (Note that the place where the window is "created" is determined by the location of the cursor when this command and option are invoked.)

/WWV (The Vertical Window Option). This option provides two vertical windows: one on the left side and the other on the right side of the screen.

/WWS (The Synchronized Window Option). This and the next option are actually subsets of The Horizontal and Vertical Window Options. The synchronized option permits the user to examine the cell contents on one side of the window and when scanning through the spreadsheet, the other window follows. In effect, this choice holds constant the rows on both sides of the spreadsheet.

/WWU (The Unsynchronized Window Option). This feature supresses the synchronized option. Some uses facilitate scanning one side without altering the other.

/WWC (The Window Clear Option). This option clears the spreadsheet of windows. The result is the single default screen.

/WS (The Status Command). This command displays the worksheet default values as a check on their current status.

Range Options

/R (The Range Menu). Although not very descriptive, the Lotus 1-2-3 user typically makes heavy use of the range command options. It is this set of options that permits fine-tuning and custom-designing of the cells within the spreadsheet.

/RF (The Format Command).　　This command permits the formatting of a range of cells. It is virtually the same as found under /WGF. Each of the options are discussed below.

> **/RFF (The Fixed Format Option).**　　This format provides a fixed number of decimal places.

> **/RFS (The Scientific Format Option).**　　This format reports values in scientific notation.

> **/RFC (The Currency Format Option).**　　This format provides output with dollar signs and commas.

> **/RF, (The Comma Format Option).**　　This format provides output with commas and parentheses.

> **/RFG (The General Format Option).**　　This format displays cell contents as entered or calculated, given the size of the cell.

> **/RF+ (The Plus and Minus Format Option).**　　This format displays values in parentheses when negative.

> **/RFP (The Percent Format Option).**　　This format displays values as percents.

> **/RFD (The Date Format Option).**　　This format uses the date option displays.

> **/RFT (The Text Format Option).**　　This format displays formulas in the range of cells.

> **/RFR (The Format Reset Option).**　　This choice enables the range's format to be reset.

/RL (The Label-Prefix Command).　　This command permits the justification of the range to vary from the global setting.

> **/RLL (The Label-Prefix Left Option).**　　This option enables left-justification.

> **/RLR (The Label-Prefix Right Option).**　　This option enables right-justification.

> **/RLC (The Label-Prefix Center Option).**　　This option enables center-justification.

/RE (The Erase Command). The Erase Command is used to clear a range of cells. It is used repeatedly in the development of templates. Note that the use of this command does not alter the format specifications for the cells.

/RN (The Name Command). Naming ranges has several purposes in Lotus 1-2-3. In the development of the real estate templates, naming is used in generating graphics, both on-line and graphics print files as well as in the development of the menus.

> **/RNC (The Create Name Option).** This option creates a named range within the spreadsheet.

> **/RND (The Delete Name Option).** This option deletes a named range within the spreadsheet.

> **/RNL (The Label Name Option).** This option labels a named range within the spreadsheet.

> **/RNR (The Name Reset Option).** This option resets all named ranges within the spreadsheet.

/RJ (The Justify Command). This option enables the user to enter long labels into the text without fear of loss of text due to extra characters which exceed the space by column.

/RP (The Protect Command). The ability to protect ranges is useful in many applications. This command also enables the user to "protect" cells once again after they have been "unprotected" in a global environment where the protection option has been elected.

/RU (The Unprotect Command). The unprotect option is valuable for data entry purposes where the global protection option is in force. In this way, the user can only modify the spreadsheet in a limited number of ways. The real estate templates make use of this option in this manner in every case.

/RI (The Input Command). This command prevents the user from moving the cursor to cells which are protected.

Copy and Move Options

/C (The Copy Command). The Copy Command is very useful since Lotus 1-2-3 permits the rapid copying of cells without retyping. A range must be indicated to inform Lotus 1-2-3 where you wish to copy. The copying may be in absolute or relative forms. Note that copying into a cell overwrites the cell.

/M (The Move Command).   The Move Command is also very useful since cell contents may be moved to different locations within the spreadsheet without the burden of retyping. Moves are made in absolute form and also overwrite into the new cell location.

File Options

/F (The File Menu).   These selections deal with the information stored on the diskette. It is in this area that results are retrieved, stored, and combined, and other options are employed.

/FR (The Retrieve Command).   This command enables the user to read and load a file from the present diskette in the computer's diskdrive. Note that Lotus will display those available to the user. Note also that the display provides options for the user but does not clear the current memory until the user chooses to retrieve one of the stored files.

/FS (The Save Command).   This command permits the user to save the contents of the spreadsheet in current memory. The user may select a new name for the file to be saved on the diskette or use an existing one. If an existing name is chosen, Lotus will ask if you really want to do that since the initial contents in the file will be erased if the existing name is chosen for the new file. (For the real estate templates, *it is strongly urged that you choose new names for your templates* and leave the existing ones intact.)

/FC (The Combine Command).   This command is useful when developing large templates and material is needed from more than one spreadsheet. The Combine Command permits the user to "pick and choose" named ranges from various spreadsheets when making new ones. Note that combining spreadsheets also overwrites cell contents.

/FX (The Xtract Command).   This feature saves named ranges in a separate worksheet file. This may be useful when developing large spreadsheets. Under this option, you have the ability to store cell contents as "F" (Formulas) or "V" (Values).

/FE (The Erase Command).   This command enables the user to erase files from the diskette. Any of the types of files may be erased. These include "W" (Worksheets), "P" (Print files), or "G" (Graph files).

/FL (The List Command). This command provides the user with a list of files on the diskette presently in the diskdrive. This may be helpful when attempting to locate a file. The command is used on all types of files: "W", "P", or "G".

/FI (The Import Command). This feature enables the user to import a print file from the diskette for use in the spreadsheet in memory. The data may be either "T" (Text) or "N" (Numbers).

/FD (The Directory Command). This feature enables the user to change the directory associated with DOS. This means going from DOS 1.1 to DOS 2.0 (or 2.1) or vice versa.

Print Options

/P (The Print Menu). The Print Menu provides a variety of options. One of the nicest features is that it is possible to use the defaults and print easily or it is possible to customize the output using several of the print options.

/PP or /PF (The Printer or File Commands). As the Lotus 1-2-3 manual says, users can "print it now" or "print it later" with these commands. By sending the spreadsheet to the printer, the user seeks hardcopy now. On the other hand, the spreadsheet may be printed to the diskette for later printing. Under either command, the following options are available.

/PPR or /PFR (The Range Option). This option is used to indicate which part of the spreadsheet should be printed. Note that the previous range is stored by Lotus 1-2-3 so that reprinting does not require range specifications each time.

/PPL or /PFL (The Line Option). This option advances the printer to the beginning of the next line.

/PPP or /PFP (The Page Option). This option advances the printer to the top of the next page. (This feature is automatically built-in to the real estate templates).

/PPO or /PFO (The Options Option). There are several printing options available. These are hidden in this "Options" option. Each are briefly identified below.

/PPOH or /PFOH (The Options Header Option). Provides header at top of each printed page of output.

/PPOF or /PFOF (The Options Footer Option). Provides footer at bottom of each printed page of output.

/PPOM or /PFOM (The Options Margins Option). Provides margin control for user, including "L" (Left), "R" (Right), "T" (Top), or "B" (Bottom).

/PPOB or /PFOB (The Options Borders Option). Provides ranges as borders from various spreadsheet locations.

/PPOS or /PFOS (The Options Setup Option). Provides for special instructions to printer. As an example, a setup string may be used to alter the print font.

/PPOP or /PFOP (The Options Page-Length Option). Provides options for various page-lengths.

/PPOO or /PFOO (The Options Other Option). Provides for special display options. These are "A" (As-Displayed), "C" (Cell-Formulas), "F" (Formatted printing), or "U" (Unformatted printing without page breaks).

/PPOQ or /PFOQ (The Options Quit Option). Provides for return to previous print menu.

/PPC or /PFC (The Clear Option). This option clears specifications. The user can choose the extent he/she wishes to clear of the print options.

/PPA or /PFA (The Align Option). This option enables the user to inform Lotus 1-2-3 that the paper has been realigned for printing at the top of the page.

/PPG or /PFG (The Go Option). This is the final option before printing. It tells Lotus 1-2-3 to print the indicated range.

/PPQ or /PFQ (The Quit Option). This option returns the user to the main Lotus menu.

Graph Options

/G (The Graph Menu). The Graph Menu enables the user to create and design one or more of several graphics options using Lotus 1-2-3.

/GT (The Type Command).   This command forces the user to select the type of graph. The following graph types are available: **"L"** (Line Graph), **"B"** (Bar Graph), **"X"** (XY Graph), **"S"** (Stacked-Bar Graph), and **"P"** (Pie Chart).

/GX (The X-Axis Command).   Provides data to be used in XY graphs.

/GA (The A Data Set Command).   Provides first data range.

/GB (The B Data Set Command).   Provides second data range.

/GC (The C Data Set Command).   Provides third data range.

/GD (The D Data Set Command).   Provides fourth data range.

/GE (The E Data Set Command).   Provides fifth data range.

/GF (The F Data Set Command).   Provides sixth data range.

/GR (The Reset Command).   Provides for resetting of graph settings.

/GV (The View Command).   Provides display of current graph.

/GS (The Save Command).   Saves current graph in a PrintGraph file.

/GO (The Options Command).   Provides for several special options for customizing graphs.

> **/GOL (The Legend Options Option).**   Provides for identification of each data set.
>
> **/GOF (The Format Options Option).**   Provides for symbols and/or lines in XY graphs.
>
> **/GOT (The Title Options Option).**   Provides for informational titles displayed on graph. Two titles at the top of the graph are permitted as well as titles for the X and Y axis.
>
> **/GOG (The Grid Options Option).**   Provides for horizontal and/or vertical grid lines in all but Pie Charts.
>
> **/GOS (The Scale Options Option).**   Provides a variety of options to set the scale of graphs. These options include the complete set of formats as well as sizes and procedures.

/GOC (The Color Options Option).   Provides displays of graphs in color (for users with RGB monitors). Also, provides option for color graphics with color plotters. (Almost all of the real estate graphs will support color monitors!)

/GOB (The Black-&-White Options Option).   Provides contrasting "crosshatch" patterns for each data set when displayed. (The PrintGraphs shown in Appendix II were generated using this option).

/GOD (The Data-Labels Options Option).   Provides opportunity to label data points within graph. (At least one of the real estate graphs makes use of this option. Can you find it?)

/GOQ (The Quit Options Option).   Provides option to return to previous graph menu.

/GN (The Name Command).   Provides a name options for display graphs. The options include "**U**" (Use an existing named graph), "**C**" (Create a new named graph), "**D**" (Delete a named graph), or "**R**" (Reset named graphs).

/GQ (The Quit Command).   Provides an option to return to basic Lotus 1-2-3 menu.

Data Options

/D (The Data Menu).   This menu provides the database management facility using Lotus 1-2-3. These commands may be useful for special applications.

/DF (The Fill Command).   Provides option to fill a range of data in ascending or descending order.

/DT (The Table Command).   Provides option to test values in a table as an approximation to "sensitivity analysis."

/DS (The Sort Command).   Provides the opportunity to sort a range of data from ascending or descending order on up to two keys of data. This is one of the most useful commands in the data menu.

/DQ (The Query Command).   Provides the user with the ability to select a sample of cells using a selection criterion. This is the most powerful of the database management commands.

/DD (The Distribution Command). Provides opportunity to analyze a data set and develop a histogram or data distribution.

Quit Option

/Q (The Quit Command). This is the final item on the basic menu and permits the user to return to the Lotus Access System and stop using the spreadsheet. With the help of the other Lotus 1-2-3 diskettes, the user can employ the Utilities programs, the PrintGraph program, or the Tutorial programs.

These (and the special keys and the preprogrammed functions noted in Appendix A) constitute Lotus 1-2-3's spreadsheet's main mode of operation. As you use Lotus 1-2-3, you will come to appreciate its design, power, and versatility. As a beginner, don't worry about the complexity of the program. Use the commands, options, special keys, and functions that you are comfortable with. Use the ones you think you need. In time, you will become familiar with nearly all of them.

The Real Estate Commands

As indicated earlier, the real estate templates have their own command structure built into the program. This facilitates the immediate usage of the templates for *anyone*. You do not need to know *anything* about the Lotus menus to use the real estate templates! This feature should help ease the apprehension many novices seem to have concerning computers and spreadsheets. It will also increase your productivity in the real estate market.

Similar to the section above, this discussion presents an overview of the custom-designed menus and options. Note that in some of the actual real estate templates, there are slight changes from the general menus presented here. This discussion is intended to provide a general overview of the menu structure.

There are basically two menus for the real estate templates: the *basic option menu* and the *menu for special user options*. (In templates with more than one graph, a separate graphs menu is also included within the template.) The basic option menu is shown below in its most general form:

Title Input(s) Output(s) Solutions Summary User Options Quit

After each option, a description is provided to help the user identify what each option means. Appendix A also provides the second lines of each option as shown on-line within the real estate template series.

T (The Title Option). This option enables the user to return to the top of the file and see the "title page" and the basic option menu.

I or 1st I (The Input(s) Options).   This option permits the user to input values for processing within the template. Note that in some cases, there are two input pages, but typically all of the inputs are entered on one page. Note also that in the event the user errs in inputting, the user can return using this option and correct the value and continue to input or stop if all of the inputs have previously been made.

O or 1st O (The Output(s) Options).   This option permits an analysis of the outputs. In some cases, the outputs extend over more than one page, but typically, the output is provided with one option. Note also that in some cases, a summary of the output is provided; some users may regard the summary as important as the output option.

S or 1st S (The Solutions Option).   Some templates have a separate option to calculate the solutions to the problem.

S or 2nd S (The Summary Option).   Many templates provide a summary of the results. Sometimes this is a summary of the output; other times, it is more of a synthesis of the template's results.

U (The User Options Option).   As discussed below, each template provides a separate menu for special options. These include graphics, printing, saving, retrieving, and quitting.

Q (The Quit Option).   This option returns the user to the Lotus Access System. *Be careful! If you haven't stored your analysis, pressing "Q" will lose your results forever!*

In response to the user selecting "**User Options**," the following menu is displayed:

Print Graph Save Retrieve Menu Index Quit

UP (The Print Option).   The template will automatically be printed with the current results intact. Notice, you do not have to save your results to print. Save if you wish to print the same results in the future (i.e., after the computer has been turned off!).

UG (The Graph Option).   The results will be shown graphically, (if you have the color/graphics board to support the software). If you do not have the hardware for graphics, a beep will occur and you will return to the "User Options" menu.

US (The Save Option).   This facility enables the user to save the results. Once again, if you wish to save your analysis, *save your results using a new file name.*

UR (The Retrieve Option).   This option retrieves other worksheet files on the diskette in the diskdrive.

UM (The Menu Option).   This option returns the user to the previous menu.

UI (The Index Option).   This option retrieves the index file (AUTO123) to permit examination of the location of files on the other real estate diskettes.

UQ (The Quit Option).   This option takes the user to the Lotus Access System.

That's it! These options are all you need to know in order to use the real estate templates!

The Lotus 1-2-3 Functions

Lotus 1-2-3 is also programmed to do a variety of calculations without the user having to develop the specific formula. These preprogrammed shortcuts are called "functions" and several are useful for real estate analysts. Many have been used in the development of the system of templates found later in this book. Some of the more useful ones are briefly discussed below. (Information about the functions not discussed is provided in the Lotus manual.)

All functions are invoked by beginning with the "@" symbol. In addition, with only a few exceptions, after the function name, the value or range must be input. In a few cases, several value inputs are required.

The following list represents several of the functions used in the development of the real estate templates. While some of the functions take a bit of practice, with experience, the Lotus function will save the user hours of time.

@ABS(value) (The Absolute Value Function).   Finding the absolute value of a formula is often useful if, for example, negative values of an expression have little or no real-world meaning.

@AVG(list) (The Average Function).   Instead of having to calculate the average of a series of numbers, this function permits the user to specify the range and calculate the average. For many users, the function will become a natural and useful option.

@CHOOSE(value, list) (The Choose Function). This is a technical function which permits the analyst to search a list of parameters and choose a value in the list according to a predetermined decision. For example, the user might wish to choose the ninth element in the list even though the user may not know what the ninth element's value is. This function facilitates those types of choices.

@COUNT(list) (The Count Function). This is similar to the Average Function except that The Count Function merely sums the number of non-blank elements in a range instead of computing its average. The Count Function is useful to keep track of observations as a check against input ommissions.

@EXP(value) (The Exponent Function). This function provides the analyst with the mathematical function of taking an exponent. This is useful in some of the rate of return calculations.

@FV(values) (The Future Value Function). The calculation of the future value of an annuity is facilitated with this function. Note that the real estate series includes a separate template for this calculation (Template lot503).

@IRR(values) (The Internal Rate of Return Function). This is the heralded internal rate of return function. It approximates the rate which equates the present value of the benefits to the present value of the costs. It is limited in that very long cash flow streams are not able to be approximated before Lotus returns the "ERR" message in some cases. Template lot1102 is devoted to the internal rate of return calculation.

@IF(logical value, value, value) (The IF Function). This is a powerful function for sophisticated programs. This function provides the facility to test logical relationships and report a result dependent upon the outcome of the test. This "if statement" represents the most implicit computer programming capability of any function in Lotus 1-2-3.

@MAX(list) (The Maximum Function). Finding the maximum value in a range when the specific parameter values are unknown or changing is a useful option. Lotus users will frequently use this function for large data problems.

@MIN(list) (The Minimum Function). Finding the minimum value in a range when the specific parameter values are unknown or changing is also a useful option.

@NPV(values) (The Net Present Value Function). This is one of the well-known financial functions of Lotus 1-2-3. (Its companion, the Internal Rate of Return Function, or @IRR(values), is also described above.) The Net Present

Value function permits the user to find the present value of inputs (for example, cash flows) and compare this sum to the cash outflow at the beginning of the investment. A discount rate is required to take into account the time value of money. This system of templates includes an entire template for Net Present Value (Template lot1101), but for some purposes, Lotus has already preprogrammed this calculation.

@PMT(values) (The Payment Function).   This function may be used to calculate the level-payment periodic payment. Template lot601 and others are devoted to this same purpose.

@PV(values) (The Present Value Function).   This calculates the present value of an annuity. Note that the real estate series includes a separate template for this calculation (Template lot504).

@ROUND(values) (The Round Function).   This function rounds values upward or downward depending upon their decimal values.

@SQRT(value) (The Square Root Function).   This function calculates the square root of a cell value.

@STD(list) (The Standard Deviation Function).   This function calculates the standard deviation found in a specified list.

@SUM(list) (The Sum Function).   This function adds a series of parameters found in the specified list.

@VAR(list) (The Variance Function).   Like the @STD Function, this is a statistical function. It is used to calculate the variance of a distribution of values. Template lot1105 is devoted to both the variance and the standard deviation calculations.

Remember, as a new Lotus 1-2-3 user, when developing your own spreadsheets, you do not have to use any of the functions. Use them only when you are comfortable with the commands and the features of Lotus. Indeed, for many simple spreadsheet applications, the functions do not add much to the spreadsheets. They should be useful to you, but never a burden.

When you use the real estate templates already designed and included with this book, you never have to worry about the functions: they are built into the spreadsheets. You benefit from Lotus' versatility and you do not have to worry about their implementation.

Special Features of Lotus 1-2-3

The discussion in Chapter 1 and so far in this chapter has already suggested that Lotus 1-2-3 represents a major accomplishment in microcomputer history. In this section, a few of the special features of Lotus 1-2-3 will be discussed, including some tips about how to get the most out of the program and the applications to real world problems.

One of the most important features is the ability to "copy" formulas from one cell to another. This is very effective and very efficient. However, perhaps the most important aspect of this process is that Lotus 1-2-3 presumes (unless told to the contrary), that the user wants to update all of the cell locations of related formulas. Thus, the user can be confident that copied formulas across various cells will be properly altered.

Similarly, if a column or row is inserted into a range of data, the @AVG or @SUM functions will *automatically* increase its range to reflect the insert. This will be true as long as the insertion is at a place other than the last row or the farthest column in the range. Lotus presumes you want to calculate the average with the insertion rather than without it.

The use of titles and windows is an extremely useful feature. I am confident that you will agree if you examine some of the longer templates provided later in this book. Also, the ability to control the order of calculation is useful, since Lotus can run into trouble in an area termed "forward referencing." This means that each time the spreadsheet is calculated, the order of execution either begins in the first row, first column and proceeds down each consecutive column or through each consecutive row. If formulas near the bottom or near the end of the spreadsheet use more than one value or result from the beginning of the spreadsheet, the order in which Lotus 1-2-3 executes its instructions may affect the answer. Therefore, it is important to recognize whether the columns or rows are the given order or recalculation. (Remember: this should not be a problem with the real estate templates.)

Lotus 1-2-3 also provides the opportunity for self-checking of the results. After all, simply because a number appears as the output does not mean the number is correct. If mistakes are made in designing the spreadsheet or the template, or if data input errors are present, the results will be misleading, incorrect, or potentially nonsensical. Experienced Lotus users can guard against this problem by designing error checks within their spreadsheets. This will provide information as to whether "errors exist" and whether the structure of the spreadsheet needs to be reexamined. Examples would include checks on the number of observations used (using the @Count Function)- or a report to see if the sum of the inputs is correct before the analysis is performed. Several of the real estate templates in this book feature these error checks.

Another feature of spreadsheets such as Lotus 1-2-3 is that the results may be stored over and over again on an inexpensive, but high-quality data diskette. It is important to recognize that floppy diskettes can be damaged and your hard work would be lost. Thus, try to remember to get in the habit of "backing up" your results by making a copy of your data diskette. In the event that something happens to the first diskette, you still have your results.

The ability to store your results means that hard copies are not essential every time you make a change. Hard copies are invaluable for many purposes, but you do not need to make a printed copy of each change. Be confident that Lotus will save your changes and return them to the screen when you are ready. If nothing else, this feature reduces the necessity of paper files; huge amounts of information can now be stored on the diskette. More importantly, when you want to make some changes to the analysis, you pick up right where you left off.

Given the well-known other features such as speed of execution, accuracy, testing "what if" questions, graphics, database management and others, Lotus 1-2-3 is a most powerful tool. But perhaps the most important feature is its friendliness. As promised in Chapter 1, individuals without any computer experience can be using Lotus 1-2-3 and the real estate (or other) templates in a matter of minutes. Computerization has become available for everyone, even those who know little about them!

A Word about the Limitations of Lotus 1-2-3

As is the case with everything, there are some aspects of Lotus that seem to get in the way. However, many users can find virtually nothing wrong with Lotus! This is additional testimonial to how superior this program is to most products on the market.

Some of us forget and quickly become spoiled as new products are introduced and as we become complacent with what we can do. We forget how difficult it is to perform a complex chain of calculations as Lotus 1-2-3 routinely calculates them for us in seconds. We forget how we marveled at the color graphics generated right before our eyes. We forget how long it takes to sort numbers of labels by hand.

In any case, the following is a brief overview of some of the items which appear on my "wish list" for future releases or new products.

For example, newer products are attempting to provide multiple windows for "multi-tasking" environments. The Lotus Development Corporation has recently announced its new product "Symphony" which permits this type of option. It is a limitation of Lotus 1-2-3 that only one window or title can be used at any one time and that graphics cannot be done on the screen at the same time as other activities.

A more serious problem is that sloppy importing of data into cells where formulas exist can destroy the template. When new characters are combined or imported into a cell, what formerly occupied the cell is gone. (Of course, if the spreadsheet with the erased formula is still stored on the diskette, the current spreadsheet may be cleared and the original one reloaded.) One way to deal with this problem is to combine in columns where no data exists and then move the data within the worksheet.

I find the method for moving formulas with absolute addresses cumbersome and tedious. It seems it would have been a lot easier had the designers chosen a submenu to specify either relative, absolute, or mixed addresses.

Also, while the graphics options are very nice and easy to use, it is a bit disappointing that some of the extra features are not available. For example, the ability to "paint" Pie Charts or Line Graphs would have been a nice touch. Also, I am a sucker for three-dimensional bar and stacked-bar graphs. Finally, more than three colors would also have been nice, especially with the recent development of newer, higher quality graphics monitors.

In the area of database management, many users have noted that the Lotus 1-2-3 facility is limited. In addition, it is often difficult to make use of these options within well-developed templates. Symphony has solved these deficiencies to a great extent.

One other complaint: when the logical @IF Function is used, Lotus returns "1" if the equation is "true" and "0" if the equation is "false." It would have been helpful if the words could have been returned, as is typically done in other products. It would also have been nice to be able to return labels in general.

But after all, one can always wish for what one doesn't have! Lotus 1-2-3 is an incredible package, even for the most picky and tough-to-please user. The power of the program is almost limitless. The value for the money is outstanding to say the least. It has been and continues to be the best-selling software by far. It will provide service for literally hundreds of thousands of users over the next ten years! It will also be available to solve *your* problems, if you spend a little time, a little effort, and a little creativity.

PART II
REAL ESTATE APPLICATIONS

Part II forms the major part of this book and is devoted exclusively to real estate applications using Lotus 1-2-3. There are ten chapters in this part which contain 41 models or "templates". Each is discussed in detail and without confusing terms or mathematics. One of the major advantages of using Lotus 1-2-3 over calculators and other methods is that the computer worries about the mathematics; you concern yourself with the inputs and the interpretation of the results.

Each chapter is devoted to a different area in real estate analysis. These include household decisions, brokerage applications, financial calculations and creative financing, lending decisions, property management tasks, investment analysis, tax planning and analysis, financial ratio analysis, discounted cash flow models, and real estate appraising applications. Each chapter builds upon the previous chapter in term of skills and models using Lotus 1-2-3. In some cases, templates are extended to include additional considerations from earlier ones. In this manner, the entire set of templates represent a system of analysis for real estate users and decision makers.

Chapter 3 is devoted to household decisions and financial statements, including income statements and balance sheets, a rent versus buy analysis, and a record of investment holdings. Chapter 4 provides applications for real estate salespersons and brokers. These templates include a table of properties for sale, an estimate of cash required for closings, and a settlement statement. Chapter 5 provides a number of compound interest calculators. The formulas include present and future values, annuity calculations, sinking funds, and mortgage constants.

Chapter 6 continues the development of real estate financial factors by providing methods of calculating debt service, amortization schedules, and methods for measuring the effective cost of borrowing and the lender's yield on mortgage loans. Chapter 7 is devoted to the measurement of financial leverage and some of the new mortgages which have become popular in the last few years. These include the adjustable rate mortgage (ARM), the growing equity mortgage (GEM), and wraparound mortgage financing. Chapter 8 provides analyses of important items in any real estate property: income and expenses. The templates concentrate on the rent roll calculation and projection, operating expense budgeting and monitoring, the calculation of before-tax cash flow, and forecasting income and expenses for financial planning.

Chapter 9 is devoted to taxation and includes the calculation of depreciation allowances using the 1984 ACRS system. It includes tables for both the traditional straight-line method as well as the 175% declining balance method. In addition, taxable income is calculated and a template is provided for the measurement of after-tax cash flow, an important measure in real estate investment analysis. Given the results in the previous chapters, Chapter 10 provides three templates of financial ratios. These include a number of rates of return, income statement and balance sheet ratios, and the measurement of the effective rate of return from an investment. Chapter 11 is devoted entirely to discounted cash flow models. These have become increasingly popular in many real estate markets. These models include the net present value (NPV), the internal rate of return (IRR), the profitability index (PI), the net terminal value (NTV), and the use of the variance and standard deviation as measures of risk. These modern techniques are easily understood and serve as useful tools for any type of financial analysis.

Finally, the last chapter in this part is devoted to real estate appraisal applications using market data. A model of the sales comparison adjustment grid is provided. This is one of the three approaches to real estate market value estimation and can now be done on-line with Lotus and this book. The remaining two templates are statistical in nature and provide descriptive statistics and simple linear regression applications for real estate.

3 Household Tools for Financial Decisions

Overview

This chapter provides four comprehensive tools to provide assistance in financial planning for all households, especially those beginning to consider the purchase of a new home. These templates permit the user to develop financial statements, examine the ability of a family to qualify for mortgage financing, evaluate the rent versus buy decision, and keep a record of investments in a family or investment portfolio. These same tools may also be used by partnerships, small businesses, and firms when faced with the same decisions. The models used in this chapter are fundamental to sound financial planning and money management. They are also the first step toward developing a real estate investment portfolio.

FINANCIAL STATEMENTS
(Template: lot301)

There are two important statements in most real estate firms and other businesses. These are the *Balance Sheet* (or *Statement of Financial Position*) and the *Income Statement*. This template is designed to enable the user to develop both of these statements with ease.

Principles.   Traditionally, accountants have separated assets from liabilities and income from expenses. This helps to identify, measure, and control the wealth of individuals and firms as well as assist in planning for future contingencies. Assets represent value to their owner; liabilities represent claims against the owner's assets. The difference between assets and liabilities is called *equity* or *net worth*. Changes in net worth represent changes in the wealth of the entity.

Similarly, income is measured by the dollars expected over a relevant period of time, which are expected to accrue to the owner of the assets. As indicated in the template, there are several types of income an individual can earn. Expenses are outflows and require payment for goods or services. For most people, expenses occur because we purchase goods and services willingly; although we do not like to pay these expenses, we would be worse off without the products.

For any budget, the difference between income and expenses represents a surplus or a deficit position. If the analysis is done on an expected basis, the estimated income and expenses result in an expected budgetary surplus or deficit. If the analysis is done using actual past data, the purpose is to measure the results of recent economic activity. Using past data to forecast future budgets is a valuable tool for financial planning purposes.

Using the Template.   This template enables the user to input a variety of balance sheet and income statement items. If every item does not apply, the user may skip some by pressing "Enter" and the template will automatically skip to the next space. The templates are programmed to enable the user to enter data and press "Enter" to move on or press "Enter" by itself and leave the item blank. In addition, there are miscellaneous spaces for assets and liabilities for special household needs.

In Table II, the inputs for the income statement should be done on an annual basis. The output in Table IV will provide both monthly and annual statements. Notice that all of the inputs are entered by the user in either Tables I or II. *(Generally, most of the templates in this book use a single table, typically Table I, for inputting all of the data.)* The menu system permits the user to enter data in each table consecutively or independently. Also, if you make a mistake, you are free to go back and "repair" the error.

Table III provides net worth. As indicated, this is important since it provides a measure of the value of the wealth of the household, individual investor, partnership, or firm. Notice in Table IV that income and expense items have been grouped and summed. Note also that the difference between income and expenses will result in a surplus or deficit. This is shown automatically using the Lotus 1-2-3 logical value functions of "TRUE" or "FALSE". Lotus

1-2-3 shows "0" when the answer is "FALSE" and "1" when the answer is "TRUE".

As in all of the templates in this book, this one has been designed to facilitate easy and extensive usage. The user is encouraged to become familiar with these easy ones before attempting to master the more complex models. For example, all of the templates provide a Table of Contents for easy template access. The user can always return to the table of contents by pointing to "Title" in the custom-designed menu. This will return the user to the top of the template on the first menu. (The user is encouraged to refer to Appendix A for more discussion of the Lotus 1-2-3 and the specially designed menus found in every template.)

The table of contents provides information to direct the user through each template. Each table within the template is consecutively numbered and generally can be viewed by pointing to sequential spaces in the menu. For example, suppose the menu says "Title" "Input" "Output" "Summary" across the top of the screen. The user can be confident that there are three "tables": input, output and summary tables. They are also typically situated one right after the other on the template.

Note also that within each menu is an item called "User Options." This is the gateway to another menu of specialized activity such as printing, graphing, saving, retrieving, returning to the index, and others. The structure of the system is to input and output from the first menu; specialized activities are directed from the User Options menu. Note also that you may switch back and forth between the menus. If you are using the first menu, go to the special menu by pointing to "User Options" (or pressing the letter "u"). If you are on the second or in some cases, third menus, return to the previous menu by pointing to "Menu" (or press the letter "m"). Notice that the second line of each menu provides a description of what each item will do when chosen.

You should learn to become familiar with the menu system. It is very easy and convenient. Indeed, you do not have to know anything about the operation or even the usage of Lotus 1-2-3 to use these templates. The menus do all of the work; you get the results. Experience and experimentation will bring forth greater familiarity with the design of these templates. In a short time, the user will "feel" right at home.

An Example.   For each template in this book, an example is provided, using hypothetical data. Each example provides an illustration regarding the use of the model to solve the particular problem. If you obtain your own copies of the diskettes, you may obtain the same results as shown in the illustrations by retrieving the template and inputting the numbers indicated in each example. All of the templates which accompany this book are available in a package as indicated on the coupon attached to the book. All are "empty" of data but have been tested to provide the identical answers when data is supplied in the appropriate spaces by the user.

Graphics.   One of the very best features of Lotus 1-2-3 is the superb graphics capability which is available to support the numerical analysis. However, in order to use the graphics facility, your hardware must contain a color/graphics board. If you do not have one, you cannot use the graphics feature of the system.

There are actually two types of graphics options with Lotus 1-2-3. First, the user may create graphics representations of analysis. Then with the touch of a single button, a graph in black-and-white or color appears. Change the numbers in the template and the graph is automatically updated. With built-in options such as titles, legends, grid systems, and several types of graphs available, this feature alone gets users excited about Lotus 1-2-3!

The other type of graphics is used with the Lotus 1-2-3 PrintGraph diskette. This enables users to save graphics files for special and high-quality printing at a later time. There are several options at this point as well, but the reader need not be kept in suspense. Whether or not you have a color-graphics board, you will not be stopped from scanning through Appendix B to look at the various graphs. All have been produced with an ordinary, standard dot-matrix printer and Lotus 1-2-3. Not only are there several types, but they are all proportionately spaced and centered. All use the same data as found in the templates in the spreadsheet. All were developed using the same data as reported in each example.

As nice as the graphs are in Appendix B, the user is in for a treat if he/she has a color monitor and the color/graphics board. For each template, there is a graph (in some cases, more than one!) in color automatically waiting for the user to call it to the screen. The graphics capability of Lotus 1-2-3 is outstanding and these templates make use of the facility as much as possible. For this template, the family expenses are broken down into categories and compared. Both monthly and annual expenses are shown. Note also that the dimensions on the y-axis are automatically set to accommodate the level of the data input by the user. Try it out; I'm confident you will be pleased.

Possible Modifications.   This template is relatively simple and as a result, few modifications are likely. The user is free to modify the items listed as assets, liabilities, income, or expenses. It is important, however, to understand that changing the templates should only be attempted by an experienced user. At a minimum, the custom-designed macros will have to be modified and while it is not difficult, an inexperienced Lotus 1-2-3 user will not be able to make the changes. In addition, the cells must first be "unprotected" to accept changes, the formulas should not be changed unless you are precise about the change, and so on. If cells with formulas are modified and the new template is stored in place of the old one, the original template will be lost. Therefore, until you become a seasoned Lotus 1-2-3 user, *never* revise a template until you are certain you wish to do so. Always store the new template under a new name on your data diskette.

Another suggestion is to make backup copies of all of the diskettes with Lotus 1-2-3 templates. This may be done quickly using the DOS "diskcopy" command. It may also be accomplished using the DOS "copy" command. In this way, you may feel at ease when using the templates.

As with many of the templates, this first template works quickly and easily. The user may find it useful to change data and examine the impact on the outputs. This is often called "sensitivity analysis" and is one of the strongest features of spreadsheets such as Lotus 1-2-3. For example, changing jobs may result in your salary increasing by 20%, but your travel expenses may rise by 30%. What impact will these changes have on your budget? For Lotus 1-2-3, this is a simple problem to answer. Check the output with your current salary and travel expenses and check it with the proposed job. In this way, you can quickly see how and if you should make the job switch.

A useful aid in this type of sensitivity analysis is to use the Lotus 1-2-3 "window" convention. This permits the user to view two parts of the spreadsheet at once. I prefer the horizontal window for most analysis, especially since most of the templates in this book make use of the first eight columns. If you wish to create a window, hit "Ctrl-Break" to get out of the Command mode. (This disables the menu and can always be used if you get out of synch with the movement of the cursor on the spreadsheet. Press "Control" and "Break" together and you are back to the generic Lotus 1-2-3 menu. To return to the custom menu, at any time, press "Alt" and "M". These instructions are frequently shown at the bottoms of pages throughout most of the real estate templates.)

If you are adventurous, center the input table on the top and the output table on the bottom. Move the cursor to the top half of the page (use the Function Key F6). Press "Alt M" to get the real estate menu. Input the data as you normally would. In most cases, you will be able to see the effects of the data as soon as you enter it. In some cases, when you begin to look at the output page, the spreadsheet begins the series of calculations. In the first case, each time you enter new data or in the second case, each time you begin to evaluate the output, the computer proceeds to recalculate the spreadsheet. In this manner, you can take control of the spreadsheet, the computer, and your financial situation.

EXAMPLE TEMPLATE 3.1
Financial statements.

```
lot301x                                      Real Estate Diskette #1
===================================================================
FINANCIAL STATEMENTS             Copyright (C) Reston Pub. Co., 1985
===================================================================

~~~~~~~~~~~~~~~~~~~~~~~~~~~~~~~~~~~~~~~~~~~~~~~~~~~~~~~~~~~~~~~~~~~~~~~

                   ***   TABLE OF CONTENTS   ***
                       ==================
             Table                                    Page
             -----                                    ----

      I.    INPUTS FOR BALANCE SHEET STATEMENT          1

     II.    INPUTS FOR INCOME STATEMENT                 2

    III.    OUTPUT FOR FAMILY BALANCE SHEET             3

     IV.    OUTPUT FOR FAMILY INCOME STATEMENT          4


~~~~~~~~~~~~~~~~~~~~~~~~~~~~~~~~~~~~~~~~~~~~~~~~~~~~~~~~~~~~~~~~~~~~~~~
```

```
         I. INPUTS FOR BALANCE SHEET STATEMENT
         =======================================

    Enter the following balance sheet items:

            ASSETS:
              Cash                            $        100
              Savings Accounts           ,    $         10
              Checking Accounts              $         10
              Money Market Funds             $         10
              Treasury Bills                 $         25
              U.S. Govt Bonds                $         25
              Other Short Term Investments   $         50
              Common Stock                   $        200
              Long Term Bonds                $        100
              Accounts Receivable            $         50
              Notes Receivable               $         50
              Retirement & Pensions          $        450
              House                          $     50,000
              Automobiles                    $      1,000
              Furniture                      $      5,000
              Personal Property              $        500
              Valuables                      $        250
              Other Assets                   $        250

            LIABILITIES:
              Charge Accounts                $         56
              Bank Loans                     $        125
              Car Loans                      $        145
              Consumer Loans                 $      1,000
              Personal Loans                 $         50
              Accounts Payable               $      1,000
              Notes Payable                  $      1,000
              Mortgages                      $     40,000
              Other Liabilities              $         78


  Press  [Alt] M  for MENU        Press  [Ctrl] [Break]  for READY

  ~~~~~~~~~~~~~~~~~~~~~~~~~~~~~~~~~~~~~~~~~~~~~~~~~~~~~~~~~~~~~~~~~~~~
```

II. INPUTS FOR INCOME STATEMENT
==================================

Enter the following income statement items:

```
        INCOME:
            Your Annual Earnings              $   10,000
            Your Spouse's Annual Earnings     $    4,000
            Income from Investments           $    1,000
            Supplementary Business Income     $    1,000
            Other Income                      $    1,000

        EXPENSES:
            Monthly Payments on Liabilities   $      500
            Food                              $      100
            Utilities                         $      100
            Medical                           $      100
            Education                         $      100
            Transportation                    $       45
            Insurance                         $       57
            Recreation                        $      100
            Maintenance                       $      100
            Income Taxes                      $      600
            Social Security                   $      250
            Other Taxes and Fees              $       25
            Contributions                     $       10
            Savings                           $       50
            Investments                       $       60
            Miscellaneous Living Expenses     $       50
            Other Expenses                    $       25
```

Press [Alt] M for MENU   Press [Ctrl] [Break] for READY

~~~~~~

III. OUTPUT FOR FAMILY BALANCE SHEET
=======================================

ASSETS:			LIABILITIES:		
Cash Reserves	$	130	Charge Accounts	$	56
Receivables	$	100	Loans	$	1,320
Short Term Investments	$	100	Payables	$	2,000
Stocks and Bonds	$	300	Mortgages	$	40,000
Real Estate	$	50,000	Other Liabilities	$	78
Other Fixed Assets	$	6,000			
Personal Assets	$	1,000			
Retirement Assets	$	450			
		------			------
TOTAL ASSETS............$		58,080	TOTAL LIABILITIES.....$		43,454
			NET WORTH............$		14,626

Press [Alt] M for MENU   Press [Ctrl] [Break] for READY

~~~~~~

```
        IV. OUTPUT FOR FAMILY INCOME STATEMENT
        ========================================

                                Monthly           Annually

    INCOME:

        Family Earnings          $    1,167      $   14,000
        Investment Income        $       83      $    1,000
        Supplementary Income     $       83      $    1,000
        Other Income             $       83      $    1,000
                                     ------           ------
            TOTAL FAMILY INCOME.......$   1,417  ......$   17,000

    EXPENSES:

        Debt Payments            $      500          6,000
        Household Living Expenses        650          7,800
        Income Taxes and Social Security $  850      10,200
        Transportation                    45            540
        Insurance                         57            684
        Savings and Investments          110          1,320
        Contributions                     10            120
        Other Expenses                    50            600
                                      ------           ------
            TOTAL FAMILY EXPENSES.....$   2,272  ......$   27,264

            INCOME MINUS EXPENSES.....$    (855)  ......$  (10,264)


    $$$$$$$$$$$$$$$$$$$$$$$$$$$$$$$$$$$$$$$$$$$$$$$$$$$$$$

        There is a BUDGET SURPLUS..        0 !!

        There is a BUDGET DEFICIT..        1 !!

    -----(Computer returns 0 if FALSE, 1 if TRUE)-----

    $$$$$$$$$$$$$$$$$$$$$$$$$$$$$$$$$$$$$$$$$$$$$$$$$$$$$$

Press  [Alt] M  for MENU          Press  [Ctrl] [Break]  for READY

~~~~~~~~~~~~~~~~~~~~~~~~~~~~~~~~~~~~~~~~~~~~~~~~~~~~~~~~~~~~~~~~~~~~~~~~~~
```

BUYER'S QUALIFICATION STATEMENT
(Template: lot302)

One of the difficult parts of buying real estate for many people is qualifying, especially as a first-time buyer, for long-term financing. Since many individuals and investors lack enough equity capital (cash) to settle at the closing without mortgage financing, or in some cases, *prefer* the use of debt financing rather than using equity, it is useful to determine whether or not a prospective purchaser will qualify for loan acceptance, given the lending guidelines applicable in the market in which the transaction takes place. This template helps the loan applicant, loan officer, or counselor of a prospective purchaser by performing the necessary numerical calculations to test whether the buyer is "qualified" for the mortgage financing.

Principles. Traditionally, lenders established housing "rules of thumb" to provide guidelines for residential loan applicants. These included a maximum ratio of housing expenses to income and a maximum ratio of total expenses to income. Household income includes both the husband's and wife's income. The template shows the suggested ratios from the Federal Home Loan Mortgage Corporation (FHLMC) as 25 percent and 33 percent respectively. Note that these ratios are only guidelines, not complete underwriting criteria.

In addition, the purchaser might also want to see if his or her housing budget will be able to support a housing purchase, given housing prices, mortgage terms, the amount of downpayment available, and household income. Clearly, it is difficult if not impossible to come to a rational conclusion to this important question, without looking at the numbers carefully. This template enables the user to evaluate this decision using all of the relevant data.

Using the Template. All of the inputs are entered in Table I. These include income and expenses, lender's guidelines for qualification, and property characteristics. Note that the income is annual and the non-housing expenses are entered on a monthly basis. The lender's guidelines may be the same as those suggested by FHLMC or any other. The important point is that the guidelines used should be those which apply to the specific market conditions at the time the analysis is being done. Call your local lender to find out current guidelines. Finally, details of the property under consideration should also be entered. These include sales price of the property and equity downpayment. Since the difference between the sales price and the downpayment will be financed, the mortgage interest rate and term are also required.

Table II presents the output of the analysis. Both monthly and annual figures are provided. Given the available income, the guideline is applied to show the maximum amount available for total payments. Subtracting out other expenses including utilities, alimony, child support payments, property insurance, and property taxes, the analysis shows the net amount available for housing. This amount is compared to the fully amortized housing payment, given the mortgage interest rate and term of the loan. The difference results in a budget deficit or surplus.

The results of the analysis are shown in Table III. Actual ratios can be compared to the lender's limits. In addition, the budgeted amount can be compared to the required expenditure. With this information, three tests are provided, each of which are critical for qualifying for the loan.

The results of these tests directly impact the conclusion. In the template, if the user fails to meet any of the tests, the computer will report a "zero" (or FALSE) in Table III (i.e., one or more of the tests will not be satisfied). If all of the tests are satisfied, the template shows that "THIS HOUSEHOLD WILL SOON BE A HOMEOWNER!!!" In this manner, the template reports the results in English, with limited algebra ("0" or "1"); interpretation is a simple matter.

An Example.   Notice that in this case, the ratios of housing expenses to income and total payments to income fall within the guidelines. In addition, the family estimates that $900.00 can be budgeted for housing expenditures. The analysis shows that $841.00 is the monthly amount the family would be expected to pay toward housing expenses. Therefore, in this case, it appears that the buyer would qualify for the loan.

Graphics.   There is limited graphics associated with this template. However, note that a graph can show the magnitude within which the buyer meets the lending tests. The graph shows that all three tests are met. In the last case, the budgeted amount exceeds that which is required for the house under consideration.

Possible Modifications.   This analysis is based upon a number of assumptions such as good credit records, a sufficient appraised value to warrant the mortgage, and other assumptions. Some of these items may be included into the analysis. In addition, the analysis allows for only one conventional mortgage at a fixed interest rate. Adjustable rate mortgages could also be included. Finally, the analysis concentrates on the income and expenses in the first year. More sophisticated methods could expand the analysis to include these considerations.

This template also works well with a "window". It is very useful to see how sensitive the ratio budget tests are to changes in income and expenses. The user is invited to test the limits of how the applicant will be able to qualify for the maximum amount, given the set of guidelines. Similarly, the guidelines can be changed to see the point at which the buyer will qualify.

EXAMPLE TEMPLATE 3.2
Buyer's qualification statement.

```
lot302x                                    Real Estate Diskette #1
================================================================
BUYER'S QUALIFICATION STATEMENT     Copyright (C) Reston Pub. Co., 1985
================================================================


~~~~~~~~~~~~~~~~~~~~~~~~~~~~~~~~~~~~~~~~~~~~~~~~~~~~~~~~~~~~~~~~~~~~~~

                 ***   TABLE OF CONTENTS   ***
                       =================
              Table                              Page
              -----                              ----

     I.   INPUTS TO EVALUATE BUYER'S FINANCIAL
          CAPACITY                                 1

    II.   OUTPUT OF BUYER'S QUALIFICATION
          STATEMENT                                2

   III.   CONCLUSION OF BUYER'S CAPACITY           3


~~~~~~~~~~~~~~~~~~~~~~~~~~~~~~~~~~~~~~~~~~~~~~~~~~~~~~~~~~~~~~~~~~~~~~
```

I. INPUTS TO EVALUATE BUYER'S FINANCIAL CAPACITY

Enter the following assumptions:

INCOME:

Current Annual "Primary" Household Income	>>>	$ 35,000
Current Annual "Experienced" Other Household Income	>>>	$ 7,000

LIABILITIES: (Before Housing Expenses)

Current Monthly Utility Bills	>>>	$ 150.00
Current Monthly Alimony and Child Support Payments	>>>	$ 0.00
Estimated Annual Property Insurance Expense (if owner)	>>>	$ 250.00
Estimated Annual Property Tax Expense (if owner)	>>>	$ 600.00
Maximum Desired Housing Expenses (includes prin, int, tax, ins)	>>>	* 900.00

LENDING GUIDELINES:

Ratio of "Housing Expenses" to "Stabilized Income" (FHLMC=25%)	>>>	25.00 %
Ratio of "Total Payments" to "Stabilized Income" (FHLMC=33%)	>>>	33.00 %

DETAILS OF PROPERTY UNDER CONSIDERATION:

Sales Price	>>>	$ 75,000
Downpayment	>>>	$ 10,000
Mortgage Interest Rate	>>>	14.00 %
Mortgage Term	>>>	30 years

Press [Alt] M for MENU   Press [Ctrl] [Break] for READY

```
         II. OUTPUT OF BUYER'S QUALIFICATION STATEMENT
         ==============================================

                           Monthly              Annually


Stabilized Household Income      $    3,500       $   42,000
Times Guideline Limit Percentage
    for Total Payments                33.00%            33.00%
Equals Amount Available for
    Total Payments:.........................$    1,155   ......$   13,860

Less Current Utility Bills       $      150       $    1,800
Less Current Alimony and
    Child Support Payments       $        0       $        0
Equals Amount Available for
    Housing Expenses........................$    1,005   ......$   12,060

Less Estimated Property Ins-
    urance Expense (if owner)    $       21       $      250
Less Estimated Property Tax
    Expense (if owner)           $       50       $      600
Equals Net Amount Available
    for Housing Finance...................$      934   ......$   11,210

Less Mortgage Payment for
    Property Under Consideration $      770       $    9,242
Equals Household Budget
    Surplus or (Deficit)..................$      164   ......$    1,968


Press   [Alt] M  for MENU            Press  [Ctrl] [Break]  for READY
```

~~~~~~

III. CONCLUSION OF BUYER'S CAPACITY
=====================================

Based upon the analysis in the Buyer's Qualification Statement, the following conclusions can be made:

$$

	Household	Guideline
Ratio of Housing Expenses to Income:	24.03%	25.00%
Ratio of Total Payments to Income:	28.31%	33.00%
Comparison between Housing Budget and Required Expenditure:	$ 900	$ 841

1. The Household's Housing Payments Relative to Income
    satisfies the Lending Guideline Test: 1

2. The Household's Total Payments Relative to Income
    satisfies the Lending Guideline Test: 1

3. The Household's Housing Expense Budget Allocation
    is sufficient for the Property Under Consideration: 1

    -----(Computer returns 0 if FALSE, 1 if TRUE)-----

                        THEREFORE,

    THIS HOUSEHOLD WOULD QUALIFY FOR THE MORTGAGE!   1

    THIS HOUSEHOLD WOULD SATISFY THE BUDGET FOR HOUSING!!   1

    THIS HOUSEHOLD WILL SOON BE A HOMEOWNER!!!   1

$$

Press [Alt] M for MENU   Press   [Ctrl] [Break] for READY

RENT VERSUS BUY ANALYSIS
(Template: lot303)

This template is related to the previous one. In this case, the question to be decided is whether the user should rent rather than buy real estate. Some investors act as if one should never rent; this is foolish since under some conditions, buying is likely to be unattractive. In addition, this analysis frames the question as a financial decision; one which requires estimates of the relevant benefits and costs. Lotus 1-2-3 is an excellent tool for making this type of decision.

Principles. The rent versus buy decision involves several variables. These include a comparison between the costs and benefits of each form of housing choice. For example, as an owner, the right to sell the property in the future as well as tax shelter benefits are distinct advantages. However, the cost of operating the property may be greater than under a rental situation. In addition, as a buyer, cash is typically required as a downpayment. There are opportunity costs associated with the buyer giving up the downpayment. In effect, the renter is presumed to continue to earn interest or dividends on these funds; the buyer gives up these funds as part of the real estate purchase. It should also be pointed out that frequently, the quality of housing consumed increases as a renter moves to become a homeowner.

This model reduces to a decision rule which estimates whether or not the prospective buyer can duplicate an equivalent amount of housing and consumption in the rental market as in the buyer's market. If, as in the case of the enclosed example, it is cheaper to buy than rent, given a host of considerations, the analysis suggests that the user should buy. On the other hand, if the user cannot find property for sale at a similar comparable rent, the model suggests the individual should rent, or at least postpone buying.

Using the Template. Table I requires a number of inputs for the decision. These include information about the property under consideration, financing assumptions including the amount to be financed, the mortgage rate and the term of the loan. Since operating expenses are likely to vary between a homeowner and a renter, the difference in these expenses may be inputted. (If, for example, there would not be any difference expected, as in the case of some commercial leases, zeros may be entered in these cells.)

As an owner, one acquires the right to resell the property in the future. Thus, the benefits from economic growth as well as the costs of selling in the future become part of the decision. In the analysis, this information is included by inputting the property value growth rate, the expected selling expenses, and the expected planning horizon. The economic gain from owning property may be compared to the opportunity cost of saving the additional funds required by the investment. This calculation is also made in the model. Finally, the tax law provides incentive for individuals and firms to own rather than rent by making any interest and property tax payments tax deductible. Renters are not afforded the same treatment by the law and therefore, the tax rate of the user becomes an important aspect of the analysis.

The output is provided in Table II. Given the information provided, this table shows the sales price, mortgage used, and downpayment. In addition, the model produces the total cash required at closing of the deal. Note that if the sum of the mortgage and downpayment does not equal the sales price, an error message will appear. This indicates that the inputs must be reentered.

An amortization schedule is developed for up to ten years. This schedule shows the interest paid each year and the ending balance at the conclusion of the holding period. (See Template lot602 devoted entirely to mortgage amortizations.)

The output shows the gross and net outlays for housing. The difference is the reduction due to tax savings. An estimate of the net proceeds is provided, given the property growth rate, selling expenses, and the outstanding balance of the loan. The difference between the net proceeds at the end of the planning horizon and the after-tax savings as a renter is the buyer's advantage. Finally, the amount of funds needed to be saved is shown in order to offset the financial gain from buying.

A Summary is provided. Note that Lotus 1-2-3 can be used in the narrative form as well. The Summary walks the user through the approach step-by-step. Given the owner's input for monthly rent for comparable housing, the template indicates whether a buy or rent decision is warranted.

An Example.   In the example, a buy decision is illustrated. The net advantage to buying is estimated to be over $14,000 and the housing may be purchased for less than the estimated comparable rental housing ($568.50 versus $600.00). Therefore, the user is encouraged to purchase rather than rent, in this case.

Graphics.   A simple graph is built into this template. It shows a rental comparison of equivalent rent and the cash available for monthly rent. If the former is larger than the latter (i.e., the first data is greater than the second), the analysis suggests that the family should buy rather than rent. If not, renting is expected to be cheaper. Note that the graph is automatically sized and scaled for the amount of money used in the analysis. This is a very nice and helpful feature.

Possible Modifications.   This model has been adapted from analysis in *Foundations of Real Estate Analysis* by G. Vincent Barrett and John P. Blair (New York: Macmillan, 1981). Similar "rent versus buy" decisions are also available. This approach is very useful since it analyzes a number of related considerations. However, some improvements may be made.

For example, only conventional mortgage financing is used. While the property value growth rate is compounded for future economic activity, the rental value of the property is not. The decision rule presumes away any changes in rent over the relevant planning horizon. This may not be the case. Finally, it may be difficult to quantify every aspect of the "rent versus buy" decision. Certain psychological benefits from owning do not lend themselves very well to financial analysis, including Lotus 1-2-3 spreadsheets, but are nonetheless important to the decisionmaker. Thus, the model developed here may be refined to more complex templates by experienced users and analysts.

EXAMPLE TEMPLATE 3.3
Rent versus buy analysis.

```
lot303x                                      Real Estate Diskette #1
==================================================================
RENT VERSUS BUY ANALYSIS            Copyright (C) Reston Pub. Co., 1985
==================================================================

~~~~~~~~~~~~~~~~~~~~~~~~~~~~~~~~~~~~~~~~~~~~~~~~~~~~~~~~~~~~~~~~~~~~~~

                   ***   TABLE OF CONTENTS   ***
                         =================
                Table                              Page
                -----                              ----

      I.    INPUTS FOR RENT VS. BUY ANALYSIS          1

     II.    OUTPUT OF RENT VS. BUY ANALYSIS           2

    III.    SUMMARY OF RENT VS. BUY ANALYSIS          3


~~~~~~~~~~~~~~~~~~~~~~~~~~~~~~~~~~~~~~~~~~~~~~~~~~~~~~~~~~~~~~~~~~~~~~
```

```
            I. INPUTS FOR RENT VS. BUY ANALYSIS
            ======================================

    Enter the following assumptions:


        Purchase Inputs:
          Sales Price......................>>>      $  85,000
          Closing Costs....................>>>      $   2,000

        Financing Inputs:
          Mortgage Amount..................>>>      $  75,000
           Interest Rate on Mortgage.......>>>         13.25  %
           Mortgage Term (max.=30).........>>>            30  years

          Equity Investment (Downpayment)...>>>     $  10,000

        Monthly Operating Inputs:
          Property Taxes...................>>>      $  150.00
          Property Insurance...............>>>      $   20.00
          Maintenance and Repair...........>>>      $   15.00
          Utilities........................>>>      $   75.00

        Owner's Marginal Income Tax Rate....>>>        35.00  %

        Property Value Growth Rate.........>>>          6.00  %

        Expected Selling Expenses..........>>>          6.00  %

        Opportunity Cost of Alternative
        Investments of Savings.............>>>         15.00  %

        Monthly Rent for Comparable Housing.>>>    $  600.00

        Expected Planning Horizon (max.=10).>>>           5  years

  Press  [Alt] M  for MENU          Press  [Ctrl] [Break]  for READY


  ~~~~~~~~~~~~~~~~~~~~~~~~~~~~~~~~~~~~~~~~~~~~~~~~~~~~~~~~~~~~~~~~~~~~~~~~~
```

```
              II. OUTPUT OF RENT VS. BUY ANALYSIS
              ====================================

  Purchase and Financing:
  -----------------------

     Sales Price:...............................$  85,000

     Mortgage:                        $  75,000
     Equity (Downpayment):            $  10,000

     Additional Cash Required at Closing:........$   2,000
                                                   ------
        Total Cash Required at Closing:..........$  87,000


  Amortization of Mortgage:
  -------------------------

         Year  Beg Bal Mort Pay Interest    Amort  End Bal
         ----  ------- -------- --------    -----  -------
          1   $75,000 $10,181  $9,938     $244  $74,756
          2   $74,756 $10,181  $9,905     $276  $74,481
          3   $74,481 $10,181  $9,869     $312  $74,168
          4   $74,168 $10,181  $9,827     $354  $73,814
          5   $73,814 $10,181  $9,780     $401  $73,414
         NA      NA      NA       NA        NA     NA
         NA      NA      NA       NA        NA     NA
         NA      NA      NA       NA        NA     NA
         NA      NA      NA       NA        NA     NA
         NA      NA      NA       NA        NA     NA


  Forecast of Annual Net Housing Outlays:
  ---------------------------------------

     Operating Expenses:              $   3,120
     Mortgage Payment:                $  10,181
                                          ------
        Gross Outlays:....................................$  13,301

     Interest:                        $   9,938
     Property Taxes:                  $   1,800
                                          ------
        Tax Savings:......................................$   4,108
                                                            ------
        Net Outlays:......................................$   9,193


  Forecast of Net Proceeds at End of Holding Period:
  --------------------------------------------------

     Future Sales Price:              $ 113,749
     Selling Expenses:                $   6,825
     Outstanding Mortgage Balance:    $  73,414
                                          ------
        Net Proceeds:.....................................$  33,511
```

```
     Net Advantage from Homeownership:
     -------------------------------

         Net Proceeds:                    $  33,511
         After-Tax Savings (if Renter):   $  19,108
                                             ------
             Net Advantage from Homeownership:.................$  14,403


     Renter's Savings Needed to Offset Homeownership Advantage:
     ----------------------------------------------------------

         Amount Needed to be Accumulated:  $  14,403
         End of Accumulation Year:               5   years

             Renter's Savings Needed to Offset Advantage:.......$   2,371


  Press  [Alt] M  for MENU            Press  [Ctrl] [Break]  for READY


~~~~~~~~~~~~~~~~~~~~~~~~~~~~~~~~~~~~~~~~~~~~~~~~~~~~~~~~~~~~~~~~~~~~~~~~~~~~
```

III. SUMMARY OF RENT VS. BUY ANALYSIS
=======================================

The following findings are available from this analysis:

$$

     A potential homeowner is considering the purchase of a
home which costs $ 85,000 with a $ 75,000   mortgage and
equity $ 10,000 . The mortgage interest rate is   13.25
percent over a period of   30 years. The annual mort-
gage payment is $ 10,181 . In addition, if the home is
purchased, the buyer must also pay $ 2,000 in closing costs.

     The annual net housing outlays include $ 3,120 in oper-
ating expenses and the mortgage payment of $ 10,181 . Since
the total gross outlay is $ 13,301 , of which interest and
property taxes are tax deductible, the resulting tax savings
equals $ 4,108 , under the current tax law.

     If the house is owned   5   years and grows   6.00
percent per year, a future sales price of $ 113,749 will be
obtained. If selling expenses are $ 6,825 and the mortgage
balance owed is $ 73,414 , the net proceeds from the sale
will be $ 33,511 .

     If the house is not purchased, the downpayment and closing
costs will be saved. If this sum, $ 12,000 , is invested at a
before-tax rate of   15.00 percent and a tax rate of   35.00
percent, the savings will grow to $ 19,108 . Therefore, the
buyer's net advantage from homeownership is $ 14,403 .

     In order to compare the savings needed to offset the fin-
ancial advantages of homeowning, it is necessary to calculate
how much of the annual rental budget is required to be saved
and invested if the home is not purchased. In this case, this
amount would be $ 2,371 each year.

     Finally, the buyer has determined that the required rent
for an equivalent amount of housing and consumption as an
owner is about $ 600.00 per month. This analysis indicates
that the sum of $ 568.50 is available for monthly rent.

THEREFORE, THIS ANALYSIS INDICATES A   BUY DECISION: 1
THEREFORE, THIS ANALYSIS INDICATES A   RENT DECISION: 0

     -----(Computer returns 0 if FALSE, 1 if TRUE)-----

$$

Press [Alt] M for MENU   Press [Ctrl] [Break] for READY

RECORD OF INVESTMENT PORTFOLIO
(Template: lot304)

The final template in this chapter provides an investor the opportunity to keep track of and monitor changes in the investor's portfolio. This is really a book-keeping function, but by using Lotus 1-2-3 the investor can also use the information to monitor performance of each investment as well as the entire portfolio.

Principles.　　When an investment is purchased, a number of items are important for recordkeeping purposes. Some of these are required by the Internal Revenue Service, while others are needed in order to measure performance by the investor. Items such as date of purchase, purchase price, and current market value (as an estimate of what the property would bring if it were sold) are essential items to know for any investor. In addition, it is useful to analyze net operating income, debt service and the outstanding balance of each loan periodically and in conjunction with other information in order to see how each investment is performing and to identify the contribution of each investment to the investment portfolio.

Using the Template.　　This template enables the investor to keep track of up to 15 properties at a time. However, as shown in Table II, a number of other important aspects of the investment are also shown.

The user must input purchase price, annual net operating income (gross income minus expenses), annual debt service, the current outstanding mortgage balance, and an estimate of the current market value of the property. For recordkeeping purposes, only the purchase price, the date of purchase, and the name or number of the property would be required. The template is efficiently designed to enable the user to hop from one space to the next. Remember if you have only two properties and you are tired of stopping at each space, press "Ctrl-Break" to end the "string" and "Alt M" for the real estate menu. Then go to the next page and proceed as before.

The output shows a variety of interesting results. The "Overall Cap Rate" is defined as the annual net operating income divided by the current market value. (This is illustrated in detail in Chapter 10 in Template lot1001.) This rate is a basic rate of return used by many real estate appraisers, investors, and brokers. "BTCF" stands for "before-tax cash flow" and is equal to net operating income minus the debt service. (Before-tax cash flow is examined in detail in its own template in Chapter 8 in Template lot803.) "DCR" is the "debt coverage ratio." It is defined as the ratio of net operating income to debt service and is an important tool for lenders who are interested in mortgage security. (The debt coverage ratio is included in Chapter 10 in Template lot1002.)

The two final columns in this template show the amount of investor equity or worth in each project. This is the difference between the current market value and the outstanding mortgage. Also, the template provides the gain or loss in the project. This is calculated by taking the difference between the purchase price and the current market value. Note also that averages and totals are included for the entire portfolio and all calculations are made before any capital gains taxes.

The summary provides a thumbnail sketch of the investment portfolio including the total net operating income and debt service. In addition, the estimated market value of the portfolio is shown as well as the total of all purchases. Finally, the difference between the market value of the portfolio and the total mortgage balances represents the value of the equity. When this number becomes greater than one million, you have become one of a select group of real estate investors!

An Example.   In the example, note that each property is shown in the portfolio. Note also that the purchase price may be different than the current market value. In some cases (but hopefully, not too many!), the market value is less than the purchase price as in the North Adams property. On the other hand, Hilltop Plaza shows a sizeable gain in a short period of time. Also, note that some properties may not have any net operating income. In the case of raw land, the net operating income may be negative due to items such as real estate taxes, insurance, etc.)

In the summary of the portfolio, the cash flow is negative since the sum of the debt service requirements exceeds the sum of the net operating incomes for the projects. This means that the investor must provide a supplement to the portfolio each year in the amount of about $10,300. While this is unattractive to most investors, investments with negative cash flows might still be good investments based upon other characteristics.

Graphics.   The graph associated with this template is very nice and quite colorful (if you have the hardware). Each property is shown consecutively and comparisons can be made by property type. Clearly, graphics has the advantage over other presentations by displaying a large amount of information at one time. In this case, note the relative size of the negative before-tax cash flow for Palm Grove. The graph brings this to the investor's attention immediately! Also, as always, if you change the inputs, the output changes as well. The graph is just an elegant and colorful way of providing output.

Possible Modifications.   Certain changes are possible for this template. Investors with large portfolios may find the limit of fifteen properties too small. It would be simple to increase the number of properties in the template by expanding the size of the record. Beware that the menu must be changed as well. Do not venture into this area until you are experienced with using the generic Lotus 1-2-3 menus as well. In addition, others may wish to keep track of other values in addition to those included here. One of the advantages of

Lotus 1-2-3 is its size. This template, like most in this book, makes use of only eight standard sized columns. Lotus 1-2-3 contains 256 columns! For most investors, this provides an adequate amount of space for all of the variables they wish to record and monitor. (Don't worry if your portfolio is very large; there are 2048 rows in the Lotus 1-2-3 program! Believe it or not, some users find that they run out of space before they run out of memory!) Also, some investors may wish to do other financial calculations in addition to those provided in this template. Such investors are encouraged to review several of the templates in later chapters which have already been developed to accomplish this same purpose. Try to avoid doubling your efforts and happy investing!

EXAMPLE TEMPLATE 3.4
Record of investment portfolio.

```
lot304x                                        Real Estate Diskette #1
========================================================================
RECORD OF STATEMENTS PORTFOLIO        Copyright (C) Reston Pub. Co., 1985
========================================================================

~~~~~~~~~~~~~~~~~~~~~~~~~~~~~~~~~~~~~~~~~~~~~~~~~~~~~~~~~~~~~~~~~~~~~~~~~~~


                    ***   TABLE OF CONTENTS   ***
                          =================
              Table                                      Page
              -----                                      ----

      I.    INPUTS FOR INVESTMENT PORTFOLIO                1

     II.    OUTPUT OF INVESTMENT PORTFOLIO                 2

    III.    SUMMARY OF INVESTMENT PORTFOLIO                3


~~~~~~~~~~~~~~~~~~~~~~~~~~~~~~~~~~~~~~~~~~~~~~~~~~~~~~~~~~~~~~~~~~~~~~~~~~~
```

I. INPUTS FOR INVESTMENT PORTFOLIO
====================================

Date of Purchase	Name of Property	Purchase Price	Annual NOI	Annual Dt Ser	Outstand Mort Bal	Current Mkt Val
		($)	($)	($)	($)	($)
1-15-81	Rosebud Apts	500,000	55,000	49,600	385,700	525,000
2-1-81	The Home Office	125,000	20,000	17,020	105,600	140,000
4-1-81	5 East Main St	56,000	7,800	7,200	48,200	57,000
7-15-81	Pan Amer Apts	250,000	38,500	40,000	242,700	264,500
9-1-81	The Homestead	135,000	18,000	16,900	118,000	140,000
1-25-82	Southernview Apts	37,500	4,000	4,100	31,750	38,000
6-2-82	25 North Adams	76,900	6,900	7,550	69,200	75,000
7-30-82	Western Arms	175,000	21,900	25,000	162,550	190,000
12-20-82	Smith Offices	245,000	40,000	36,400	220,000	275,000
4-15-83	Broadway Towers	460,000	61,000	50,250	438,000	475,000
7-5-83	Eagle Apts	245,500	32,600	30,450	196,500	250,000
10-7-83	Hilltop Plaza	310,000	39,500	41,750	279,600	330,000
1-4-84	Royal Circle	189,500	22,000	19,800	181,900	190,000
5-18-84	Palm Grove	215,900	0	31,000	204,200	216,000
8-15-84	Three Oaks	136,700	16,000	16,500	129,450	136,000

Press [Alt] M for MENU   Press [Ctrl] [Break] for READY

~~~~~~

II. OUTPUT FOR INVESTMENT PORTFOLIO
======================================

Property Number	Overall Cap Rate	BTCF	DCR	Investor Equity	Est Gain (Loss)
		($)		($)	($)
1	11.00%	5,400	1.11%	139,300	25,000
2	16.00%	2,980	1.18%	34,400	15,000
3	13.93%	600	1.08%	8,800	1,000
4	15.40%	(1,500)	0.96%	21,800	14,500
5	13.33%	1,100	1.07%	22,000	5,000
6	10.67%	(100)	0.98%	6,250	500
7	8.97%	(650)	0.91%	5,800	(1,900)
8	12.51%	(3,100)	0.88%	27,450	15,000
9	16.33%	3,600	1.10%	55,000	30,000
10	13.26%	10,750	1.21%	37,000	15,000
11	13.28%	2,150	1.07%	53,500	4,500
12	12.74%	(2,250)	0.95%	50,400	20,000
13	11.61%	2,200	1.11%	8,100	500
14	0.00%	(31,000)	0.00%	11,800	100
15	11.70%	(500)	0.97%	6,550	(700)
	------	------	------	------	------
AVERAGES	12.05%	(688)	0.97%	32,543	9,567
TOTALS	----	(10,320)	----	488,150	143,500

Press [Alt] M for MENU   Press   [Ctrl] [Break] for READY

~~~~~~

```
            III. SUMMARY OF INVESTMENT PORTFOLIO
            ======================================

     This investment portfolio consists of the following:


     $$$$$$$$$$$$$$$$$$$$$$$$$$$$$$$$$$$$$$$$$$$$$$$$$$$$$$$$$$$

        Total number of properties:            15

        Total annual net operating income: $ 383,200
        Total annual debt service:         $ 393,520
                                           ---------
           ANNUAL CASH FLOW FROM PORTFOLIO..$ (10,320)


        Total estimated market value of
           investment portfolio:           $ 3301500
        Total purchase price of portfolio: $ 3158000

           ESTIMATED GAIN ON INVESTMENTS....$ 143,500


        Total estimated market value of
           investment portfolio:           $ 3301500
        Total outstanding mortgage balance:$ 2813350

           ESTIMATED VALUE OF EQUITY.......$ 488,150

     $$$$$$$$$$$$$$$$$$$$$$$$$$$$$$$$$$$$$$$$$$$$$$$$$$$$$$$$$$$


  Press  [Alt] M  for MENU           Press  [Ctrl] [Break]  for READY


~~~~~~~~~~~~~~~~~~~~~~~~~~~~~~~~~~~~~~~~~~~~~~~~~~~~~~~~~~~~~~~~~~~~
```

4 Residential Brokerage Applications

Overview

This chapter presents Lotus 1-2-3 templates useful for residential brokerage applications. There are three models presented here. These include a table which lists properties on the market, an estimate of cash required for a closing, and a closing statement. These applications are well-suited to Lotus 1-2-3 because they are important but tedious when done by hand. Lotus 1-2-3 enables the user to evaluate important data quickly and easily.

TABLE OF PROPERTIES FOR SALE
(Template: lot401)

Perhaps the most important piece of financial information in the residential real estate brokerage business is the current listing of properties "on the market." In most cities, this information is provided by a cooperative service, generally called a multi- or multiple-listing service. Periodically, typically each week or two weeks, a revised list of properties for sale is produced and distributed to members of the service. The listing may be quite extensive, especially in large cities, and contains much of the information salespeople and brokers need in order to effectively sell real estate.

Principles.   This template provides an opportunity to computerize properties which are for sale. In addition, some statistics are calculated to assist the salesperson or broker in understanding what is going on in the real estate market.

The template enables the user to enter up to 30 properties for sale at a given time. Several attributes have been included which generally appear in listings and advertisements. These include listing (asking) prices, number of rooms, number of bedrooms, number of bathrooms, building and lot sizes, the year the structure was built, property taxes, whether or not a garage or finished basement exists on the property, and others. The idea is that the user can keep track of houses for sale and watch trends as they develop in the market.

Using the Template.   Notice that this template differs in appearance from the others. Since it was useful to have many parameters included on the table, a large template was needed. In this case, each column has fewer spaces (seven instead of the usual nine) in order to get more information on the screen. (Note that Lotus 1-2-3 permits varying sizes for its columns if desired.) In addition, the example below was printed in "compressed print" (a regular feature of Lotus 1-2-3 and other spreadsheets to enable more information to be printed on each output page of hardcopy). Note that compressed print is automatically available to the user; the instructions are associated with the User Options selection of the menu. (Note also that if your printer does not support compressed print, the template will have to be printed in parts.)

In addition to the property number, there are 17 items included in this template. While most markets have more than 30 properties for sale at a given time, for manageability purposes the size of the template was limited to 30. It is suggested that the user segment the data into small areas in order to better analyze market conditions. This really means developing a set of these templates, perhaps with data for each neighborhood. It is also possible to expand the size of the template.

The Output Table reproduces the input values. (Note that labels, or non-numerical inputs, cannot be reproduced from one part of the template to another. Therefore, the property numbers are entered as "values" rather than as "labels.") Table II can then be used to find minimum, maximum, and average values. One can also use the results of this table to identify relationships between subsequent sales, listing characteristics, and market preferences. The reader is referred to Chapter 12 where statistical applications are presented.

Finally, the summary provides an accounting of the properties entered into the template, the highest and lowest price properties on the market, and average estimates for properties on the market. This is important since it is often difficult to judge what "typical" housing characteristics are available at any point in time. Lotus 1-2-3 can quickly provide this information.

An Example.   Note that in the example provided, there is a wide range of houses available for sale. There are also numerous special features associated with the houses as well as special types of financing, at least in some cases. While the highest priced house is selling for $125,000, the lowest priced house is asking for only $54,500. In this market, the average house is currently selling for almost $84,000. Note also that the average house has four bedrooms and two baths, built in 1966 with less than 13,000 square feet of land and more than 2,000 square feet of building space. The average property tax bill is about $860 per year and most houses have at least one fireplace.

Graphics.   Note that for this template, there are two graphs. These may be accessed through a third menu from the Graph option on the User Options menu. Note also that the user can move back to the preceding menu by pointing to "menu" each time. The first graph uses the stacked bar feature available with Lotus 1-2-3. This illustration places each amenity in comparison with the other properties. While it is misleading to conclude that each amenity may be added up to get the property for sale with the most features, the first graph illustrates how various properties compare to each other.

The other graph of this template plots the relationship between building size, lot size, and listing price. In effect, those properties which are listed for larger sums are not always the largest in this market; nor are they the properties with the largest lot sizes. Some are "outliers" while most fall within normal ranges. Graphs of this type are especially useful for statistical analysis, a topic discussed in some detail in Chapter 12.

Possible Modifications.   In addition to expanding the size of the template to accommodate large markets, experienced users may be able to build in other functions which would provide useful information. For example, there are several other variables which might help users understand the type of property available in the market. It would be interesting, for example, to identify the values of each of the main characteristics to buyers in the market. In other words, how important is a two-car garage in this market, or an extra room for a study? These and other questions require greater statistical methods than simply averages.

Also, it would be quite useful to monitor the average calculations over time as market conditions change. Thus, the user could modify this template (or build another one) to keep track of changes in the type of properties for sale and, especially, at what prices they sold. A particularly important item to keep would also be "time on the market." This would be relatively easy for Lotus 1-2-3 to do. Finally, really ambitious users could expand the input (and output) table, further enabling the inputting of all market characteristics of houses and other properties for sale. In this manner, an extensive data base may be developed. Lotus 1-2-3 contains data-base management capabilities. But perhaps more importantly, Lotus 1-2-3 can provide you with an on-line property search system, something that large brokerage firms are spending huge sums of money to have developed for them. With a bit of ingenuity and experience, Lotus 1-2-3 can provide the same service to you, with your own custom-designed preferences and needs!

EXAMPLE TEMPLATE 4.1
Table of properties for sale.

===
TABLE OF PROPERTIES FOR SALE   Copyright (C) Reston Pub. Co., 1985
===

```
*** TABLE  OF  CONTENTS ***
==============================
```

Table	Page
-----	----
I. INPUTS OF PROPERTIES FOR SALE	1
II. OUTPUT TABLE OF PROPERTIES FOR SALE	2
III. SUMMARY STATISTICS	3

```
I. INPUTS OF PROPERTIES FOR SALE
================================
```

Prop #	Area	LP	Style	#Rms	#Bed	#Bth	BS	LS	YrBlt	Taxes	Gar	Finish Base	Fire	Heat Sys	Spec Finan	Xtra Feat	List Brok
		($)								($)							
1003	NW	68000	Cp Cd	7.0	3.0	2.0	1,350	8,000	1959	876	1.0	0.0	1.0	Oil	Assump	Deck	Jones
1004	NE	75500	Sp Lvl	9.0	4.0	2.5	1,500	9,720	1968	900	2.0	1.0	1.0	Oil	No	Porch	Samps
1007	N	69500	Sp Lvl	8.0	4.0	2.5	1,600	12,000	1964	789	1.0	0.5	1.0	Elec	No	St Win	Benn
1008	NE	59900	2 Stor	8.0	4.0	1.5	1,952	9,840	1972	750	1.0	0.5	0.0	Elec	Yes	Refrig	Samps
1009	N	67500	Sp Lvl	8.0	4.0	2.0	1,850	14,369	1960	814	2.0	0.5	0.5	Oil	Assump	Landsc	More
1011	NW	87900	Tri Lvl	9.0	5.0	3.0	2,506	11,340	1977	970	2.0	1.0	2.0	Elec	No	WetBar	Jhnsn
1014	S	100000	2 Stor	6.0	3.0	1.5	2,227	20,091	1938	806	1.0	0.0	1.0	Oil	No	BeauLt	Jhnsn
1015	S	84900	Br&Alu	7.0	3.0	2.5	1,900	11,648	1980	780	2.0	0.0	1.0	Gas	Assump	New It	First
1019	NE	64900	Ranch	9.0	3.0	1.0	1,406	10,220	1965	669	1.0	1.0	1.0	Elec	Yes	Neigh	Samuls
1020	S	87500	Cp Cd	9.0	4.0	2.5	2,600	11,250	1947	713	1.0	0.5	1.0	Oil	No	NewFur	Benn
1025	NW	93500	Sp Lvl	10.0	5.0	2.5	2,042	9,500	1979	826	2.0	0.0	0.0	Gas	Yes	QualBt	Martin
1026	E	85000	Ranch	8.0	4.0	2.0	1,735	13,187	1977	726	2.0	0.0	0.0	Elec	Yes	SwimPl	Wllms

1028	E	80000	Ranch	10.0	4.0	2.0	2,775	11,780	1935	803	0.0	0.0	1.0 Oil	No	Range Martin
1029	NE	71900	Sp Lvl	8.0	3.0	2.0	2,286	9,000	1974	755	2.0	0.5	1.0 Elec	No	New Pt Samuls
1032	E	87900	Cp Cd	9.0	4.0	2.5	2,600	11,250	1947	913	1.0	0.0	1.0 Oil	Assump	NewFur Jhnsn
1033	S	89900	Colon	11.0	5.0	2.5	3,193	10,710	1968	879	2.0	0.5	2.0 Elec	Yes	Appl Benn
1038	W	54500	Cp Cd	7.0	3.0	1.0	1,369	9,050	1947	832	1.0	0.0	1.0 Oil	No	Rental Hamlet
1039	NW	99500	2 Stor	11.0	4.0	3.0	3,493	11,430	1966	1,040	2.0	0.0	1.0 Elec	Yes	Landsc Samps
1040	NE	124700	Colon	10.0	5.0	2.5	2,464	18,315	1975	980	2.0	1.0	2.0 Elec	No	Appl Benn
1041	NE	91900	Sp Lvl	8.0	4.0	2.5	2,200	12,750	1976	808	2.0	0.0	1.0 Elec	No	ExCond First
1043	E	84900	L-Shap	9.0	5.0	3.0	2,810	11,392	1968	1,136	2.0	0.0	0.0 Elec	Yes	Locat Wllms
1045	N	58900	Tri Lvl	9.0	4.0	1.5	1,850	15,000	1968	625	2.0	0.0	2.0 Elec	No	Landsc Jones
1046	E	84900	Colon	7.0	3.0	2.5	2,337	17,500	1977	801	2.0	0.0	1.0 Gas	No	Refrig Jhnsn
1049	S	67500	A-Frme	6.0	3.0	2.0	1,632	19,650	1976	738	0.0	0.0	1.0 Elec	Assump	2d Lot Martin
1050	NE	92900	2 Stor	8.0	4.0	2.5	2,081	12,000	1934	1,047	1.0	0.5	1.0 Oil	No	Landsc First
1052	NW	96500	2 Stor	9.0	4.0	2.5	1,941	17,500	1974	778	2.0	0.5	1.0 Oil	Yes	NewPrh Winn
1053	NW	91500	Sp Lvl	10.0	4.0	2.5	2,042	11,540	1979	899	2.0	0.0	0.0 Elec	No	QualBt Benn
1054	E	78900	Sp/Ran	7.0	3.0	2.5	2,184	13,200	1980	745	1.0	0.5	1.0 Gas	No	Nice Martin
1057	E	91900	Colon	10.0	4.0	2.5	2,108	17,677	1977	1,006	2.0	0.0	0.0 Gas	Assump	Appl Wllms
1059	NE	125000	Contem	9.0	5.0	3.5	2,090	18,700	1977	1,433	2.0	1.0	1.0 Elec	Yes	Lot Winn

Press [Alt] M for MENU   Press [Ctrl] [Break] for READY

# of Project	Prop #	LP	#Rms	#Bed	#Bth	BS	LS	YrBlt	Taxes	Gar	Finish Base	Fire
		($)							($)			
1	1003	68000	7.0	3.0	2.0	1,350	8,000	1,959	876	1.0	0.0	1.0
2	1004	75500	9.0	4.0	2.5	1,500	9,720	1,968	900	2.0	1.0	1.0
3	1007	69500	8.0	4.0	2.5	1,600	12,000	1,964	789	1.0	0.5	1.0
4	1008	59900	8.0	4.0	1.5	1,952	9,840	1,972	750	1.0	0.5	0.0
5	1009	67500	8.0	4.0	2.0	1,850	14,369	1,960	814	2.0	0.5	0.5
6	1011	87900	9.0	5.0	3.0	2,506	11,340	1,977	970	2.0	1.0	2.0
7	1014	100000	6.0	3.0	1.5	2,227	20,091	1,938	806	1.0	0.0	1.0
8	1015	84900	7.0	3.0	2.5	1,900	11,648	1,980	780	2.0	0.0	1.0
9	1019	64900	9.0	3.0	1.0	1,406	10,220	1,965	669	1.0	1.0	1.0
10	1020	87500	9.0	4.0	2.5	2,600	11,250	1,947	713	1.0	0.5	1.0
11	1025	93500	10.0	5.0	2.5	2,042	9,500	1,979	826	2.0	0.0	0.0
12	1026	85000	8.0	4.0	2.0	1,735	13,187	1,977	726	2.0	0.0	0.0
13	1028	80000	10.0	4.0	2.0	2,775	11,780	1,935	803	0.0	0.0	1.0
14	1029	71900	8.0	3.0	2.0	2,286	9,000	1,974	755	2.0	0.5	1.0
15	1032	87900	9.0	4.0	2.5	2,600	11,250	1,947	913	1.0	0.0	1.0
16	1033	89900	11.0	5.0	2.5	3,193	10,710	1,968	879	2.0	0.5	2.0
17	1038	54500	7.0	3.0	1.0	1,369	9,050	1,947	832	1.0	0.0	1.0
18	1039	99500	11.0	4.0	3.0	3,493	11,430	1,966	1,040	2.0	0.0	1.0
19	1040	124700	10.0	5.0	2.5	2,464	18,315	1,975	980	2.0	1.0	2.0
20	1041	91900	8.0	4.0	2.5	2,200	12,750	1,976	808	2.0	0.0	1.0
21	1043	84900	9.0	5.0	3.0	2,810	11,392	1,968	1,136	2.0	0.0	0.0
22	1045	58900	9.0	4.0	1.5	1,850	15,000	1,968	625	2.0	0.0	2.0
23	1046	84900	7.0	3.0	2.5	2,337	17,500	1,977	801	2.0	0.0	1.0
24	1049	67500	6.0	3.0	2.0	1,632	19,650	1,976	738	0.0	0.0	1.0
25	1050	92900	8.0	4.0	2.5	2,081	12,000	1,934	1,047	1.0	0.5	1.0
26	1052	96500	9.0	4.0	2.5	1,941	17,500	1,974	778	2.0	0.5	1.0
27	1053	91500	10.0	4.0	2.5	2,042	11,540	1,979	899	2.0	0.0	0.0
28	1054	78900	7.0	3.0	2.5	2,184	13,200	1,980	745	1.0	0.5	1.0
29	1057	91900	10.0	4.0	2.5	2,108	17,677	1,977	1,006	2.0	0.0	0.0
30	1059	125000	9.0	5.0	3.5	2,090	18,700	1,977	1,433	2.0	1.0	1.0
MINIMUM	1003	54500	6.0	3.0	1.0	1,350	8,000	1,934	625	0.0	0.0	0.0
MAXIMUM	1059	125000	11.0	5.0	3.5	3,493	20,091	1,980	1,433	2.0	1.0	2.0
AVERAGE	----	83910	8.53	3.90	2.28	2,137	12,987	1,966	861	1.53	0.32	0.92

Press [Alt] M for MENU   Press [Ctrl] [Break] for READY

```
                        III. SUMMARY STATISTICS
                        =======================


             The real estate market currently consists of the following listings:


    $$$$$$$$$$$$$$$$$$$$$$$$$$$$$$$$$$$$$$$$$$$$$$$$$$$$$$$$$$$$$$$$$$$$$

                  Number of Properties:              30

                  Lowest Priced Property:         $ 54500
                  Highest Priced Property:        $125000

             At this time, the average property selling for  $ 83910  is a:

                            9  Room House,

                       consisting of the following:

                        4  Bedrooms
                        2  Bathroom(s)
                    2,137  Square Feet of Living Area
                   12,987  Square Feet of Lot Size
                     1966  Year Built
                 $    861  Property Taxes
                      1.5  Garage(s)
                      0.3  Finished Basement(s)
                      0.9  Fireplace(s)


    $$$$$$$$$$$$$$$$$$$$$$$$$$$$$$$$$$$$$$$$$$$$$$$$$$$$$$$$$$$$$$$$$$$$$


        Press  [Alt] M  for MENU        Press  [Ctrl] [Break]  for READY
```

ESTIMATE OF CASH REQUIREMENT AT CLOSING
(Template: lot402)

One of the most important calculations is the amount of cash required prior to closing. This is important not only to real estate buyers (without a sufficient amount of cash at closing by the buyers, the deal cannot be made), but it is also important to sellers and brokers. Sellers do not want to own the property and are anxious to obtain the money in exchange. Brokers are anxious to complete the deal and receive the commission they have worked to earn.

Principles. There are several items which affect the amount of cash required at a real estate closing. These include the purchase price of the property, the amount of the mortgage, and several types of expenses. In addition, there may be more than one type of mortgage financing used and in some cases, more than one source of equity (cash). For example, the seller of the property may provide a portion of the debt financing. Or, parents might help first-time buyers by providing a supplement to their children's downpayment.

Also, financial institutions often establish escrow accounts for certain items to ensure that funds are available ahead of time. These items include mortgage insurance premiums, property insurance and taxes escrows, and other payments. In some cases, one or more mortgage payments must also be escrowed before the closing can proceed.

Using the Template. This template is fairly straightforward to use. In Table I, spaces are indicated to enable the user to input the relevant information. (Note that throughout this book, inputs tend to occur in Table I and outputs elsewhere. Also, whenever the template shows these symbols as arrows (">>>"), the user is frequently alerted to input data for the particular item.)

Note that in addition to the sales price, up to four mortgages are available. These might include the initial, or primary mortgage, typically with the financial institution, one or two second mortgages, either with financial institutions or with individuals, and "interest-only" loans. As will be explained in Chapter 7, interest-only loans differ from conventional mortgage financing since the interest-only loans do not systematically repay the principal of the loan. This is called "amortization" and is a characteristic of level-payment loans where the periodic payment is greater than the amount of interest owed to the lender each period. In this template, the user can explicitly evaluate most types of financing arrangements.

The downpayment is also required. If more than one type of equity is used, this can also be shown. Finally, numerous cash expenses are permitted, including monthly escrow requirements.

The output provides a check to see if the sum of the debt and equity financing is equal to the sales price. If not, the property cannot be purchased (and Lotus 1-2-3 provides an error message). Also, mortgage payments are calculated for each type of mortgage, including any interest-only financing. Typically, the first month's mortgage payment is paid at the time of closing. Note that Lotus 1-2-3 can solve for the correct mortgage payment without much difficulty. This calculation will be done several times throughout this book. Also, other cash requirements are shown.

At the end of the output, the total cash requirement for settlement with the seller is provided. This is the figure you need to worry about prior to closing. Note in the summary, two numbers result from this template: the total monthly cash requirement (principal, interest, and any escrow amounts, for example, mortgage insurance, property insurance, and property taxes) and the total cash requirement for settlement (downpayment and other equity, any charges or fees, and other personal property purchases, such as refrigerators, or washing machines from the seller at the time the real property is sold).

Graphics.   In this case, a pie chart is used to highlight the breakdown between the debt financing payments. Using these numbers, the debt service from the first mortgage requires 72.8 percent of the total debt service, while the interest-only loan is only 8.8 percent of the total. Lotus 1-2-3 automatically calculates and recalculates the percentages in a pie chart. The user does not need to request this information. For users with color, you will surely note that pie charts are in black-and-white. It would have been colorful to have been able to "paint" the pieces of the pie with various colors. (Actually, since only three colors are available with Lotus 1-2-3 graphics, this may be the reason this feature was omitted.)

Possible Modifications.   This template is narrow in objective and scope. Thus, it is less likely that users will want to expand the template very much, if at all. However, there may be items to be included which do not currently appear in the list of cash expenses, for example. In addition, users might wish to compare the amount of the closing costs between institutions or even sellers if such a comparison is likely to result in an advantage for the buyer.

This template also benefits from employing a horizontal window to see dramatically how cash required at closing is changed by the addition of certain closing costs and the increases in mortgage interest rates. The user can test how high interest rates and other costs can become before the buyer runs out of cash for closing!

EXAMPLE TEMPLATE 4.2
Estimate of cash requirement at closing.

```
lot402x                                     Real Estate Diskette #1
=================================================================
ESTIMATE OF CASH REQUIREMENT AT CLOSING
                              Copyright (C) Reston Pub. Co., 1985
=================================================================


~~~~~~~~~~~~~~~~~~~~~~~~~~~~~~~~~~~~~~~~~~~~~~~~~~~~~~~~~~~~~~~~~~~~

                 ***  TABLE OF CONTENTS  ***
                 ==================

           Table                                   Page
           -----                                   ----

     I.    INPUTS TO ESTIMATE CASH REQUIREMENT       1

     II.   OUTPUT OF ESTIMATED CASH REQUIREMENT
           FOR SETTLEMENT                             2

     III.  SUMMARY OF CASH REQUIREMENT                3



~~~~~~~~~~~~~~~~~~~~~~~~~~~~~~~~~~~~~~~~~~~~~~~~~~~~~~~~~~~~~~~~~~~~

                I. INPUTS TO ESTIMATE CASH REQUIREMENT
                =====================================

     Enter the following assumptions:

       TRANSACTION AND FINANCING DETAILS:

           Sales Price of Real Estate    >>>  $   75,000

           Debt Financing:

               Mortgage #1               >>>  $   50,000
                 Interest Rate           >>>      12.00  %
                 Term of Mortgage        >>>         30  years

               Mortgage #2               >>>  $   10,000
                 Interest Rate           >>>      13.50  %
                 Term of Mortgage        >>>         15  years

               Mortgage #3               >>>  $   _____
                 Interest Rate           >>>      _____  %
                 Term of Mortgage        >>>      _____  years

               Interest-Only Loans       >>>  $    5,000
                 Interest Rate           >>>      15.00  %
                 Term                    >>>          5  years
```

```
          Equity Financing:

              Downpayment                  >>>  $   10,000

              Other Equity Sources         >>>  $   _____


      ESTIMATED CASH EXPENSES FROM PURCHASE:

              Loan Origination Fee         >>>  $   _____
              Mortgage Placement Fee       >>>  $ 1,500.0
              Title Fee                    >>>  $   265.0
              Title Insurance              >>>  $   _____
              Appraisal Fee                >>>  $    50.0
              Credit Report                >>>  $    25.0
              Escrow Fee                   >>>  $   _____
              Legal Fees                   >>>  $   100.0
              Mortgage Recording Fee       >>>  $     8.5
              Deed Recording Fee           >>>  $     8.5
              Release Fees                 >>>  $   _____
              Notary Fee                   >>>  $   _____
              Survey Fee                   >>>  $   _____
              Inspection Fee               >>>  $    35.0
              Document Preparation Fee     >>>  $   _____
              Transfer Tax                 >>>  $   750.0
              Other Taxes                  >>>  $   _____
              Property Insurance (pro-rated) >>> $   180.0
              Property Tax (pro-rated)     >>>  $   700.0
              Interest on Loan (pro-rated) >>>  $   _____
              Other Prorates               >>>  $   _____
              Fuel Oil Reimbursement       >>>  $   300.0
              Other Reimbursements         >>>  $   _____
              Other Expenses               >>>  $   _____
              Sales Price of Seller's
                 Personal Property         >>>  $ 1,000.0

      ESTIMATED MONTHLY CHARGES:

              Mortgage Insurance Premium   >>>  $   _____
              Property Insurance           >>>  $    15.0
              Property Taxes               >>>  $    58.3
              Other Escrow Payments        >>>  $   _____


  Press  [Alt] M  for MENU          Press  [Ctrl] [Break]  for READY
```

~~~~~~

```
    II. OUTPUT OF ESTIMATED CASH REQUIREMENT FOR SETTLEMENT
    =========================================================

    SALES PRICE AND FINANCING DETAILS

            Sales Price      $  75,000    (if ERROR, check inputs)

            Debt Financing   $  65,000    (if ERROR, check inputs)
            Equity Financing $  10,000    (if ERROR, check inputs)


    CASH REQUIREMENT EACH MONTH

            Monthly Mort. Pay. #1    $   514.31
            Monthly Mort. Pay. #2    $   129.83
            Monthly Mort. Pay. #3    $     0.00
            Monthly Int-Only Pay     $    62.50

              Total Financing Payments.........$  706.64

            Mortgage Insur. Premium  $     0.00
            Monthly Prop. Insurance  $    15.00
            Monthly Prop. Taxes      $    58.33
            Monthly Escrow Payments  $     0.00

              Total Insur. and Taxes...........$   73.33

              ESTIMATED TOTAL MONTHLY CASH
              REQUIREMENT...............................$  779.97


    CASH REQUIREMENT AT CLOSING

            Downpayment in Cash      $  10,000
            Other Equity in Cash     $       0

              Total Equity....................$  10,000

            Financing Charges        $ 1,500.0
            Title Charges            $   265.0
            Fees                     $   227.0
            Taxes                    $   750.0
            Prorates                 $   880.0
            Seller's Reimbursements  $   300.0
            Other Expenses           $     0.0

              Total Charges and Fees..........$   3,922

            Seller's Personal Prop.  $ 1,000.0

              Total Personal Prop. Purchases...$   1,000

              ESTIMATED TOTAL CASH REQUIREMENT
              FOR SETTLEMENT...........................$  14,922


 Press  [Alt] M  for MENU          Press  [Ctrl] [Break]  for READY
```

```
            III. SUMMARY OF CASH REQUIREMENT
            ==================================

      Based upon the Estimated Cash Requirement for Settlement,
                the following summary can be made:


$$$$$$$$$$$$$$$$$$$$$$$$$$$$$$$$$$$$$$$$$$$$$$$$$$$$$$$$$$$$$

           Estimated Monthly Payment:         $   779.97

           Estimated Total Cash Requirement
           for Settlement:                    $    14,922

$$$$$$$$$$$$$$$$$$$$$$$$$$$$$$$$$$$$$$$$$$$$$$$$$$$$$$$$$$$$$


 Press  [Alt] M  for MENU          Press  [Ctrl] [Break]  for READY


~~~~~~~~~~~~~~~~~~~~~~~~~~~~~~~~~~~~~~~~~~~~~~~~~~~~~~~~~~~~~~~~~~~~~~~
```

HUD SETTLEMENT STATEMENT
(Template: lot403)

This is the most formal template in the book. It was developed as a direct computerization of the standard form used by federally insured savings and loan associations and other institutions to record the flows of funds between buyer, seller, and third parties at the time of closing. This template permits the user to enter the relevant data and have Lotus 1-2-3 calculate the closing statement. It is perhaps the best example of the use of Lotus 1-2-3 as a form generator.

Principles. The closing statement used here is based directly on the form advocated by the U.S. Department of Housing and Urban Development. It is Document OMB No. 63-R-1501 and is the standard instrument used for this purpose in the industry. It is quite extensive and requires a considerable amount of memory on the computer. (Some others, however, later in the book, require even more!) In its present form, it is considerably user-friendly and almost foolproof to use. Experienced real estate purchasers may know that financial institutions hire several clerks to complete these statements by hand. Now, Lotus 1-2-3 enables the completion of this statement much more quickly and accurately.

Using the Template. The HUD document provides for separate columns for buyers and sellers. Each line is numbered and each series of numbers corresponds to the category of the item. For example, series 100 provides space for the amounts due from the borrower; series 400 provides space for the amounts due from the seller.

This template is developed in two pages on Lotus 1-2-3 just as in the actual document. Note that the Page 2 of the document results in inputs which are needed for Page 1. There are two of these inputs: one for the buyer (Line 103) and the other for the seller (Line 502). Since the computer must obtain these inputs from Page 2 before it can complete Page 1 (in technical computerese, this is called "forward referencing"), earlier spreadsheets had difficulty with this problem. However, Lotus 1-2-3 handles this problem easily and quickly when making the calculations.

As in real market transactions, most closings do not use every item in the document. Thus, a Lotus 1-2-3 user should put inputs into only those items which apply; the computer will place zeros in all other items. Finally, note that the Lotus 1-2-3 template is designed so the computer will calculate as much as possible. (This is the general rule. The computer can calculate much faster and better than the individual. The individual needs to work on inputting accurate information without worrying about the calculations. The computer also does things like try to keep you from entering data "off the lines". It does this by "protecting" the cells. This is evidenced by the green or dark shade on monochrome monitors for "unprotected" cells. Thus, the computer refuses to accept data in the wrong places!)

As an example of the underlying complexity of the computer's instructions, note that on Page 2, Line 801 shows the loan origination fee. This is frequently stated in terms of percentage points on the loan. The user need not calculate the dollar amount; only the number of points is required. Lotus 1-2-3 will provide the calculation. Similarly, insurance inputs may be per day or per month and the template will provide the appropriate dollar amounts.

Graphics. The graph for this template compares various categories for buyer and seller. In this case, while the purchase price is the same, the closing costs are different. The seller pays more settlement charges than the buyer.

Possible Modifications. Since this template is a reproduction of a formal document which is used every day in practice, it would be ill-advised to suggest changing the document in any way. This is especially true in this case since there are two pages of inputs and outputs. This is unusual compared to other templates in this set. Most have separate input and output tables.

In this case, as with many others, the use of a window to see the effects of changes in closing costs on cash required at closing may be helpful. In addition, another feature of Lotus 1-2-3 might also be used with this template. Lotus 1-2-3, like other spreadsheets has a feature called "titles". This command enables the user to mark a horizontal, vertical, or both lines in the template under which the template will scroll. In this case, it is useful to create a horizontal title when entering the data to retain the borrower and seller headings on the columns. This facilitates easy data entry and avoids the problem of keeping the column headings in your own memory. If you wish to use the title command, learn how to use it and experiment. Be careful not to destroy the original template, however. But have fun in current memory. And one more thing, Lotus 1-2-3 tries to help when it can—just give it a chance!

EXAMPLE TEMPLATE 4.3
HUD settlement statement.

```
lot403x                                      Real Estate Diskette #1
=====================================================================
HUD SETTLEMENT STATEMENT          Copyright (C) Reston Pub. Co., 1985
=====================================================================

~~~~~~~~~~~~~~~~~~~~~~~~~~~~~~~~~~~~~~~~~~~~~~~~~~~~~~~~~~~~~~~~~~~~~~~~

                  ***   TABLE OF CONTENTS   ***
                      ==================
            Table                                   Page
            -----                                   ----

     I.   INPUTS/OUTPUT FOR SETTLEMENT STATEMENT
                   (PAGE 1)                           1

     II.  INPUTS/OUTPUT FOR SETTLEMENT STATEMENT
                   (PAGE 2)                           2


~~~~~~~~~~~~~~~~~~~~~~~~~~~~~~~~~~~~~~~~~~~~~~~~~~~~~~~~~~~~~~~~~~~~~~~~

            I. INPUTS/OUTPUT FOR SETTLEMENT STATEMENT
            =========================================
                         (PAGE 1)

   This template is based upon the document: OMB No. 63-R-1501

        U.S. DEPARTMENT OF HOUSING AND URBAN DEVELOPMENT

                   SETTLEMENT STATEMENT




    --------------------------------------------------------------

                                            Borrower    Seller
     SUMMARY OF BORROWER'S TRANSACTION

        100 GROSS AMOUNT DUE FROM BORROWER:

        101 Contract sales price          >>>    $   57,500
        102 Personal property             >>>    $    1,500
        103 Settlement charges to borrower.. >>>  $    1,763
        104 _____ >>>  $    -----
        105 _____ >>>  $    -----
```

```
ADJUSTMENTS FOR ITEMS PAID BY SELLER
IN ADVANCE

    106 City/town taxes        to        >>>   $   _____
    107 County taxes           to        >>>   $   575.78
    108 Assessments            to        >>>   $   _____
    109 _____    >>>   $   _____
    110 _____    >>>   $   _____
    111 _____    >>>   $   _____
    112 _____    >>>   $   _____

    120 GROSS AMOUNT DUE FROM BORROWER.........$   61,339

    200 AMOUNTS PAID BY OR IN BEHALF OF BORROWER:

    201 Deposit or earnest money          >>>   $    1,000
    202 Principal amount of new loan(s)   >>>   $   50,000
    203 Existing loan(s) taken subj. to   >>>   $   _____
    204 _____    >>>   $   _____
    205 _____    >>>   $   _____
    206 _____    >>>   $   _____
    207 _____    >>>   $   _____
    208 _____    >>>   $   _____
    209 _____    >>>   $   _____

ADJUSTMENTS FOR ITEMS UNPAID BY SELLER

    210 City/town taxes        to        >>>   $   _____
    211 County taxes           to        >>>   $   _____
    212 Assessments            to        >>>   $   _____
    213 _____    >>>   $   _____
    214 _____    >>>   $   _____
    215 _____    >>>   $   _____
    216 _____    >>>   $   _____
    217 _____    >>>   $   _____
    218 _____    >>>   $   _____
    219 _____    >>>   $   _____

    220 TOTAL PAID BY/FOR BORROWER...... >>>   $   51,000

    300 CASH AT SETTLEMENT FROM/TO BORROWER

    301 Gross amount due from borrower..........$   61,339
    302 Less amounts paid by/for borrower.......$   51,000

    303 CASH FROM (TO) BORROWER.................$   10,339


SUMMARY OF SELLER'S TRANSACTION

    400 GROSS AMOUNT DUE FROM SELLER:

    401 Contract sales price              >>>   $        57,500
    402 Personal property                 >>>   $         1,500
    403 _____    >>>   $        _____
    404 _____    >>>   $        _____
    405 _____    >>>   $        _____
```

```
ADJUSTMENTS FOR ITEMS PAID BY SELLER
IN ADVANCE

    406 City/town taxes        to        >>>    $         0.00
    407 County taxes           to        >>>    $       575.78
    408 Assessments            to        >>>    $         0.00
    409 _____  >>>    $         0.00
    410 _____  >>>    $         0.00
    411 _____  >>>    $         0.00
    412 _____  >>>    $         0.00

    420 GROSS AMOUNT DUE TO SELLER..............$      59,576

    500 REDUCTIONS IN AMOUNT DUE TO SELLER:

    501 Excess deposit                   >>>    $      _____
    502 Settlement charges to seller.... >>>    $       4,308
    503 Existing loan(s) taken subj. to  >>>    $         0.00
    504 Payoff of first mortgage loan    >>>    $      14,269
    505 Payoff of second mortgage loan   >>>    $      _____
    506 (Earnest Money)       _____  >>>    $       1,000
    507 _____  >>>    $      _____
    508 _____  >>>    $      _____
    509 _____  >>>    $      _____

ADJUSTMENTS FOR ITEMS UNPAID BY SELLER

    510 City/town taxes        to        >>>    $         0.00
    511 County taxes           to        >>>    $         0.00
    512 Assessments            to        >>>    $         0.00
    513 _____  >>>    $         0.00
    514 _____  >>>    $         0.00
    515 _____  >>>    $         0.00
    516 _____  >>>    $         0.00
    517 _____  >>>    $         0.00
    518 _____  >>>    $         0.00
    519 _____  >>>    $         0.00

    520 TOTAL REDUCTION AMOUNT DUE
        SELLER......................... >>>    $      19,577

    600 CASH AT SETTLEMENT TO/FROM SELLER

    601 Gross amount due to seller..............$      59,576
    602 Less reductions in amount due seller....$      19,577

    603 CASH TO (FROM) SELLER...................$      39,998
_____


Press  [Alt] M  for MENU        Press  [Ctrl] [Break]  for READY

~~~~~~~~~~~~~~~~~~~~~~~~~~~~~~~~~~~~~~~~~~~~~~~~~~~~~~~~~~~~~~~~~~~~~~~~~~
```

```
                II. INPUTS/OUTPUT FOR SETTLEMENT STATEMENT
                ===========================================
                              (PAGE 2)

        This template is based upon the document: OMB No. 63-R-1501

            U.S. DEPARTMENT OF HOUSING AND URBAN DEVELOPMENT

                        SETTLEMENT STATEMENT



    ----------------------------------------------------------------------


                                           Borrower    Seller
        SETTLEMENT CHARGES

           700  TOTAL SALES/BROKER'S COMMISSION
                based on price:     $  57,500
                commission rate:       7.00  %

           Division of Commission as follows:
           701 $ _____  to  _____
           702 $ _____  to  _____
           703 Commission paid at Settlement  >>>  $  _____     4,025
           704 _____  >>>  $  _____     _____

           800  ITEMS PAYABLE IN CONNECTION WITH LOAN

           801 Loan Orig. Fee     2.00  %      >>>  $1,000.00   _____
           802 Loan Discount      ____  %      >>>  $   0.00    _____
           803 Appraisal Report        to      >>>  $  50.00    _____
           804 Credit Report           to      >>>  $  25.00    _____
           805 Lender's Inspection Fee          >>>  $  _____    _____
           806 Mortgage Insur. Application Fee  >>>  $  _____    _____
           807 Assumption Fee                   >>>  $  _____    _____
           808 _____  >>>  $  _____    _____
           809 _____  >>>  $  _____    _____
           810 _____  >>>  $  _____    _____
           811 _____  >>>  $  _____    _____

           900  ITEMS REQUIRED BY LENDER TO BE PAID IN ADVANCE

           901 Interest from Jan 20      to   Feb 1    :
                No. of days:       12
                $    19.18   per day            >>>  $  230.16   _____
           902 Mortgage Insurance Premium:
                For   12.00   months
                To _____ :          >>>  $  195.00   _____
           903 Hazard Insurance Premium:
                For  _____   years
                To _____ :          >>>  $  _____    _____
           904 _____  >>>  $  _____    _____
           905 _____  >>>  $  _____    _____
```

```
1000  RESERVES DEPOSITED WITH LENDER

1001  Hazard Insurance:
              _____       months
      $  _____            per month      >>>    $    0.00
1002  Mortgage Insurance:
              _____       months
      $  _____            per month      >>>    $    0.00
1003  City property taxes:
              _____       months
      $  _____            per month      >>>    $    0.00
1004  County property taxes:
              _____       months
      $  _____            per month      >>>    $    0.00
1005  Annual assessments:
              _____       months
      $  _____            per month      >>>    $    0.00
1006  _____
              _____       months
      $  _____            per month      >>>    $    0.00
1007  _____
              _____       months
      $  _____            per month      >>>    $    0.00
1008  _____
              _____       months
      $  _____            per month      >>>    $    0.00

1100  TITLE CHARGES

1101  Settlement or closing fee        >>>    $   _____      _____
1102  Abstract or title search         >>>    $   _____      _____
1103  Title examination                >>>    $   _____      _____
1104  Title insurance binder           >>>    $   _____      _____
1105  Document preparation             >>>    $   _____      _____
1106  Notary fees                      >>>    $   _____      _____
1107  Attorney's fees                  >>>    $   75.00      _____

1108  Title insurance                  >>>    $  131.00    262.00

1109  Lender's coverage    $   50,000
1110  Owner's coverage     $   57,500
1111  _____  >>>   $   _____      _____
1112  _____  >>>   $   _____      _____
1113  _____  >>>   $   _____      _____

1200  GOVERNMENT RECORDING AND TRANSFER CHARGES

1201  Recording Fees:
      Deed        $    4.75
      Mortgage    $   17.50
      Releases    $   21.00
                                        >>>   $   22.25     21.00
1202  City/county tax/stamps:
      Deed        $   _____
      Mortgage    $   _____
                                        >>>   $   _____      _____
```

```
      1203 State tax/stamps:
           Deed        $    _____
           Mortgage    $    _____

                                        >>>    $   _____      _____
      1204 _____   >>>  $   _____      _____
      1205 _____   >>>  $   _____      _____

      1300 ADDITIONAL SETTLEMENT CHARGES

      1301 Survey                        >>>    $   _____      _____
      1302 Pest inspection               >>>    $   35.00      _____
      1303 _____   >>>  $   _____      _____
      1304 _____   >>>  $   _____      _____
      1305 _____   >>>  $   _____      _____

      1400 TOTAL SETTLEMENT CHARGES...............$   1,763      4,308
      _____


      Press  [Alt] M  for MENU          Press  [Ctrl] [Break]  for READY
```

5 Compound Interest Calculators

Overview

In this chapter, a number of financial tables are developed. All of the tables deal with the calculation of future or present values. In some cases, the question to be answered deals with calculating the value of a single sum in the future or the present. In other cases, a future or present value is sought from a given set of periodic payments. Finally, in the remaining cases, other factors are sought. In any of these problems, given three of the values, the remaining variable can be solved for.

When these and other financial calculations are typically performed by hand, the analyst solves for the answer with a given interest rate and a given period of time. However, since Lotus 1-2-3 is much more powerful than even a hand calculator, it is only a bit more difficult to calculate a series of solutions for a range of interest rates and time periods. Therefore, for the six types of calculations in this chapter, each equation generates a set of answers. The result produces a table of output for each function. Therefore, the term *table generator* has been given to each of these templates.

FUTURE VALUE TABLE GENERATOR
(Template: lot501)

If a saver has a sum of money today, how large will the sum grow if the saver earns a rate of interest over a period of time? This is the type of question this template has been designed to answer. In addition, the template will automatically show how large the sum will become for different interest rates and longer periods of time.

Principles.   The future value of a single sum is best viewed as an accumulation of interest earned each year at a certain rate of interest and the initial sum put on deposit at the beginning of the savings period. However, it is not correct to simply multiply the interest rate times the initial sum and then multiply by the number of years on deposit. (This is sometimes called "simple interest".) It is a poor measure of how much a saver can accumulate because it does not count any interest which would be earned as a result of leaving the previously earned interest in the account. In effect, if the first year's interest is left to earn its own interest, we would want the "interest on the interest" to be included when we estimate what the future sum would be. The method which does this is called "compound interest."

Figure 5-1 displays the cash inflows and outflows for future value calculations. Note that the future value is directly related to the time and interest

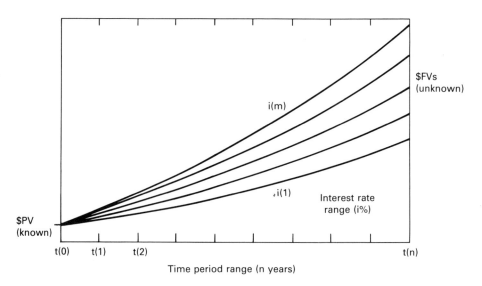

FIGURE 5-1
Future values of initial sum.

rate. As shown in Figure 5-1, the longer the time period, the greater the future value. In addition, the higher the interest rate, the greater the future value.

An attractive attribute of the compound interest formula is the "interest on the interest" feature and as a result, it is preferred overwhelmingly when making loans, investments, and other financial contracts. In addition, the measure of the rate of return from the investment (sometimes called *yield*) will not vary with the length of the investment period when compound interest is used. If simple interest was used, this would not be the case.

All of the financial calculations in this book make use of compound rather than simple interest. In the case of this template, future values are calculated assuming compound interest.

Using the Template.   The template is easy to use and provides a wealth of information. The user is required to input the initial sum (for example, the amount the saver has today on deposit). In addition, the user can decide the interest rate range and the time period range. If only one interest rate and/ or time period is needed, only those should be input. Thus, the user has the option to generate a variety of tables: from a single number to a large table with up to seven different interest rates and up to 15 different years. Note also that the model automatically adds 2.5 percentage points to the initial input up to the limit placed on the model by the user. Similarly, the model adds five-year increments to the initial future year input by the user. Thus, the template is limited to a span of 15 percentage points and 70 years. For most types of analysis, this will be more than satisfactory.

Of course, the user can quickly regenerate a new table by changing one or more of the inputs. Try it; this is when Lotus 1-2-3 performs at its best. Watch the numbers change before your very eyes.

The output table is shown in Table II. It provides a repeat of the inputs and automatically sets up the output table for the factors you have requested. Note that if the table you have requested is smaller than the available space, "NA" is inserted by the computer.

This template generates a future value table for any single sum. In financial books, if a future value table is provided, it typically is designed for $1.00. When the user finds the appropriate factor, the initial sum is multiplied by the tabled factor to arrive at the answer. Doing the same task using Lotus 1-2-3, the user can automatically multiply the initial sum by all of the factors, internally, every time, without error. This is the power of Lotus 1-2-3! You are now free from the printed tables!

Two caveats are in order. This template, like most of those in this chapter, performs a bit slower than most of the others in this book. The reason for this is that there are so many calculations to be done to generate a full table. Lotus 1-2-3 is up to six times faster than other spreadsheets. However, if, for some applications, speed becomes a problem, limit the ranges of interest rates or time periods. The computer works faster when there are fewer calculations to be performed. Also, if the values become greater than the space allowed in each cell, a greater than sign is shown in the cell (" ********* "). This is more annoying than a problem. It makes the output less attractive, but it does not alter the calculations. Even though the number is larger than can be displayed, the precise number is stored in the computer and used in any subsequent calculation. Therefore, one solution is to reduce the size of initial sum by for example, 10, or 100, or 1,000 in order to see the precise future value. Another might be to increase the column width to accommodate large numbers.

An Example.   In the example, a future value table is calculated for an initial deposit of $10.00 with an interest rate range from 5 to 15 percent, for a period from 5 to 70 years. Note that these are the only required inputs. The table shows interest rates at 5, 7.5, 10, 12.5, and 15 percent for every five years from 5 to 70, as requested. In each cell, the future value of $10.00 is shown.

Graphics.   There are a special set of graphics throughout Chapter 5. For each template, three graphs are available. This also means that a separate graphics menu awaits the user. The three graphs divide the data sets into two parts. The first three sets of factors are shown in the first graph; the last three sets in the second graph. (Lotus 1-2-3 only permits a maximum of six data sets per graph.) Finally, the third graph combines all data sets in the template, to the constrained maximum of six.

Note that if a very wide range of interest rates are chosen, there may be seven sets of data in this template. In such a case, only the first six will be used in generating the graphs. Note also in Appendix B, the first two graphs for each template in this chapter are smaller in size and shape; this is because they have been printed by the Lotus PrintGraph program this way. The third and comprehensive graph is full size throughout the chapter.

The templates in this chapter are well-suited for graphics. In this case, note that the longer the period and the higher the interest rate, the greater the future value. Note also that, due to compound interest, the future sum grows at a geometric rate (the functions are curved) so "interest is earned on the interest."

Possible Modifications.   Experienced users may wish to modify the formulas for narrower ranges of interest rates or years. Lotus 1-2-3 will generally accommodate all reasonable requests. For example, if a user wanted to see the difference between very small interest rates over long periods of time, it would be relatively easy to modify the formulas from the 2.5 percentage point increments to something smaller, say 0.1 percentage points. However, you might want to rename that template rather than revise the existing one to ensure that the one discussed in the book is always available. Remember also to remove the protection device if you seek to make changes.

This template is also designed for annual compounding only. Some others in later chapters deal with compounding at various periods, (e.g., monthly compounding). If the user wanted to compound other than annually, the appropriate adjustments could be made. However, do not try this, unless you are very familiar with the formulas used to calculate these numbers!

EXAMPLE TEMPLATE 5.1
Future value table generator.

```
lot501x                                    Real Estate Diskette #1
=================================================================
FUTURE VALUE TABLE GENERATOR      Copyright (C) Reston Pub. Co., 1985
=================================================================

~~~~~~~~~~~~~~~~~~~~~~~~~~~~~~~~~~~~~~~~~~~~~~~~~~~~~~~~~~~~~~~~~~~~~

                 ***  TABLE OF CONTENTS  ***
                      ==================
              Table                             Page
              -----                             ----

    I.   INPUT ASSUMPTIONS                        1

   II.   OUTPUT TABLE OF FUTURE VALUES            2


~~~~~~~~~~~~~~~~~~~~~~~~~~~~~~~~~~~~~~~~~~~~~~~~~~~~~~~~~~~~~~~~~~~~~

                     I. INPUT ASSUMPTIONS
                     ====================

   Enter the following assumptions:


       Initial Sum (PV)                >>>    $   10.00

       Interest Rate Range [i(1)...i(m)]

               From i(1)               >>>       5.00   %
                 To i(m)               >>>      15.00   %

       Time Period Range [t(1)...t(n)]

               From t(1)               >>>          5   years
                 To t(n)               >>>         70   years

 Press  [Alt] M  for MENU         Press  [Ctrl] [Break]  for READY


~~~~~~~~~~~~~~~~~~~~~~~~~~~~~~~~~~~~~~~~~~~~~~~~~~~~~~~~~~~~~~~~~~~~~
```

II. OUTPUT TABLE OF FUTURE VALUES
==

For any single sum,

if the PV is: $ 10.00 ,

if the [i(1)...i(m)] is: 5.00   %   to   15.00   % ,

if the [t(1)...t(n)] is: 5   yrs to   70   yrs ,

the Future Value Table is provided as follows:

$$$

Interest Rates

Years	5.00	7.50	10.00	12.50	15.00	NA	NA
5	12.76	14.36	16.11	18.02	20.11	NA	NA
10	16.29	20.61	25.94	32.47	40.46	NA	NA
15	20.79	29.59	41.77	58.52	81.37	NA	NA
20	26.53	42.48	67.27	105.45	163.67	NA	NA
25	33.86	60.98	108.35	190.03	329.19	NA	NA
30	43.22	87.55	174.49	342.43	662.12	NA	NA
35	55.16	125.69	281.02	617.08	1331.76	NA	NA
40	70.40	180.44	452.59	1111.99	2678.64	NA	NA
45	89.85	259.05	728.90	2003.84	5387.69	NA	NA
50	114.67	371.90	1173.91	3610.99	10836.57	NA	NA
55	146.36	533.91	1890.59	6507.12	21796.22	NA	NA
60	186.79	766.49	3044.82	11726.04	43839.99	NA	NA
65	238.40	1100.40	4903.71	21130.70	88177.87	NA	NA
70	304.26	1579.77	7897.47	38078.21	********	NA	NA
NA	NA	NA	NA	NA	NA	NA	NA

$$$

Press [Alt] M for MENU   Press [Ctrl] [Break] for READY

~~~~~~

PRESENT VALUE TABLE GENERATOR
(Template: lot502)

This template is very similar to the previous one: the difference is that a present value is sought, given a future sum. Previously, the future value was the unknown and the present sum was known. For example, suppose you are lucky enough to have a million dollar inheritance available for you at your 35th birthday! However, if you are only 20 years old, you cannot use the money for an additional 15 years. This template will help you calculate how much the inheritance is worth to you *today*.

Principles.   In effect, you need to find out how much money you would need to place in an investment earning a given interest rate to obtain one million dollars in precisely, in this case, 15 years. Formally, the question may be phrased, what is the present value of a known future sum?

Figure 5-2 presents a picture of the concept of present value calculations. Note that the present values are inversely related to the size of the discount rate. This means that as the discount rate increases, the present value of the future sum falls. The reason is because as the discount rate increases, the present value is lowered since it is more costly to "wait for the future to become the present."

It is not coincidental that this template is closely related to the previous one. In fact, relating present and future values is easy since these two relationships are *reciprocal* to one another. This means that when finding the

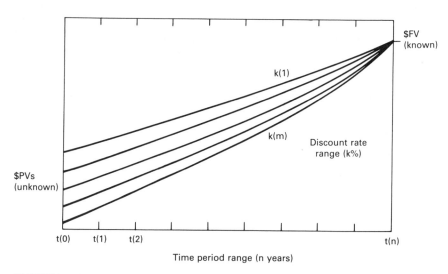

FIGURE 5-2
Present values of future sum.

future value from a present sum, the analyst is "compounding"; when the reverse situation occurs and the analyst seeks a present value from a future sum, the process is called "discounting." These two relationships are the converse of each other. (In mathematical terms, if one has the factor for one, by taking the reciprocal of the factor, the other table's factor is obtained. Test this for yourself!)

Using the Template.   Notice that the format of this template is identical to the previous one: the user is required to put in the "future" sum (or $1.00 for a "generic" table), the discount rate range, and the time period range. The computer and Lotus 1-2-3 do the rest!

Notice that the numbers get smaller the larger the discount rate and the farther the period in the future. Don't get confused; you are calculating present values. The model presumes that the future sum will be in each or any of the future periods. Thus, if you expect to receive $10.00 in 60 years, using a discount rate of 7.5 percent, it is worth only $.13 today. (As a check, test what the future value of 13.04644 cents will be compounding at 7.5 percent for 60 years. Right? It is exactly $10.00!)

An Example.   The example uses the same numbers as the previous table except the initial sum is now presumed to be the future sum. See how present value factors are smaller than the present value amounts. That is because the saver must wait to receive the future sum and this lowers the amount in present value terms.

Graphics.   These graphs show higher values in near years. This is because the sooner the future payoff period, the greater the value. Note that these curves also reflect compound interest.

Possible Modifications.   As before, in special cases, analysts may wish to modify the parameters on the scope of the table. This can easily be done once the user becomes familiar with Lotus 1-2-3, the template system, and the present value formula.

EXAMPLE TEMPLATE 5.2
Present value table generator.

```
lot502x                                       Real Estate Diskette #1
=====================================================================
PRESENT VALUE TABLE GENERATOR       Copyright (C) Reston Pub. Co., 1985
=====================================================================

~~~~~~~~~~~~~~~~~~~~~~~~~~~~~~~~~~~~~~~~~~~~~~~~~~~~~~~~~~~~~~~~~~~~~~~~~


                   ***  TABLE OF CONTENTS  ***
                        ==================
              Table                                   Page
              -----                                   ----

     I.   INPUT ASSUMPTIONS                              1

     II.  OUTPUT TABLE OF FUTURE VALUES                  2


~~~~~~~~~~~~~~~~~~~~~~~~~~~~~~~~~~~~~~~~~~~~~~~~~~~~~~~~~~~~~~~~~~~~~~~~~


                        I. INPUT ASSUMPTIONS
                        ====================

      Enter the following assumptions:


          Future Sum (FV)                  >>>     $   10.00

          Discount Rate Range [k(1)...k(m)]

                  From k(1)                >>>         5.00   %
                    To k(m)                >>>        15.00   %

          Time Period Range [t(1)...t(n)]

                  From t(1)                >>>            5   years
                    To t(n)                >>>           70   years


  Press  [Alt] M  for MENU          Press  [Ctrl] [Break]  for READY


~~~~~~~~~~~~~~~~~~~~~~~~~~~~~~~~~~~~~~~~~~~~~~~~~~~~~~~~~~~~~~~~~~~~~~~~~
```

II. OUTPUT TABLE OF PRESENT VALUES

For any single sum,

if the FV is: $ 10.00   ,

if the [k(1)...k(m)] is: 5.00   %   to   15.00   % ,

if the [t(1)...t(n)] is: 5   yrs to   70   yrs ,

the Present Value Table is provided as follows:

$$

Discount Rates

Years	5	7.5	10	12.5	15	NA	NA
5	7.835261	6.965586	6.209213	5.549289	4.971767	NA	NA
10	6.139132	4.851939	3.855432	3.079461	2.471847	NA	NA
15	4.810170	3.379660	2.393920	1.708882	1.228944	NA	NA
20	3.768894	2.354131	1.486436	0.948308	0.611002	NA	NA
25	2.953027	1.639790	0.922959	0.526243	0.303776	NA	NA
30	2.313774	1.142210	0.573085	0.292027	0.151030	NA	NA
35	1.812902	0.795616	0.355841	0.162054	0.075088	NA	NA
40	1.420456	0.554193	0.220949	0.089928	0.037332	NA	NA
45	1.112965	0.386028	0.137192	0.049904	0.018560	NA	NA
50	0.872037	0.268891	0.085185	0.027693	0.009228	NA	NA
55	0.683264	0.187298	0.052893	0.015367	0.004587	NA	NA
60	0.535355	0.130464	0.032842	0.008528	0.002281	NA	NA
65	0.419464	0.090876	0.020392	0.004732	0.001134	NA	NA
70	0.328661	0.063300	0.012662	0.002626	0.000563	NA	NA
NA	NA	NA	NA	NA	NA	NA	NA

$$

Press [Alt] M for MENU   Press [Ctrl] [Break] for READY

~~~~~~

FUTURE VALUE OF AN ANNUITY TABLE GENERATOR
(Template: lot503)

This template is similar to the first one in this chapter in that both seek future values. However, in the first future value template (lot501), a single, present sum was compounded to a future value. In this case, the situation is different. In this model, the future value of a series of equal payments is calculated. The series is called an *annuity* and this template calculates the future values of annuities for a set of interest rates and a set of time periods.

Principles.   The future value of an annuity calculation is used to calculate how much money can be accumulated at some future period, given an interest rate, assuming that a periodic payment, R, is made at the *end* of each year. For example, suppose a saver wanted to see how much money he would accumulate by age 65 if he opened an IRA at age 30. The limit for an individual under the current federal regulations for Individual Retirement Accounts is $2,000 (or $2,250 with a non-working spouse) per year. The question to be answered is "how large will the IRA account grow at, say 10 percent, if on December 31 of each year, the saver put $2,000 into the account for the next 35 years?" The future value of an annuity solves this problem directly.

Figure 5-3 illustrates the principle of a future value of an annuity. The future value of an annuity represents the sum of the *future* values of each R payment. In this case, there are eight payments of R at the end of each year. For a given interest rate, the future value of the annuity may be calculated.

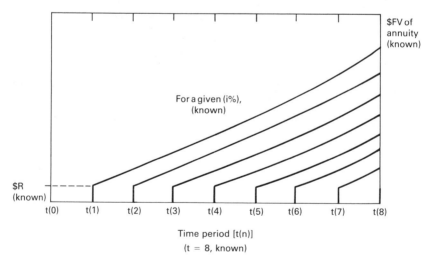

FIGURE 5-3
Future value of an annuity.

Note that this template calculates the future values of several annuities, not simply the one illustrated in Figure 5-3. For each set of time periods (and annuity payments), a new future value of an annuity value is obtained. Also, as the interest rate changes, the annuity value changes. As with the future value of the initial sum, the higher the interest rate, the higher the future value of the annuity.

Using the Template.   The Future Value of an Annuity Table Generator not only solves the problem for a specific rate of interest and a given number of years, but also, like the others in this chapter, shows how sensitive the sum is to changes in interest rates and shorter or longer periods of time. Although a large template like this takes a bit longer than some of the others, Lotus is well-suited to this type of table generation: difficult and messy by hand, but relatively quick and easy with Lotus.

The format of the input and output tables is identical to the previous models, with a few noted exceptions. Instead of future or present sums, annuity calculations presume a periodic payment. This is the amount accumulated (or in the case of the next template, discounted) each year. The interest rate range and range of years can be identical to the previous inputs.

The output table shows a range of future values that rise quickly in size. This is because the impact of the periodic payment has a sizable effect on the future value. A brief look at the numbers illustrates this point.

An Example.   The example shows the future values of depositing $5.00 into an investment or savings account or similar vehicle each year for from three to 68 years. (Note that 69 years was requested so the model will not output values greater than at 69 years in increments of five years.) The interest rates chosen were 4, 6.5, 9, 11.5, 14, 16.5, and 19 percent. As before, the increments are in 2.5 percentage point differences. The table produces the desired results.

For example, if $5.00 were placed into a savings account every year *and the interest was left on deposit* (this is important!) for a period of 43 years, if the interest rate earned on the account was 9 percent (compounded annually), the value of the account would be $2,204.23 at the end of the period. Note that if the interest earned was taxable, the taxes would have to be paid from other funds, because if they were taken from the savings account, the value would be considerably lower. (If it was an IRA account, of course, the interest would not be taxable until you withdrew the money . . . at the end of 43 years.) If you deposited $50.00 per year, the sum would be $22,042.28 (multiply the previous results by ten, since the payment is now ten times higher than $5.00). Similarly, if $500 was deposited, the sum would then be $220,422.83.

It is interesting to see the power of compound interest, especially with annuities. Look at the example for a moment. Even with *only $5.00 per year*, at high rates of interest and over a long time period, several of the cells show accumulations of greater than $100,000! What are you waiting for? Get started and harness the power of compound interest. Lotus 1-2-3 can help you monitor your program and show you various possible patterns of accumulation.

Graphics.   The graphs for this template show that annuities can quickly amount to sizeable future sums if the interest rate assumed is high. Note that the level of the interest rate over a long period of time can have an extremely large impact on the final, future value.

Possible Modifications.   If the user desires only one calculation, as before, limit the range of interest rates and years to one level. This will hasten the calculations and provide the answer with the same precision. If other numbers are useful for comparison purposes, this template can be used with a dual-window format. Create a horizontal window in the middle of the screen with the inputs on the top and the relevant portion of the output table at the bottom. Change the inputs and examine the effect on the outputs. Do this a few times and make Lotus 1-2-3 work for you.

EXAMPLE TEMPLATE 5.3
Future value of an annuity table generator.

```
lot503x                                    Real Estate Diskette #1
=================================================================
FUTURE VALUE OF AN ANNUITY TABLE GENERATOR
                                Copyright (C) Reston Pub. Co., 1985
=================================================================

~~~~~~~~~~~~~~~~~~~~~~~~~~~~~~~~~~~~~~~~~~~~~~~~~~~~~~~~~~~~~~~~~~~~

                  ***   TABLE OF CONTENTS   ***
                        =================
            Table                              Page
            -----                              ----

     I.   INPUT ASSUMPTIONS                      1

     II.  OUTPUT TABLE OF FUTURE ANNUITY VALUES  2


~~~~~~~~~~~~~~~~~~~~~~~~~~~~~~~~~~~~~~~~~~~~~~~~~~~~~~~~~~~~~~~~~~~~

                    I. INPUT ASSUMPTIONS
                    ====================

     Enter the following assumptions:


        Periodic Payment (R)          >>>      $    5.00

        Interest Rate Range [i(1)...i(m)]

              From i(1)               >>>          4.00   %
                To i(m)               >>>         19.00   %

        Time Period Range [t(1)...t(n)]

              From t(1)               >>>             3   years
                To t(n)               >>>            69   years


   Press  [Alt] M  for MENU        Press  [Ctrl] [Break]  for READY


~~~~~~~~~~~~~~~~~~~~~~~~~~~~~~~~~~~~~~~~~~~~~~~~~~~~~~~~~~~~~~~~~~~~
```

II. OUTPUT TABLE OF FUTURE ANNUITY VALUES
===

For any level payment annuity,

if the R is: $ 5.00   ,

if the [i(1)...i(m)] is: 4.00   %   to   19.00   % ,

if the [t(1)...t(n)] is: 3   yrs to   69   yrs ,

the Future Value of an Annuity Table is provided as follows:

$$$

Interest Rates

Years	4	6.5	9	11.5	14	16.5	19
3	15.61	16.00	16.39	16.79	17.20	17.61	18.03
8	46.07	50.38	55.14	60.39	66.16	72.52	79.51
13	83.13	97.50	114.77	135.52	160.44	190.36	226.22
18	128.23	162.05	206.51	265.00	341.97	443.23	576.33
23	183.09	250.49	347.66	488.13	691.49	985.90	1411.81
28	249.84	371.66	564.84	872.68	1364.45	2150.48	3405.56
33	331.05	537.68	899.00	1535.38	2660.18	4649.65	8163.35
38	429.85	765.13	1413.15	2677.45	5154.99	10012.88	19517.12
43	550.06	1076.77	2204.23	4645.64	9958.54	21522.36	46611.24
48	696.32	1503.73	3421.40	8037.53	19207.38	46221.69	*********
53	874.26	2088.71	5294.17	13882.96	37015.21	99226.46	*********
58	1090.75	2890.19	8175.67	23956.70	71302.68	******************	******************
63	1354.14	3988.28	12609.20	41317.31	***************************		
68	1674.60	5492.75	19430.74	71235.78	****************************		
NA	NA	NA	NA	NA	NA	NA	NA

$$$

Press [Alt] M for MENU   Press [Ctrl] [Break] for READY

~~~~~~

PRESENT VALUE OF AN ANNUITY TABLE GENERATOR
(Template: lot504)

Guess what? This is a similar calculation to the previous one except in this case, a present value sum is sought where in the last case, a future value was calculated. The present value of an annuity is useful for a different set of situations. In real estate, there may be numerous times when the present value of an annuity is essential to valuing leases, debt payment receipts, and other financial flows where the payment is fixed in size.

Principles.   The present value of an annuity provides the answer to the following question: "Given a set of annuity payments for a number of years and at a certain *discount* rate, how much is this set of payments worth *today*?" With this template and Lotus 1-2-3 an entire table of present value annuity factors can be generated.

Figure 5-4 provides a graphic view of the present value of an annuity. The present value of an annuity represents the sum of the *present* values of each R payment. As before, in this case, there are eight payments of R at the end of each year. For a given discount rate, the present value of an annuity may be calculated.

Note that this template calculates several present values of annuities in addition to the one shown in Figure 5-4. For each set of time periods in-

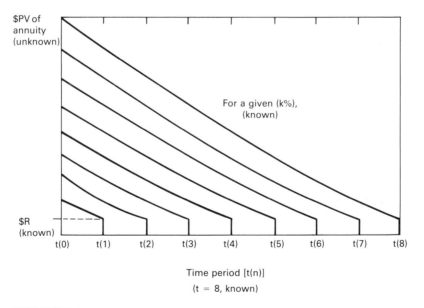

FIGURE 5-4
Present value of an annuity.

putted, a new present value of an annuity is obtained. Changes in the size of the payment, discount rates, or the number of payments will affect the result.

Using the Template.   The format of the template is identical to the previous one. In this case, the rates are used to discount the payments over a particular time span. As before, the span for discount rates is 15 percentage points; the span for years is 70. The increments in rates and years is the same as before: 2.5 percentage points and 5 years, respectively.

Notice that as the discount rates become larger, the values in the table become smaller. This is because a discount rate may be interpreted as being costly to wait for the "future to come." A high discount rate means money is relatively valuable to have now, for reinvestment purposes or for some other reason. Note also that the present values become greater with additional years. This is because with annuities each year means two things: additional periodic payments and more interest on the existing sum. Therefore, an eight year contract to receive a $5.00 payment each year at 14 percent is worth only $23.19, while a 48 year contract, everything else the same, is worth $35.65.

An Example.   As another example, if $1,000 is promised to you (in writing!) for the next 25 years, how much is this promise worth if you use a discount rate of 13.5%? (Can you calculate this answer using the template? Clearly the numbers would have to be changed from the example in the book: $1,000 is the payment, 25 years lies between 23 and 28, and 13.5 percent lies between 11.5 and 14 percent.) The answer is $7,094.97. Note that this result is considerably less than $1,000 times the 25 payments. Why? It is because the owner of this contractual promise does not receive more than $1,000 per year. If $25,000 were to be paid all at once today, this would be a much more valuable promise.

Graphics.   These graphs show that high discount rates for long annuity streams are very valuable contracts. Note also that the discount rate accounts for more of the difference in present values than does the number of years the payments are made after the annuity is extended for more than about 25 years.

Possible Modifications.   The experienced user may make modifications for special problems which need to be solved. Otherwise, the template is well-suited to a wide variety of problems.

EXAMPLE TEMPLATE 5.4
Present value of an annuity table generator.

```
lot504x                                    Real Estate Diskette #1
=================================================================
PRESENT VALUE OF AN ANNUITY TABLE GENERATOR
                              Copyright (C) Reston Pub. Co., 1985
=================================================================


~~~~~~~~~~~~~~~~~~~~~~~~~~~~~~~~~~~~~~~~~~~~~~~~~~~~~~~~~~~~~~~~~~~~

                    ***  TABLE OF CONTENTS  ***
                         =================
               Table                              Page
               -----                              ----

      I.   INPUT ASSUMPTIONS                        1

      II.  OUTPUT TABLE OF PRESENT ANNUITY VALUES    2


~~~~~~~~~~~~~~~~~~~~~~~~~~~~~~~~~~~~~~~~~~~~~~~~~~~~~~~~~~~~~~~~~~~~

                    I. INPUT ASSUMPTIONS
                    ====================

      Enter the following assumptions:

         Periodic Payment (R)           >>>     $    5.00

         Discount Rate Range [k(1)...k(m)]

                From k(1)               >>>          4.00   %
                  To k(m)               >>>         19.00   %

         Time Period Range [t(1)...t(n)]

                From t(1)               >>>             3   years
                  To t(n)               >>>            69   years


Press  [Alt] M  for MENU         Press  [Ctrl] [Break]  for READY


~~~~~~~~~~~~~~~~~~~~~~~~~~~~~~~~~~~~~~~~~~~~~~~~~~~~~~~~~~~~~~~~~~~~
```

II. OUTPUT TABLE OF PRESENT ANNUITY VALUES
==

For any level payment annuity,

if the R is: $ 5.00 ,

if the [k(1)...k(m)] is: 4.00   %   to   19.00   % ,

if the [t(1)...t(n)] is: 3   yrs to   69   yrs ,

the Present Value of an Annuity Table is provided as follows:

$$

Discount Rates

Years	4	6.5	9	11.5	14	16.5	19
3	13.88	13.24	12.66	12.11	11.61	11.14	10.70
8	33.66	30.44	27.67	25.28	23.19	21.37	19.77
13	49.93	43.00	37.43	32.92	29.21	26.14	23.57
18	63.30	52.16	43.78	37.35	32.34	28.36	25.17
23	74.28	58.85	47.90	39.92	33.96	29.40	25.83
28	83.32	63.73	50.58	41.41	34.80	29.88	26.11
33	90.74	67.30	52.32	42.28	35.24	30.11	26.23
38	96.84	69.90	53.45	42.78	35.47	30.21	26.28
43	101.85	71.79	54.19	43.08	35.59	30.26	26.30
48	105.98	73.18	54.67	43.24	35.65	30.28	26.31
53	109.36	74.19	54.98	43.34	35.68	30.29	26.31
58	112.15	74.93	55.18	43.40	35.70	30.30	26.31
63	114.44	75.47	55.31	43.43	35.70	30.30	26.32
68	116.32	75.86	55.40	43.45	35.71	30.30	26.32
NA	NA	NA	NA	NA	NA	NA	NA

$$

Press [Alt] M for MENU   Press [Ctrl] [Break] for READY

~~~~~~

SINKING FUND TABLE GENERATOR
(Template: lot505)

This template and the last one in this chapter which follows are closely related to the previous two. This template generates a series of factors called *sinking fund factors*. Sinking fund factors can be used to calculate the size of the periodic payment so that a future value of an annuity can be accumulated.

Principles. In effect, the formulas in this template are the same as the ones in Template lot503 (Future Value of an Annuity Table Generator). The difference is that in this case, the future value of an annuity is known; the unknown is the payment necessary to accumulate to the future value.

For example, suppose an individual wished to accumulate one million dollars in 40 years by making annual deposits into a savings account. This method shows what the precise annual payment should be, given an interest rate, in order to reach the saver's goal. Similarly, for a given payment, the user can search the table in order to see how high the interest rate must be in order to accumulate enough funds.

Figure 5-5 presents the sinking fund factor. Notice that this illustration is very similar to Figure 5-3: Future Value of an Annuity. Indeed, the only difference is what is "known" and "unknown" to the user; the formulas are identical.

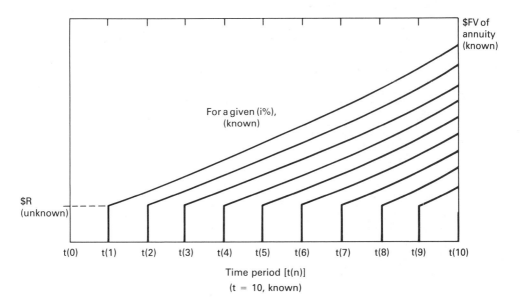

FIGURE 5-5
Sinking fund factor.

The sinking fund factor is used to find the appropriate value of R, the payment, given an interest rate to accumulate a known future value. In effect, while the future value of an annuity asked for the future value, given the payment, the time period, and the interest rate, the sinking fund asks the converse question: what is the payment, given the desired future value, the time period, and the interest rate?

Using the Template.   As before, this template requires only a minimal number of inputs: the future value to be accumulated, the interest rate or range of rates, and the time period or range of periods, in years. The same convention is adopted here with respect to limits on the table: up to seven different interest rates are permitted at 2.5 percentage point increments and up to 15 different accumulation periods are possible at 5 year increments.

An Example.   In the example provided, annual payments are provided to accumulate $10,000 at interest rates from 5 to 20 percent for periods from 5 to 70 years. Note that the higher the rate of interest, the lower the required payment. Also, the longer the time period, the lower the payment. For example, at 7.5 percent for 25 years, annual payments of $147.11 are required to accumulate $10,000 (assuming no taxes). If a higher interest rate is assumed, say, 15 percent, the required payments fall to only $46.99. If the interest rate remains at 7.5 percent, but the payments are made for 50 instead of 25 years, the payments become $47.77 each year. The user is invited to investigate other possibilities of these principles.

Graphics.   In this case, all of the functions are similar in results. In other words, different interest rates require different sinking fund payments. Over long periods of time, the payments are very similar.

Possible Modifications.   The same modifications are possible with this template as with the others. Changes in the increments to rates or years may be useful, depending upon the specific needs of the user.

EXAMPLE TEMPLATE 5.5
Sinking fund table generator.

```
lot505x                                 Real Estate Diskette #
================================================================
SINKING FUND TABLE GENERATOR       Copyright (C) Reston Pub. Co., 198!
================================================================

~~~~~~~~~~~~~~~~~~~~~~~~~~~~~~~~~~~~~~~~~~~~~~~~~~~~~~~~~~~~~~~~~~~


             ***  TABLE OF CONTENTS  ***
                  =================
         Table                                  Page
         -----                                  ----

   I.   INPUT ASSUMPTIONS                          1

   II.  OUTPUT TABLE OF SINKING FUND VALUES         2


~~~~~~~~~~~~~~~~~~~~~~~~~~~~~~~~~~~~~~~~~~~~~~~~~~~~~~~~~~~~~~~~~~~

                  I. INPUT ASSUMPTIONS
                  ====================

   Enter the following assumptions:


      Future Value of an Annuity [FV(a)]  >>>     $  10,000

      Interest Rate Range [i(1)...i(m)]

           From i(1)                   >>>        5.00   %
             To i(m)                   >>>       20.00   %

      Time Period Range [t(1)...t(n)]

           From t(1)                   >>>           5   years
             To t(n)                   >>>          70   years


   Press  [Alt] M  for MENU          Press  [Ctrl] [Break]  for READY


~~~~~~~~~~~~~~~~~~~~~~~~~~~~~~~~~~~~~~~~~~~~~~~~~~~~~~~~~~~~~~~~~~~
```

II. OUTPUT TABLE OF SINKING FUND VALUES
===

For any level payment annuity,

if the [FV(a)] is: $ 10,000   ,

if the [i(1)...i(m)] is: 5.00   %   to   20.00   % ,

if the [t(1)...t(n)] is: 5   yrs   to   70   yrs ,

the Sinking Fund Table is provided as follows:

$$$

Interest Rates

Years	5	7.5	10	12.5	15	17.5	20
5	1809.75	1721.65	1637.97	1558.54	1483.16	1411.63	1343.80
10	795.05	706.86	627.45	556.22	492.52	435.73	385.23
15	463.42	382.87	314.74	257.64	210.17	170.98	138.82
20	302.43	230.92	174.60	130.96	97.61	72.43	53.57
25	209.52	147.11	101.68	69.43	46.99	31.61	21.19
30	150.51	96.71	60.79	37.60	23.00	13.98	8.46
35	110.72	64.83	36.90	20.59	11.35	6.21	3.39
40	82.78	44.00	22.59	11.34	5.62	2.77	1.36
45	62.62	30.11	13.91	6.27	2.79	1.23	0.55
50	47.77	20.72	8.59	3.47	1.39	0.55	0.22
55	36.67	14.32	5.32	1.92	0.69	0.25	0.09
60	28.28	9.91	3.30	1.07	0.34	0.11	0.04
65	21.89	6.88	2.04	0.59	0.17	0.05	0.01
70	16.99	4.78	1.27	0.33	0.08	0.02	0.01
NA	NA	NA	NA	NA	NA	NA	NA

$$$

Press   [Alt] M   for MENU   Press   [Ctrl] [Break]   for READY

~~~~~~

MORTGAGE CONSTANT TABLE GENERATOR
(Template: lot506)

The final template in this chapter is an important one for real estate analysts. It solves for the payment which relates to the present value of an annuity. It is closely related to that present value calculation, except rather than solving for the present sum, it finds the appropriate payments, given the interest rate and the time period to obtain the present sum.

Principles.   This template is called the *mortgage constant table generator* because the calculation of the mortgage constant means the calculation of a periodic payment which when discounted to the present represents the present value of an annuity. In this case, the present sum may be one dollar (as in the typical financial tables) or any other value; the computer and Lotus 1-2-3 will do the rest.

Figure 5-6 illustrates the calculation of the mortgage constant. In this case, the result is very similar to Figure 5-4: Present Value of an Annuity. The difference is that the mortgage constant presumes a present value amount and solves for the payment, given a time period and a discount rate.

This calculation is very useful in real estate. This is the calculation which provides the precise payment which when made at the end of each period will completely repay a lender with interest and principal for the entire balance of the loan.

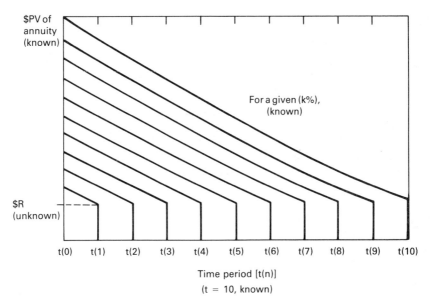

FIGURE 5-6
Mortgage constant factor.

Using the Template. As throughout this chapter, this template will calculate not only a single answer, but will also generate an entire table of mortgage constants. (In the case of the actual present sum, or actual mortgage, the table will generate mortgage payments. Why? This is because mortgage payments are annuities, the present value of which represent the present value of an annuity. This sum is the amount borrowed at the time the loan is originated.)

The dimensions on the table are the same as elsewhere in this chapter. The only difference is that the interest rates are now called discount rates since present values are calculated when solving for mortgage constants (amortizing mortgage loans). Note additional discussion and new templates are also provided for loan amortization in Chapter 6.

An Example. In this example, a loan of $10,000 is assumed with discount rates from 5 to 20 percent and time periods from 5 to 70 years. Note that as the time period is extended, the required payment falls quickly and then very slowly over long periods of time. To repay this loan at 5 percent over 10 years would require $1,295.05 each year compared to only $547.77 per year over 50 years. Also as the discount rate rises, the payments increase and over time the difference between the rates narrows. Note how for long-term loans at relatively high rates, there is very little difference between repaying the loans over 35 or 70 years. This observation is very important for many real estate financing and investment decisions.

Graphics. These graphs show the relationship between required mortgage payments and different interest rates on the mortgage (discount rates) over time. Note that if the mortgage would have a very long repayment period, (although most are limited to 25 or 30 years by various state laws), the difference between annual payments falls to pennies. This is shown graphically by the nearly horizontal functions after about 40 or 50 years.

Possible Modifications. Users may wish to concentrate on a smaller range of values, especially if a specific project is under analysis. This, as indicated previously is possible by altering the template. Also, limiting the range of parameter values may help to hasten the calculations, if necessary.

EXAMPLE TEMPLATE 5.6
Mortgage constant table generator.

```
lot506x                                      Real Estate Diskette #2
=====================================================================
MORTGAGE CONSTANT TABLE GENERATOR    Copyright (C) Reston Pub. Co., 1985
=====================================================================

~~~~~~~~~~~~~~~~~~~~~~~~~~~~~~~~~~~~~~~~~~~~~~~~~~~~~~~~~~~~~~~~~~~~~~~~~

                    ***   TABLE OF CONTENTS   ***
                    ==================
            Table                                       Page
            -----                                       ----

    I.   INPUT ASSUMPTIONS                                1

    II.  OUTPUT TABLE OF MORTGAGE CONSTANT VALUES          2


~~~~~~~~~~~~~~~~~~~~~~~~~~~~~~~~~~~~~~~~~~~~~~~~~~~~~~~~~~~~~~~~~~~~~~~~~

                       I. INPUT ASSUMPTIONS
                       ====================

    Enter the following assumptions:

        Present Value of an Annuity [PV(a)] >>>      $  10,000

        Discount Rate Range [k(1)...k(m)]

            From k(1)                   >>>          5.00   %
            To  k(m)                    >>>         20.00   %

        Time Period Range [t(1)...t(n)]

            From t(1)                   >>>             5   years
            To  t(n)                    >>>            70   years


    Press  [Alt] M  for MENU        Press  [Ctrl] [Break]  for READY


~~~~~~~~~~~~~~~~~~~~~~~~~~~~~~~~~~~~~~~~~~~~~~~~~~~~~~~~~~~~~~~~~~~~~~~~~
```

II. OUTPUT TABLE OF MORTGAGE CONSTANT VALUES
===

For any level payment annuity,

if the [PV(a)] is: $ 10,000 ,

if the [k(1)...k(m)] is: 5.00 %   to   20.00 % ,

if the [t(1)...t(n)] is: 5 yrs to   70 yrs ,

the Mortgage Constant Table is provided as follows:

$$$

Discount Rates

Years	5	7.5	10	12.5	15	17.5	20
5	2309.75	2471.65	2637.97	2808.54	2983.16	3161.63	3343.80
10	1295.05	1456.86	1627.45	1806.22	1992.52	2185.73	2385.23
15	963.42	1132.87	1314.74	1507.64	1710.17	1920.98	2138.82
20	802.43	980.92	1174.60	1380.96	1597.61	1822.43	2053.57
25	709.52	897.11	1101.68	1319.43	1546.99	1781.61	2021.19
30	650.51	846.71	1060.79	1287.60	1523.00	1763.98	2008.46
35	610.72	814.83	1036.90	1270.59	1511.35	1756.21	2003.39
40	582.78	794.00	1022.59	1261.34	1505.62	1752.77	2001.36
45	562.62	780.11	1013.91	1256.27	1502.79	1751.23	2000.55
50	547.77	770.72	1008.59	1253.47	1501.39	1750.55	2000.22
55	536.67	764.32	1005.32	1251.92	1500.69	1750.25	2000.09
60	528.28	759.91	1003.30	1251.07	1500.34	1750.11	2000.04
65	521.89	756.88	1002.04	1250.59	1500.17	1750.05	2000.01
70	516.99	754.78	1001.27	1250.33	1500.08	1750.02	2000.01
NA	NA	NA	NA	NA	NA	NA	NA

$$$

Press [Alt] M for MENU   Press [Ctrl] [Break] for READY

~~~~~~

6 Lending/Borrowing Decisions

Overview

One of the most important tools of financing is the ability to calculate lending and borrowing costs correctly. A number of important calculations are used by lenders every day. These include calculating loan payments, mortgage constants, and amortization schedules, but also include calculating the effective cost of borrowing as well as the yield on the loan (the rate of return on the lender's investment). It also follows that if these considerations are important for lenders, they are likely to be important for borrowers. This is especially true for the calculations developed in this chapter's templates.

CALCULATING DEBT SERVICE
(Template: lot601)

This is a relatively simple and short template, but one which is very useful in a variety of applications. The calculation of debt service is a procedure which a surprisingly large number of real estate practitioners have difficulty performing. Many use rough approximations to obtain the annual or monthly debt service (or mortgage payment) amount. Others search through preprinted tables of financial factors and hope they choose the right number in a sea of small print. Still others tell their clients to wait until after lunch when the boss returns and he/she will be able to make the appropriate multiplication.

If you learn little else from this book, you should be able to learn how to calculate the debt service using Lotus 1-2-3 and as shown in the next template, how to amortize the mortgage. Note also that any fixed rate loan payment is calculated the same way. Conversely, new loans with variable and changing rates begin with the same calculation but are modified in one or more ways. The discussions and demonstrations of some of the new loans are postponed until Chapter 7.

Principles.   Using the same principles introduced in the last chapter, it is possible to find the appropriate periodic payment which "amortizes" (i.e., pays back the initial loan in full with interest) in equal payments over a given period of time and given a fixed interest rate. This is the same as saying the solution to this problem is to find the equal set of payments, the present value of which is equivalent to the beginning balance of the loan, at a certain interest rate. In this case, it is presumed that the mortgage amount, interest rate on the loan, and the repayment period are known. The unknown is the periodic payment.

It is also important to recognize that the periodic payment period need not be defined as "annually." Indeed, most mortgage payments are required and due monthly. (It is interesting to note that land transactions and rental payments under leases in the 18th and 19th centuries frequently required semi-annual payments.) Therefore, it is important to consider the *period* of the required payment. This template provides payments for five well-known payment periods: annual, semi-annual, quarterly, monthly, and daily.

Using the Template.   The user simply enters the three inputs: the mortgage amount, the interest rate, and the term of the loan. That's it! The output repeats the inputs and automatically shows the debt service payments for the five periods. It is very important to note that the number of payments per year (or sometimes called the rate of compounding) will affect the size of the debt service payments. This means that one *cannot* take, for example, the annual debt service payment and divide by 12 to get the monthly payment. (Test this for yourself!) If monthly payments are used, the presumption in this template is that the interest rate on the loan is also compounded monthly. Therefore, taking the annual rate divided by twelve neglects the effects of compounding *between each monthly payment* and as a result introduces an error into the calculations.

An Example.   In the example, the mortgage is $75,000, the interest rate is 13.50 percent over a term of 30 years. The output shows the following mortgage payment possibilities:

- Annual Debt Service: $10,356.93
- Semi-Annual Debt Service: $5,165.07
- Quarterly Debt Service: $2,579.29
- Monthly Debt Service: $859.06
- Daily Debt Service: $28.23

Note that once the frequency of payment period is chosen, all of the payment schedules would result in a complete repayment of the $75,000 loan. The difference would be in the frequency of payment and more importantly, in the effective rate of interest charged on the loan. Specifically, the more frequent the rate of payments (and the rate of compounding), the higher the effective interest rate is on the loan, everything else being the same. This means that 13.50 percent on a mortgage with annual repayments is less expensive than 13.50 percent on a mortgage with monthly repayments, everything else the same.

Graphics.   The bar graph shows the relative sizes of each of the five periodic payments. Note also that this graph makes use of data labels, in this case, above each debt service payment. You can also see that twelve times the monthly payment does not equal the annual payment. Nor does 365 times the daily payment equal the yearly amount. While the graph is simple and easy, it is informative and helpful when comparing several debt services.

Possible Modifications.   This template is very fast and easy to use. It is well-suited to sensitivity testing by changing values of the inputs and testing the impact on the output. This may also be done with the use of windows or titles. Also, other repayment periods can be introduced by modifying the template. For most purposes, however, these five periods should adequately describe most real-world loans and required repayment frequencies.

EXAMPLE TEMPLATE 6.1
Calculating debt service.

```
lot601x                                    Real Estate Diskette #2
==================================================================
CALCULATING DEBT SERVICE        Copyright (C) Reston Pub. Co., 1985
==================================================================

~~~~~~~~~~~~~~~~~~~~~~~~~~~~~~~~~~~~~~~~~~~~~~~~~~~~~~~~~~~~~~~~~~~~~~

            ***   TABLE OF CONTENTS   ***
                  =================

            Table                              Page
            -----                              ----

   I.   INPUT ASSUMPTIONS                        1

   II.  SOLUTIONS                                2


~~~~~~~~~~~~~~~~~~~~~~~~~~~~~~~~~~~~~~~~~~~~~~~~~~~~~~~~~~~~~~~~~~~~~~

                  I. INPUT ASSUMPTIONS
                  ====================

      Enter the following assumptions:


          Mortgage Amount (Mort)        >>>     $  75,000

          Interest Rate (i)             >>>        13.50   %

          Term of Loan (n)              >>>           30   years


   Press  [Alt] M  for MENU         Press  [Ctrl] [Break]  for READY


~~~~~~~~~~~~~~~~~~~~~~~~~~~~~~~~~~~~~~~~~~~~~~~~~~~~~~~~~~~~~~~~~~~~~~
```

```
                    II. SOLUTIONS
                    =============

    For any fully-amortized, level-payment, ordinary annuity loan,


                if Mort is:              $  75,000 ,

                if i is:                    13.50  percent,

                and if n is:                   30  years,


    $$$$$$$$$$$$$$$$$$$$$$$$$$$$$$$$$$$$$$$$$$$$$$$$$$$$$$$$$$$$$$

    the Annual Debt Service will be:            $10356.93

    the Semi-Annual Debt Service will be:       $ 5165.07

    the Quarterly Debt Service will be:         $ 2579.29

    the Monthly Debt Service will be:           $  859.06

    the Daily Debt Service will be:             $   28.23

    $$$$$$$$$$$$$$$$$$$$$$$$$$$$$$$$$$$$$$$$$$$$$$$$$$$$$$$$$$$$$$


Press  [Alt] M  for MENU          Press  [Ctrl] [Break]  for READY


~~~~~~~~~~~~~~~~~~~~~~~~~~~~~~~~~~~~~~~~~~~~~~~~~~~~~~~~~~~~~~~~~~~~
```

CALCULATING AMORTIZATION SCHEDULES
(Template: lot602)

In addition to calculating the debt service, it is very useful to provide an amortization schedule of the entire loan. This is true for several reasons. First, since few loans are paid out over the scheduled lives (most are prepaid), at the time of sale, refinancing, or early prepayment, it is necessary to know the outstanding balance of the loan. Second, the IRS permits investors to deduct interest as a business expense. (Similarly, homeowners are permitted to deduct mortgage interest paid during each year from their individual tax returns, if the long Form 1040 is used and the individual chooses to itemize deductions.) Third, investors can measure the amount of repayment of the loan (typically called *equity buildup*) to see how much equity has been added to the down-payment and any appreciation in the property since it was purchased. Fourth, the amount of interest changes each period. For these reasons, developing an amortization schedule is an important tool for anyone owning or investing in real estate.

Principles. The calculation of an amortization schedule requires understanding of a number of basic principles. Once the proper calculation of the debt service is made, the amortization procedure goes as follows: First, the beginning balance of the loan is recorded. (This is the amount borrowed at the time of loan origination.) Second, the amount of interest is calculated for the first period. Note that amortization schedules may be calculated for any set of payments (monthly, quarterly, annually, etc.). The amount of interest, for example, of a loan with annual compounding and annual repayments will be equal to the interest rate on the loan times the beginning balance of the mortgage. Since the mortgage payment includes interest and principal payments, for any loan with a finite life, the mortgage payment will be greater than the amount of interest owed. Therefore, the difference between the interest owed and the mortgage payment is the principal repayment.

Finally, the principal repayment is used to reduce the amount owed such that the difference between the beginning balance of the loan and the principal repayment is the ending balance of the loan for the period. The ending balance of the loan for the period is defined as the beginning balance of the loan for the next period. (If the repayment period is annually, the periods are yearly. If the repayment periods are monthly, the ending balance after month five, for example, becomes the beginning balance of month six.)

Thus, this procedure is performed until the ending balance of the loan is zero (i.e., the borrower has completely repaid the note to the lender). At that point, assuming all payments have been made on time (and the debt service has been calculated correctly), the term of the loan has expired. In other words, the formula used to calculate the debt service finds the precise amount of periodic (i.e., monthly, quarterly, annually, etc.) payment such that after subtracting the amount of interest owed and applying the remaining amount of the payment to the balance owed on the loan and proceeding each period with this calculation, the outstanding balance of the loan will be equal to zero (or about zero with rounding a few dollars over a long period) at the desired end of the loan (typically 25 or 30 years).

Using the Template. This template, like some others later in the book, permits the user to recalculate if more than 30 payments are requested. For example, if annual payments are used, as long as the loan is amortized over 30 years or less, the entire schedule will be shown. However, suppose the user wanted to look at monthly payments over a 30-year period. In this case, there would be 360 payments. The template is designed to enable the user to continue to amortize the loan in 30 payment steps. Thus, the user can continue, using the automatic menu as long as necessary. This programming feature makes for an attractive template and improves the appearance and usefulness of the tool.

Enter the mortgage amount, the interest rate on the loan, and the term of the loan in the Input table. In addition, this template enables the user to decide what rate of compounding to use. In other words, how often the interest will be compounded and how often the payments will be made per year. (For example, annual compounding periods means 1.00 should be entered; monthly compounding periods require that 12.00 be entered; and so on.) Lotus 1-2-3 will automatically match the appropriate period to your request. If monthly periods are specified, the output will show 30 months; if daily periods are requested, 30 days payments will be provided.

The output page repeats the inputs and calculates the appropriate debt service. An amortization schedule is provided automatically and quickly for up to 30 periods. Note also that the current and cumulative totals are provided for the total mortgage payments, interest and amortization (principal repayments). Note also that the outstanding balance at the end of each 30 periods is shown.

If additional amortization is required, follow the directions of the recalculation option and Lotus 1-2-3 and the template will do all of the work. The template will automatically update the period column (31, 32, 33, and so on) but will also recalculate the rest of the amortization schedule for the next 30 periods. This sounds a bit complicated, but it is really quite simple and easy to do.

An Example. In this example, a mortgage is amortized with annual payments over a 25-year period. Note that zeros are reported when the amortization period is over. Note also that the ending balance at the end of year 25 is zero as required by the inputs. The annual payment is $10,570.88 for each and every year. Part of the payment is interest; the remaining part principal repayment.

Note that the amount of interest paid falls each year and the amount of principal increases. This is because the interest is based on the remaining balance of the loan. Since the previous year's principal payment serves to reduce the outstanding balance of the loan, less and less interest is paid (more and more principal reduction is applied) since a smaller and smaller balance is owed the lender. Thus, in each subsequent period, the borrower pays fewer dollars of interest and more dollars of principal out of the same, equal mortgage payment.

It is often pointed out that over the entire life of a mortgage a huge amount of interest is paid. This template shows that the amount of interest paid in this case is $189,272, or the sum of the interest column. Since the borrower also repays the original amount borrowed, in this case $75,000, it is easy to see that another way of calculating the total amount of interest to be paid is to take the total amount of dollars paid to the lender and subtract the initial amount borrowed. The difference is equal to the total interest paid.

Graphics. The graph for this template is one of the cleanest and most colorful (if you are using a color monitor). It shows the "slow process of equity build-up." This is due to the fact that interest is paid first out of the debt service payment. Any remaining dollars reduce the amount outstanding. It takes several years for the percentage of debt service to be greater for amortization than for interest. (In this example, it is not until the twenty-first year of the 25 year loan.) You are encouraged to experiment with various repayment schedules and examine the equity build-up process for each potential loan.

Possible Modifications. Since the template is designed to amortize for any number of years and with any number of payments per year, the potential types of loans are almost infinite. Thus, a small window at the top of the screen might be convenient. In the bottom, place the amortization schedule. Then, it is quite easy to watch the new outstanding balance in the top cell after each 30 periods. Try it and you will see how easy it is to do it! No longer do you have to wait for the mainframe computer to do these tasks!

EXAMPLE TEMPLATE 6.2
Calculating amortization schedules.

```
lot602x                                     Real Estate Diskette #2
===================================================================
CALCULATING AMORTIZATION SCHEDULES   Copyright (C) Reston Pub. Co., 1985
===================================================================

~~~~~~~~~~~~~~~~~~~~~~~~~~~~~~~~~~~~~~~~~~~~~~~~~~~~~~~~~~~~~~~~~~~~~~~

                  ***  TABLE OF CONTENTS  ***
                  ==================

              Table                              Page
              -----                              ----

       I.  INPUT ASSUMPTIONS                       1

      II.  SOLUTIONS                                2

     III.  RECALCULATION                            3


~~~~~~~~~~~~~~~~~~~~~~~~~~~~~~~~~~~~~~~~~~~~~~~~~~~~~~~~~~~~~~~~~~~~~~~

                      I. INPUT ASSUMPTIONS
                      ====================

     Enter the following assumptions:


         Mortgage Amount (Mort)        >>>      $  75,000

         Interest Rate (i)            >>>         13.50   %

         Term of Loan (n)             >>>            25   years

         Rate of Compounding/
           Payments per Annum (m)     >>>          1.00  times/yr


  Press  [Alt] M  for MENU          Press  [Ctrl] [Break]  for READY


~~~~~~~~~~~~~~~~~~~~~~~~~~~~~~~~~~~~~~~~~~~~~~~~~~~~~~~~~~~~~~~~~~~~~~~

                      II. SOLUTIONS
                      =============

     For any fully-amortized, level-payment, ordinary annuity loan,


             if Mort is:          $  75,000  ,

             if i is:                13.50  percent,

             if n is:                   25  years,

             and if m is:             1.00  times per year,
```

```
$$$$$$$$$$$$$$$$$$$$$$$$$$$$$$$$$$$$$$$$$$$$$$$$$$$$$$$$$$$$$

              the Debt Service is:    $10570.88

                          and

          the Mortgage is amortized as follows:

    ---------------------------------------------------------
    Period Beg Bal Mort Pay Interest   Amort    End Bal
    ---------------------------------------------------------
            ($)        ($)       ($)      ($)       ($)

         1  75000  10570.88  10125.00    445.88    74554
         2  74554  10570.88  10064.81    506.07    74048
         3  74048  10570.88   9996.49    574.39    73474
         4  73474  10570.88   9918.94    651.93    72822
         5  72822  10570.88   9830.93    739.94    72082
         6  72082  10570.88   9731.04    839.83    71242
         7  71242  10570.88   9617.66    953.21    70289
         8  70289  10570.88   9488.98   1081.90    69207
         9  69207  10570.88   9342.92   1227.95    67979
        10  67979  10570.88   9177.15   1393.73    66585
        11  66585  10570.88   8989.00   1581.88    65003
        12  65003  10570.88   8775.44   1795.43    63208
        13  63208  10570.88   8533.06   2037.82    61170
        14  61170  10570.88   8257.96   2312.92    58857
        15  58857  10570.88   7945.71   2625.16    56232
        16  56232  10570.88   7591.31   2979.56    53252
        17  53252  10570.88   7189.07   3381.80    49871
        18  49871  10570.88   6732.53   3838.35    46032
        19  46032  10570.88   6214.35   4356.52    41676
        20  41676  10570.88   5626.22   4944.65    36731
        21  36731  10570.88   4958.70   5612.18    31119
        22  31119  10570.88   4201.05   6369.83    24749
        23  24749  10570.88   3341.12   7229.75    17519
        24  17519  10570.88   2365.11   8205.77     9314
        25   9314  10570.88   1257.33   9313.55        0
        26      0      0.00      0.00      0.00        0
        27      0      0.00      0.00      0.00        0
        28      0      0.00      0.00      0.00        0
        29      0      0.00      0.00      0.00        0
        30      0      0.00      0.00      0.00        0

    ---------------------------------------------------------
    CURRENT TOTAL        264,272   189,272    75,000
    CUMULATIVE TOTAL     264,272   189,272    75,000


   The outstanding balance is:   $        0    after period:       30

$$$$$$$$$$$$$$$$$$$$$$$$$$$$$$$$$$$$$$$$$$$$$$$$$$$$$$$$$$$$$

 Press  [Alt] M  for MENU          Press  [Ctrl] [Break]  for READY

~~~~~~~~~~~~~~~~~~~~~~~~~~~~~~~~~~~~~~~~~~~~~~~~~~~~~~~~~~~~~~~~~~~~
```

CALCULATING MORTGAGE CONSTANTS
(Template: lot603)

Some borrowers and lenders are used to using mortgage constants instead of interest rates and mortgage terms in calculating debt service amounts. This is not a problem, especially with Lotus 1-2-3 since it is just as easy to calculate mortgage constants as debt services. (By definition, debt service is equal to the mortgage amount times the mortgage constant.)

Principles. For any combination of an interest rate and a term of the loan, a mortgage constant can be produced. This number, given a compounding period, can then be used to calculate the debt service once the mortgage amount is chosen. As a result, mortgage constants are a function of *both* mortgage interest rates and mortgage terms. Raising the interest rate raises the mortgage constant and the debt service. Shortening the term of the mortgage raises the mortgage constant and the debt service. Raising the interest rate and shortening the term of the mortgage both raise the mortgage constant and the debt service.

The reverse is also true. Mortgage constants and debt services can be lowered by lowering the interest rate on the loan or by lengthening the term of the loan. While many people recognize that lowering the interest rate results in a lower cost of borrowing, some also believe that lengthening the repayment period also lowers the cost of borrowing. (They reason that by lengthening the term, the cost is lowered since the mortgage constant falls.) This is dangerous since lengthening the term means more payments over a longer period of time. In effect, lengthening the repayment period may not be an advantage to some borrowers.

Using the Template. Only two inputs are required: the interest rate and the term of the loan. The output provides mortgage constants for the same five rates of compounding as before: annual, semi-annual, quarterly, monthly, and daily. Each are calculated automatically by Lotus 1-2-3. (Recall also that in Chapter 5, the Mortgage Constant Table Generator also showed how sensitive mortgage payments are to changes in interest rates and mortgage terms.)

Note also that because of compounding between the payment periods, the semi-annual mortgage constant will always be *less* than two times the annual mortgage constant, for example. Similarly, the annual mortgage constant will always be *more* than 365 times the daily mortgage constant.

Finally, the summary table compares the mortgage constants with the interest rates used to generate the mortgage constants. Note that the mortgage constants will always exceed the interest rates used in the calculations (for example, an interest rate of 1.04 percent compounded monthly is equal to 12.50 percent annually), if the loans are finite in length. If a loan had an infinite life, it would never be repaid. The mortgage payment for a loan with an infinite life must therefore be one where the entire payment is interest. Thus, the only time when the difference between the mortgage constant and the interest rate was zero would be when the term of the loan was infinity, assuming the same interest rates are used in both calculations and the loans are repaid in level, equal payments.

Graphics. The graph of this template emphasizes the difference between the interest rate on the loan and the mortgage constant. If the loan is finite in length, and all else is the same, the mortgage constant will always exceed the interest rate on the loan.

Possible Modifications. Users interested in making changes to this template can add numerous other elements for their own purposes. For example, some users might like to include portions of amortization schedules with the mortgage constant calculations. The idea of this template is to provide a fast method of calculating mortgage constants (note that Template lot506 already has calculated mortgage constants in an amortization setting). Thus, it may be useful to examine various combinations of interest rates and terms and see how the mortgage constants vary with the changes.

EXAMPLE TEMPLATE 6.3
Calculating mortgage constants.

```
lot603x                                     Real Estate Diskette #2
=================================================================
CALCULATING MORTGAGE CONSTANTS      Copyright (C) Reston Pub. Co., 1985
=================================================================

~~~~~~~~~~~~~~~~~~~~~~~~~~~~~~~~~~~~~~~~~~~~~~~~~~~~~~~~~~~~~~~~~~~~~

                *** TABLE OF CONTENTS ***
                    ==================

                Table                           Page
                -----                           ----

    I.  INPUT ASSUMPTIONS                         1

   II.  SOLUTIONS                                  2

  III.  SUMMARY OF CALCULATIONS                    3


~~~~~~~~~~~~~~~~~~~~~~~~~~~~~~~~~~~~~~~~~~~~~~~~~~~~~~~~~~~~~~~~~~~~~

                    I. INPUT ASSUMPTIONS
                    ====================

    Enter the following assumptions:

        Interest Rate (i)          >>>       12.50   %

        Term of Loan (n)           >>>          30   years

 Press  [Alt] M  for MENU       Press  [Ctrl] [Break]  for READY


~~~~~~~~~~~~~~~~~~~~~~~~~~~~~~~~~~~~~~~~~~~~~~~~~~~~~~~~~~~~~~~~~~~~~

                      II. OUTPUT
                      ==========

    For any fully-amortized, level-payment, ordinary annuity loan,

            if i is:                12.50   percent,

            and if n is:               30   years,
```

```
$$$$$$$$$$$$$$$$$$$$$$$$$$$$$$$$$$$$$$$$$$$$$$$$$$$$$$$$$$$$$$$$$$$$$$$$$$$$$$$$

   the Annual Mortgage Constant will be:            12.87601  percent

   the Semi-Annual Mortgage Constant will be:       6.418937  percent

   the Quarterly Mortgage Constant will be:         3.204823  percent

   the Monthly Mortgage Constant will be:           1.067257  percent

   the Daily Mortgage Constant will be:             0.035071  percent

$$$$$$$$$$$$$$$$$$$$$$$$$$$$$$$$$$$$$$$$$$$$$$$$$$$$$$$$$$$$$$$$$$$$$$$$$$$$$$$$
```

Press [Alt] M for MENU   Press [Ctrl] [Break] for READY

~~~~~~

III. SUMMARY OF CALCULATIONS

This summary calculates the difference between the
mortgage constant and the interest rate:

```
$$$$$$$$$$$$$$$$$$$$$$$$$$$$$$$$$$$$$$$$$$$$$$$$$$$$$$$$$$$$$$$$$$$$$$$$$$$$$$$$
```

Payments/Compounds Per Annum	Mortgage Constant	Interest Rate	Diff in Basis Pts
Annually	12.88 %	12.50 %	37.60155
Semi-Annually	6.42 %	6.25 %	16.89378
Quarterly	3.20 %	3.13 %	7.982311
Monthly	1.07 %	1.04 %	2.559109
Daily	0.04 %	0.03 %	0.082534

```
$$$$$$$$$$$$$$$$$$$$$$$$$$$$$$$$$$$$$$$$$$$$$$$$$$$$$$$$$$$$$$$$$$$$$$$$$$$$$$$$
```

Press [Alt] M for MENU   Press [Ctrl] [Break] for READY

~~~~~~

MEASURING THE EFFECTIVE COST OF BORROWING
(Template: lot604)

The final two templates in this chapter measure the loan cost to the borrower (the effective cost of borrowing) and the rate of return to the lender (the lender's yield) from making the type of loans analyzed in this chapter. In effect, previous templates in this chapter have measured the debt service, the portion of interest of the debt service, the outstanding balance at various points in time in the amortization process, and the dual effects of combinations of interest rates and terms of the loan. In these two templates, the interest rate on the loan is sought. In the first case, the question is what does the loan cost the borrower. In the second case, the question is how much does the lender earn by making the loan. You may be surprised to learn that these seem similar, but are very different questions.

Principles. Measuring the cost of borrowing is a very important question since most borrowers seek to find the cheapest loan available at the time the money is needed. One of the important issues is what is meant by "cheapest." In this book, the cheapest loan for a borrower is the one where the effective interest rate on the loan is the lowest. (Note that it is not always true that the loan with the lowest interest rate is the same as the loan with the lowest mortgage constant. The reader is referred to other texts where this is explained in more detail.)

The cost of borrowing in all of the prior templates in this chapter was equal to the interest rate when annualized. This means if the payments were made on an annual basis, the interest rate used to amortize the loan represented the effective cost of borrowing for the loan. If a monthly payment period was used, the effective cost of borrowing was the monthly interest rate multiplied by 12. This number will always be greater than the annual interest rate for level-payment loans.

In the template, the same story applies, except now some additional considerations are introduced. In real world markets, lenders include some special loan provisions which can affect the effective cost of borrowing. Some of these are closing costs (expenses and fees which are paid by the borrower at the time the loan is originated), discount points (extra charges set by the lender which are also paid at closing), prepaid interest (interest expenses to be prepaid by the borrower), mortgage insurance premiums (private insurance premiums paid by the borrower at the lender's request to shift the default risk of the loan from the lender to the insurance company), and others. In this template, these provisions can be included into the analysis.

Using the Template. The user is required to enter the typical parameters including the mortgage amount, interest rate, term of the loan, and rate of compounding. In addition, four special loan provisions are entered as they apply. Closing costs and prepaid interest may be input as a dollar amount. Discount points are entered as the number of points. (The convention is to quote these charges in "points" where each point is equal to a percentage of the loan borrowed. Thus, 3 points on a $50,000 loan is equal to $1,500. This template is designed for the user to merely enter the points; Lotus will do the multiplying.) Finally, the mortgage insurance premium is also entered as a percentage of the loan. (Note that the mortgage insurance premium in this case constitutes only the initial premium. In many cases, there is an additional charge each payment period. This charge has been omitted in this template.)

The reason these special loan provisions are important is because they are additional charges above and beyond the interest charged to the borrower. In effect, the borrower pays not only the interest and principal each period, but also any of the charges under these special provisions. Thus, the *effective* rate paid by the borrower is higher than the rate of interest on the loan whenever these charges apply. In almost every mortgage, one or more of these charges apply.

An Example.   Consider a loan for $75,000 at 13.50 percent for 30 years, compounded annually. In addition, suppose $2,000 of closing costs are required, as well as 3 discount points, $1,000 in prepaid interest, and a 1.00 percent mortgage insurance premium. The template shows that the debt service would be $10,357 for this loan and would also require $6,000 in charges (typically, these are paid at the time of origination in addition to the downpayment). Note that the effective cost of borrowing without the provisions would be equal to the interest rate on the loan, or 13.50%. However, with the loan provisions, the effective cost rises.

This template will not solve directly for the rate, but it has been designed so as to approximate the rate. The template uses the interest rate on the loan as a beginning point and increases the rate by .20 percentage points several times. The range is 3.80 percentage points. Note also that the template asks whether the effective cost of borrowing is less than each rate. If the computer produces a zero ("FALSE"), the impact of the special loan provisions is to increase the effective cost of borrowing even higher.

When the tested rate is high enough, the statement will change to a one ("TRUE"). At this point, the user knows that the effective cost of borrowing is less than the current rate and greater than the previous rate.

In the example shown here, the effective cost of borrowing, given the loan provisions, is greater than 14.70 percent and less than 14.90 percent. Note that the interest rate on the loan is 13.50 percent!

Lotus 1-2-3 has the capability of solving for rates such as this one with the use of the @IRR Function. This will be demonstrated in a template in Chapter 11.

Graphics. A pie chart has been designed to accompany this template. It presents the breakdown of special loan provisions by percentages. In this case, note that the discount points are a little more than one-third of the fees, the closing costs are exactly one-third and prepaid interest and the mortgage insurance premium account for the rest.

Possible Modifications. There are several possibilities for changes to this template. First, it is possible to increase the number and type of loan provisions. For example, prepayment penalties are frequently used by lenders and affect the effective cost of borrowing on loans. Also, as mentioned, only the initial mortgage insurance premium was included; typically there is also a monthly premium charge in most residential mortgages. Other examples are also possible.

The band which limits the rates has been set at .20 percentage points. For some purposes, this is close enough. However, if more precise rates are desired, it is possible to narrowly define these rates for closer approximations. Only an experienced Lotus 1-2-3 user should try to do this, however.

In addition, the user can try to develop a part of the output using the @IRR Function. However, this should be done on a separate diskette until it is perfected and then imported to this template. Also, see Template lot1102 for an example of how this function is used. The reason it was omitted here was to demonstrate the impact that these loan provisions can have on the effective cost of borrowing in table form. More precise needs can be implemented.

EXAMPLE TEMPLATE 6.4
Measuring the effective cost of borrowing.

```
lot604x                                      Real Estate Diskette #2
=====================================================================
MEASURING THE EFFECTIVE COST OF BORROWING
                              Copyright (C) Reston Pub. Co., 1985
=====================================================================


~~~~~~~~~~~~~~~~~~~~~~~~~~~~~~~~~~~~~~~~~~~~~~~~~~~~~~~~~~~~~~~~~~~~~~~~~


              ***   TABLE OF CONTENTS   ***
                    =================

              Table                           Page
              -----                           ----

     I.   INPUT ASSUMPTIONS                    1

    II.   SOLUTIONS                            2

   III.   SUMMARY OF EFFECTIVE COST OF BORROWING    3


~~~~~~~~~~~~~~~~~~~~~~~~~~~~~~~~~~~~~~~~~~~~~~~~~~~~~~~~~~~~~~~~~~~~~~~~~


                    I. INPUT ASSUMPTIONS
                    ====================

     Enter the following assumptions:


          Mortgage Amount (Mort)      >>>     $  75,000

          Interest Rate (i)           >>>        13.50   %

          Term of Loan (n)            >>>           30   years

          Rate of Compounding/
          Payments per Annum(m)       >>>         1.00   times/yr

          Special Loan Provisions:
          ------------------------

            Closing Costs (cc)        >>>     $   2,000

            Discount Points (dp)      >>>        3.00   points

            Prepaid Interest (ppi)    >>>     $   1,000

            Mortgage Insurance (mi)
              (Initial Premium Only)  >>>        1.00   %

  Press  [Alt] M  for MENU        Press  [Ctrl] [Break]  for READY


~~~~~~~~~~~~~~~~~~~~~~~~~~~~~~~~~~~~~~~~~~~~~~~~~~~~~~~~~~~~~~~~~~~~~~~~~
```

II. SOLUTIONS

==============

For any fully-amortized, level-payment, ordinary annuity loan,

if Mort is:	$ 75,000	,
if i is:	13.50	percent,
if n is:	30	years,
and if m is:	1.00	times per year,

and

if cc is:	$ 2,000	,
if dp is:	$ 2,250	,
if ppi is:	$ 1,000	,
if mi is:	$ 750	,

$$

```
                    the Debt Service is:            $   10,357

           the Special Loan Provisions equal: $    6,000

                               and

           the Effective Cost of Borrowing is:
    ---------------------------------------------------------
       Less than   13.50   percent  ... >          0      !!
       Less than   13.70   percent  ... >          0      !!
       Less than   13.90   percent  ... >          0      !!
       Less than   14.10   percent  ... >          0      !!
       Less than   14.30   percent  ... >          0      !!

       Less than   14.50   percent  ... >          0      !!
       Less than   14.70   percent  ... >          0      !!
       Less than   14.90   percent  ... >          1      !!
       Less than   15.10   percent  ... >          1      !!
       Less than   15.30   percent  ... >          1      !!

       Less than   15.50   percent  ... >          1      !!
       Less than   15.70   percent  ... >          1      !!
       Less than   15.90   percent  ... >          1      !!
       Less than   16.10   percent  ... >          1      !!
       Less than   16.30   percent  ... >          1      !!

       Less than   16.50   percent  ... >          1      !!
       Less than   16.70   percent  ... >          1      !!
       Less than   16.90   percent  ... >          1      !!
       Less than   17.10   percent  ... >          1      !!
       Less than   17.30   percent  ... >          1      !!


    ---------------------------------------------------------
         -----(Computer returns 0 if FALSE, 1 if TRUE)-----

    $$$$$$$$$$$$$$$$$$$$$$$$$$$$$$$$$$$$$$$$$$$$$$$$$$$$$$$$$$$$$$


  Press  [Alt] M  for MENU        Press  [Ctrl] [Break]  for READY


~~~~~~~~~~~~~~~~~~~~~~~~~~~~~~~~~~~~~~~~~~~~~~~~~~~~~~~~~~~~~~~~~~~~
```

III. SUMMARY OF EFFECTIVE COST OF BORROWING
===

Since the interest rate on the $ 75,000 mortgage is
13.50 percent, given the other assumptions, the impact of
the loan provisions is to reduce the amount borrowed by the
mortgagor by $ 6,000 . Therefore, the mortgagor receives
the difference in this case or $ 69,000 .

The impact of these loan provisions on the cost of borrowing
can be dramatic. The effective cost of borrowing will be
greater than the interest rate on the mortgage whenever the
special loan provisions are applied. In this case, the
effective interest rate exceeds the stated rate: 1

    -----(Computer returns 0 if FALSE, 1 if TRUE)-----

To approximate the effective interest rate, review the
solution table above. When the results change from FALSE
(0) to TRUE (1), the answer is provided. For example, if at
14.70 percent, "0" is shown and at 14.90 percent, "1" is
indicated, the effective rate of interest is greater than
14.70 percent and less than 14.90 percent.

Press [Alt] M for MENU   Press [Ctrl] [Break] for READY

~~~~~~

MEASURING THE LENDER'S YIELD
(Template: lot605)

In the previous template, it was shown that if one or more of several special loan provisions are used in mortgages or other loans, the effective cost of borrowing will increase above the interest rate on the mortgage. An increase in the effective cost of borrowing may or may not result in an increase in the yield to the lender. While it always results in an additional cost to the borrower, the key question is what happens to the extra funds paid by the borrower. If the funds go to the lender for fees such as title insurance, credit reports, phone expenses, etc., these payments are collected by the lender but are used to pay the costs of these services. In such cases, these fees will *not* affect the rate of return the lender earns from making the loan. On the other hand, charges such as discount points, prepaid interest, or loan origination fees (another type of charge that many lenders use in the residential and commercial mortgage market), will affect the lender's yield. As a result, the lender needs to see if and how much the yield from the loan will rise as a result of which and how much extra funds are charged to borrowers.

Principles.   As indicated, some of the special charges will affect the rate of return the lender earns and others will not. The test is whether the funds are collected to pay for services or not. If so, the lender simply dispenses the funds to the appropriate source (telephone company, title insurance company, etc.). If not, the lender retains the money and counts it as part of the return from the loan.

Using the Template.   This template is very similar to Template lot604 except the only provisions included here are those which increase the lender's yield. In effect, those fees which are paid by the borrower and dispersed to third parties by the lender are irrelevant to the calculation of the lender's yield. Thus, this template allows for discount points, prepaid interest, and loan origination fees.

As in the previous template, the calculation is approximated within .20 percentage points. As a general rule, the greater the amount of charges to the lender, the higher the lender's yield, all else the same. Note also that a summary is provided which explains the interpretation of the template.

An Example.   In this case, the lender would receive an additional $3,750 at closing for a 30-year loan of $75,000, at 13.50 percent interest compounded annually. Instead of the lender expecting to earn 13.50 percent per year, in this case, the impact of the extra charges drives the true yield up to somewhere between 14.10 and 14.30 percent. Thus, the extra charges are far from immaterial. It is not surprising that lenders like these fees and borrowers would rather avoid them.

Graphics.   In this pie chart, there are three special features to increase the yield to the lender. These are discount points (dp), prepaid interest (ppi), and loan origination fees (f). Note that here as in most cases, a majority of the special lender features charged to the borrower consists of the discount points.

Possible Modifications.   Similar types of modifications can be made regarding the range on the approximations and the number and types of loan provisions in the template. It is especially important to note that in the real world's markets, several other loan provisions also affect the lender's yield. Some of these are required to be included in the APR rate on every mortgage contract, but *some are not*. Perhaps the best example is the impact of early repayment of the loan, even if there are no prepayment penalties. If there are *any* initial charges or fees, the impact of early repayment *always* results in a higher cost of borrowing to the borrower and a higher yield to the lender! This is not included in the official APR rate in any mortgage. Why not? It is unknown when the loan is originated when and if the loan will be prepaid. As a result, it is not possible to include it for every mortgage.

The point is that this effect occurs and it is important to recognize it from either side of the market. As a borrower, the probability of prepaying the loan is an element which must be included when measuring the effective cost of borrowing when additional charges are included as part of the loan. As a lender, the likelihood of early repayment of the loan will favorably affect the yield on the loan as long as some extra charges occur at the commencement of the loan. As a result, more sophisticated models which estimate the likelihood of prepayment and the resulting impact may be very useful.

EXAMPLE TEMPLATE 6.5
Measuring the lender's yield.

```
lot605x                                    Real Estate Diskette #2
=====================================================================
MEASURING THE LENDER'S YIELD      Copyright (C) Reston Pub. Co., 1985
=====================================================================

~~~~~~~~~~~~~~~~~~~~~~~~~~~~~~~~~~~~~~~~~~~~~~~~~~~~~~~~~~~~~~~~~~~~~~~~

                   ***   TABLE OF CONTENTS   ***
                       =================
              Table                              Page
              -----                              ----

       I.   INPUT ASSUMPTIONS                      1

      II.   SOLUTIONS                               2

     III.   SUMMARY OF LENDER'S YIELD               3


~~~~~~~~~~~~~~~~~~~~~~~~~~~~~~~~~~~~~~~~~~~~~~~~~~~~~~~~~~~~~~~~~~~~~~~~

                      I.  INPUT ASSUMPTIONS
                      ====================

     Enter the following assumptions:


          Mortgage Amount (Mort)        >>>     $  75,000

          Interest Rate (i)             >>>        13.50   %

          Term of Loan (n)              >>>           30   years

          Rate of Compounding/
            Payments per Annum(m)       >>>         1.00   times/yr

          Special Features to Increase Yield
          -----------------------------------

            Discount Points (dp)        >>>         3.00   points

            Prepaid Interest (ppi)      >>>     $   1,000

            Loan Origination Fees (f)   >>>     $     500

 Press  [Alt] M  for MENU          Press  [Ctrl] [Break]  for READY


~~~~~~~~~~~~~~~~~~~~~~~~~~~~~~~~~~~~~~~~~~~~~~~~~~~~~~~~~~~~~~~~~~~~~~~~
```

II. SOLUTIONS
==============

For any fully-amortized, level-payment, ordinary annuity loan,

if Mort is: $ 75,000 ,

if i is: 13.50 percent,

if n is: 30 years,

and if m is: 1.00 times per year,

                    and

if dp is: $ 2,250 ,

if ppi is: $ 1,000 ,

if f is: $ 500 ,

$$$

                    the Debt Service is: $ 10,357

              the Special Features equal: $ 3,750

                          and

              the Effective Yield to the Lender is:

    Less than   13.5   percent ... >   0   !!
    Less than   13.7   percent ... >   0   !!
    Less than   13.9   percent ... >   0   !!
    Less than   14.1   percent ... >   0   !!
    Less than   14.3   percent ... >   1   !!

    Less than   14.5   percent ... >   1   !!
    Less than   14.7   percent ... >   1   !!
    Less than   14.9   percent ... >   1   !!
    Less than   15.1   percent ... >   1   !!
    Less than   15.3   percent ... >   1   !!

    Less than   15.5   percent ... >   1   !!
    Less than   15.7   percent ... >   1   !!
    Less than   15.9   percent ... >   1   !!
    Less than   16.1   percent ... >   1   !!
    Less than   16.3   percent ... >   1   !!

    Less than   16.5   percent ... >   1   !!
    Less than   16.7   percent ... >   1   !!
    Less than   16.9   percent ... >   1   !!
    Less than   17.1   percent ... >   1   !!
    Less than   17.3   percent ... >   1   !!

      -----(Computer returns 0 if FALSE, 1 if TRUE)-----

    $$$

Press [Alt] M for MENU   Press [Ctrl] [Break] for READY

~~~~~~

III. SUMMARY OF LENDER'S YIELD

Since the interest rate on the $ 75,000 mortgage is 13.50 percent, given the other assumptions, the impact of the special features raises the yield to the mortgagee. In this case, the mortgagee receives payments based upon a mortgage of $ 75,000 , but disperses $ 71,250 . This results in a cash benefit of $ 3,750 at the time of origination.

The impact of this benefit to the mortgagee can be substantial. The effective yield to the lender will be greater than the interest rate on the mortgage whenever the special features are applied. In this case, the lender's yield exceeds the stated mortgage interest rate: 1 .

-----(Computer returns 0 if FALSE, 1 if TRUE)-----

To approximate the lender's yield, review the solution table above. When the results change from FALSE (0) to TRUE (1), the answer is provided. For example, if at 14.10 percent, "0" is shown and at 14.30 percent, "1" is indicated, the effective yield to the lender is greater than 14.10 percent and less than 14.30 percent.

Press [Alt] M for MENU   Press [Ctrl] [Break] for READY

7 Financial Leverage and Alternative Mortgage Instruments

Overview

Financial leverage is one of the "prime movers" of real estate and as such warrants special attention. In this chapter, two templates are devoted to the analysis of financial leverage. One provides a test for favorable or unfavorable leverage (if borrowing debt financing is expected to increase or decrease the wealth of investors). The other template measures the impact of debt financing on the rate of return to the equity investor.

The remaining three templates in this chapter provide opportunities to analyze some of the new "creative" financing instruments. These include the adjustable rate mortgage, the growing equity mortgage, and the more well-known wraparound mortgage financing.

TESTING FOR FAVORABLE LEVERAGE
(Template: lot701)

Some investors act as if borrowing is always advantageous in real estate. However, common sense tells us that borrowing will only be worthwhile if the benefits associated with the use of debt exceed the costs of using debt. If the opposite is true, the investor will be worse off. However, if the investor benefits more than it costs the investor to borrow, there will be financial gains associated with the decision. This template provides a simple but effective test for conditions in which borrowing will be expected to be beneficial (favorable leverage) and conditions in which borrowing will be expected to be detrimental (unfavorable leverage).

Principles. In order to test whether leverage is expected to be favorable or unfavorable, a comparison needs to be made between the expected rate of return on the investment (the benefits) and the expected effective cost of borrowing (the costs). In addition, since income from real estate is subject to the federal income tax, the return should be measured after taxes have been taken into account. Similarly, since interest is tax deductible, according to present IRS regulations, interest costs after tax deductions should be used as a better measure of borrowing cost.

Thus, the determination of favorable or unfavorable leverage is a comparison between expected after-tax returns versus the after-tax cost of borrowing. Mathematically, this relationship may be represented as follows:

The investor can expect favorable leverage if:

$$ROI(1\text{-}t) \geq K(1\text{-}t),$$

and the investor can expect unfavorable leverage if:

$$ROI(1\text{-}t) < K(1\text{-}t),$$

where:

$$ROI = \text{expected return on investment,}$$
$$K = \text{expected effective cost of borrowing,}$$
$$t = \text{investor's marginal tax rate.}$$

Using the Template. The user is required to input three assumptions: the expected (before-tax) return on investment, the effective (before-tax) cost of borrowing, and the marginal tax rate of the investor. The computer and Lotus 1-2-3 will solve the rest of the problem.

ROI may be estimated by dividing the expected before-tax cash flow into the acquisition cost of the investment, (or the sum of the mortgage obtained at the time of sale plus the amount of equity or downpayment used). K represents the expected effective cost of borrowing as discussed in the previous chapter, and t is the investor's marginal tax rate. The marginal tax rate is the rate charged on the investor's last dollar of income. This rate is used to ensure that the analysis captures the complete impact of taxes for the investor as a result of this acquisition.

The output page repeats the inputs and applies the test using the above decision rules. In every case, the results indicate whether leverage is expected to increase the wealth of the investor (i.e., be favorable) or reduce the investor's wealth (i.e., be unfavorable).

An Example. In the example, note that an 18 percent return on investment is sufficiently higher than a 12.5 percent before-tax cost of borrowing with a 25 percent tax rate so as to result in favorable leverage. For a real estate investor, this is good news and suggests that the investor will be better off by borrowing funds at 12.5 percent in order to earn 18 percent.

Graphics. The graph associated with this template is simple but illustrates the important point of the analysis. A comparison of the after-tax cost of borrowing to the after-tax ROI indicates the presence or absence of favorable leverage. Graphically, it is quite easy to identify which measure is greater than the other.

Possible Modifications. The decision rule developed in this template is easy to apply and use. More sophisticated analysis suggests that other factors could be taken into account. For example, if some of the return from holding real estate is expected to come from capital gains, the tax rate on capital gains income is 40 percent lower than ordinary income. As a result, this provision in the federal tax law will lower the tax burden on the investment and raise the after-tax rate of return to a level higher than simply the before-tax rate of return times one minus the marginal tax rate on ordinary income. Also, the user might be interested in building in some of the special provisions which can affect the cost of borrowing as shown in Template lot604 in the previous chapter. Finally, experienced users may wish to integrate this template into others in the area of real estate investment analysis where the determination and measurement of financial leverage is a critical factor.

EXAMPLE TEMPLATE 7.1
Testing for favorable leverage.

```
lot701x                                    Real Estate Diskette #2
=================================================================
TESTING FOR FAVORABLE LEVERAGE      Copyright (C) Reston Pub. Co., 1985
=================================================================

~~~~~~~~~~~~~~~~~~~~~~~~~~~~~~~~~~~~~~~~~~~~~~~~~~~~~~~~~~~~~~~~~~~~~

                 ***   TABLE OF CONTENTS   ***
                       ==================
           Table                                    Page
           -----                                    ----

     I.   INPUT ASSUMPTIONS                           1

     II.  SOLUTIONS                                    2


~~~~~~~~~~~~~~~~~~~~~~~~~~~~~~~~~~~~~~~~~~~~~~~~~~~~~~~~~~~~~~~~~~~~~

                      I. INPUT ASSUMPTIONS
                      ====================

      Enter the following assumptions:


         Expected Return on Investment (ROI) >>>       18.00 %

         Effective Cost of Borrowing (K)     >>>       12.50 %

         Marginal Tax Rate (t)               >>>       25.00 %


   Press  [Alt] M  for MENU          Press  [Ctrl] [Break]  for READY


~~~~~~~~~~~~~~~~~~~~~~~~~~~~~~~~~~~~~~~~~~~~~~~~~~~~~~~~~~~~~~~~~~~~~
```

```
                        II. SOLUTIONS
                        ==============

    For any real estate investment project,


                  if ROI is expected to be:      18.00 percent,

                  if K is:                        12.50 percent,

                  and if t is:                    25.00 percent,


    $$$$$$$$$$$$$$$$$$$$$$$$$$$$$$$$$$$$$$$$$$$$$$$$$$$$$$$$$$$$$$$$$$$$$$$$$$

      then the investment provides FAVORABLE leverage:              1

      then the investment provides UNFAVORABLE leverage:            0

    $$$$$$$$$$$$$$$$$$$$$$$$$$$$$$$$$$$$$$$$$$$$$$$$$$$$$$$$$$$$$$$$$$$$$$$$$$

            -----(Computer returns 0 if FALSE, 1 if TRUE)-----


  Press  [Alt] M  for MENU            Press  [Ctrl] [Break]  for READY


  ~~~~~~~~~~~~~~~~~~~~~~~~~~~~~~~~~~~~~~~~~~~~~~~~~~~~~~~~~~~~~~~~~~~~~~~~~~~~
```

MEASURING THE IMPACT OF LEVERAGE
(Template: lot702)

In addition to determining the existence of favorable or unfavorable leverage, it is also useful to measure the magnitude of the impact. This template permits the analyst to demonstrate the impact of favorable leverage on the rate of return on equity. The rate of return on equity is a major concern of most real estate investors since it is a rate of return on the investor's own capital.

Principles. The use of leverage can be beneficial or detrimental, as shown in the last template. However, if leverage is expected to be beneficial, how much will it impact the investor's rate of return? This template provides a method for demonstrating the expected impact of favorable or unfavorable leverage.

The return on equity can be thought of as two parts: the return on the investment and the gain (or loss) associated with using debt to finance the purchase of the property. The relationship may be represented, mathematically as follows:

$$ROE = ROI + [(ROI-K)*(L/E)],$$

where:

$$ROE = \text{expected return on equity,}$$
$$ROI = \text{expected return on investment,}$$
$$K = \text{effective cost of borrowing,}$$
$$L = \text{amount of mortgage,}$$
$$E = \text{amount of downpayment.}$$

Note that the first term on the right side of the equation represents the return on the investment and the second term measures the financing gain. Note also that the difference between the return on the investment and the effective cost of borrowing will determine whether the financing impact is favorable (a gain) or unfavorable (a loss). This impact is multiplied by the debt-to-equity ratio to reflect the extent of debt financing as well as the relative cost. Finally, note that this method uses before-tax measures; no tax rates are used in this analysis.

Using the Template. This template is similar to the previous template but here the emphasis is on the return on equity. The user must input the expected return on the investment, the expected effective cost of borrowing, and the amount of two types of financing: debt and equity.

The output repeats the inputs as a check and shows that the sum of the debt portion and the equity portion must equal the total investment cost. In addition, the loan-to-value ratio is calculated and shown. Finally, the return on equity is shown using the above formula. Lotus 1-2-3 performs the calculation, of course; the user does the interpretation.

As a final note, recall that this analysis always uses expected returns and expected costs of borrowing. The same method can be used to measure past returns and borrowing costs. The emphasis on the expected flows is done because once the results have occurred, while it may be interesting to learn about past performance, there really is not much one can do about it. However, on an expected basis, if leverage is expected to be unfavorable, it suggests that the investor might reconsider this financing program, or this particular investment, or both.

An Example.   The example shows that an $85,000 project financed with $75,000 at 13.50 percent will result in a financing gain if the rate of return on the investment is higher than 13.50 percent. In this case, the expected return on investment is 15 percent and with a loan-to-value ratio of 88.24 percent, the expected rate of return on equity would be 26.25 percent. The reader is invited to try a variety of combinations, including those where the difference between the return on investment and the effective cost of borrowing is negative.

Graphics.   The graph partitions the return on equity into its two components: the return on the asset and the return from favorable leverage or the so-called "financing gain." Note how the graph changes when unfavorable leverage exists.

Possible Modifications.   One likely modification which can be made to this template is to introduce federal income taxes into the analysis. Another interesting change would be to test how accurately this model predicts what the return on equity will be, given actual market returns and costs of borrowing. Finally, as in the previous case, it might be useful to integrate this analysis into other templates which deal with investment analysis and financing decisions of real estate properties.

EXAMPLE TEMPLATE 7.2
Measuring the impact of leverage.

```
lot702x                                    Real Estate Diskette #2
====================================================================
MEASURING THE IMPACT OF FINANCIAL LEVERAGE
                              Copyright (C) Reston Pub. Co., 1985
====================================================================

~~~~~~~~~~~~~~~~~~~~~~~~~~~~~~~~~~~~~~~~~~~~~~~~~~~~~~~~~~~~~~~~~~~~~~~~


              ***   TABLE OF CONTENTS   ***
                    ==================
              Table                              Page
              -----                              ----

      I.   INPUT ASSUMPTIONS                       1

      II.  SOLUTIONS                                2



~~~~~~~~~~~~~~~~~~~~~~~~~~~~~~~~~~~~~~~~~~~~~~~~~~~~~~~~~~~~~~~~~~~~~~~~

                      I. INPUT ASSUMPTIONS
                      ====================

      Enter the following assumptions:


         Expected Return on Investment (ROI) >>>      15.00 %

         Effective Cost of Borrowing (K)     >>>      13.50 %

         Amount of Mortgage Borrowed (L)     >>>   $  75,000

         Amount of Downpayment (E)           >>>   $  10,000


  Press  [Alt] M  for MENU        Press  [Ctrl] [Break]  for READY


~~~~~~~~~~~~~~~~~~~~~~~~~~~~~~~~~~~~~~~~~~~~~~~~~~~~~~~~~~~~~~~~~~~~~~~~
```

```
                            II. SOLUTIONS
                            =============

         For any real estate investment project,


                  if ROI is expected to be:          15.00   percent,

                  if K is:                           13.50   percent,


             the Investment Cost (L + E) is:     $   85,000 ,

             the Loan-to-Value Ratio (L/V) is:      88.24   percent,

                                and


     $$$$$$$$$$$$$$$$$$$$$$$$$$$$$$$$$$$$$$$$$$$$$$$$$$$$$$$$$$$$$$$

             the Return on Equity (ROE) will be:     26.25   percent.

     $$$$$$$$$$$$$$$$$$$$$$$$$$$$$$$$$$$$$$$$$$$$$$$$$$$$$$$$$$$$$$$


     Press  [Alt] M  for MENU           Press  [Ctrl] [Break]  for READY


     ~~~~~~~~~~~~~~~~~~~~~~~~~~~~~~~~~~~~~~~~~~~~~~~~~~~~~~~~~~~~~~~~~~~~~~~~
```

ADJUSTABLE RATE MORTGAGE (ARM)
(Template: lot703)

The remaining three templates in this chapter deal with alternative methods of financing the purchase of real estate. Each are popular methods of using debt finance other than with a traditional, fixed-rate, long-term mortgage.

The first type of mortgage is called the *adjustable rate mortgage* or ARM. It is a very popular alternative mortgage instrument because it is the one adopted by the Federal Home Loan Bank Board for use by federally chartered savings and loan associations. It is also fairly representative of a number of variable rate mortgage proposals.

Principles.   The ARM enables the borrower to obtain long-term financing with interest rates on the loan able to change every six months. The type of loan is thus easier for lenders to make since it is less risky to offer this loan than a fixed rate loan when there is uncertainty about future interest rate levels. Generally, there are limits placed on the maximum increases permitted over time. These limits tend to be placed on each period of adjustment and over the entire life of the loan. As illustrated in the example, the suggested Federal Home Loan Bank limits are one percentage point adjustments per six month period and five percentage points over the entire life of the loan.

Many consumers and consumer groups state that loans of this type are "anti-consumer" instruments and serve as windfalls for lenders. These groups frequently propose that these loans be banned from financial institutions' offerings. It is important to recognize what these loans mean in relation to the traditional, fixed rate loans, how they work, and finally, whether you, as a borrower and/or investor, should use this type of loan. Since so much of the uproar in the media has been against these types of instruments, it is more important than ever to become familiar with the mechanics of these loans.

Using the Template.   The template requires that the user input a number of items needed to amortize any loan. These include the initial mortgage amount, the initial interest rate, and the term of the loan. However, since ARMs permit the altering of interest rates in the future (in this template, the financial institution retains the right to change the interest rate for the remaining balance every six months), the user is also required to enter the interest rate forecast for each six-month period. Thus, if interest rates were expected to rise one-half percentage point each period, the user must enter this information into the template.

In addition, the template requires that the remaining mortgage balance, the current interest rate, and the remaining term of the loan be input. (Note that at the beginning of the loan, the remaining mortgage balance is the same as the initial mortgage balance, the current and initial interest rates are identical, and the remaining term of the loan and the original term of the loan are the same.) These are required because the template provides a monthly amortization schedule and only three years (or 36 months) are possible without recalculation. Also, the user can enter the appropriate limits on changes if desired. Most ARMs and other variable rate mortgages have limits on interest rate changes built into them.

In Table II, the solutions are presented. The first output checks to see if your interest rate forecast has exceeded the limits placed on the instrument. If so, a "TRUE" or "FALSE" indication is provided. This serves as a useful check for the analyst. Next, the inputs are reproduced and the initial monthly debt service is provided. The amortization table follows automatically.

Note that for each month, the amortization table automatically uses the interest rate forecast input by the user. In the event of a differing interest rate level each six months, the debt service automatically changes, resulting in a different schedule of interest and principal (amortization). In addition, the new mortgage payment is shown in the last column during the first month of each six-month period.

If interest rates were not expected to change over one or more six-month period, the amortization schedule for an ARM would be identical to that of a fixed rate mortgage. (Try it and find out.) The important point, however, is that the borrowers for mortgage finance would prefer the fixed rate mortgage, *even* if interest rates were expected to be the same because they would be guaranteed a fixed rate by choosing the instrument. Therefore, it is true that whenever any interest rate risk exists at all, the interest rate of an ARM will *always* be lower than the interest rate on a fixed rate mortgage. (This is true even if interest rates are expected to fall in the future. Are you surprised by this statement? Can you figure out why this is true from the analysis above?)

Finally, because this template involves numerous calculations, the user may have to use the recalculation facility of the template. This works well in this case and the user is able to regenerate the table over and over again. Note also that the values may be reset for analyses of other projects.

An Example. In the example provided, a mortgage of $75,000 is available at an initial rate of 13.50 percent compounded monthly for a period of 25 years (or 300 payments). Note that the limits placed on the instrument are no more than one percentage point per period and no more than five percentage points over the life of the loan. (These are the current FHLB regulations as well.) Finally, the interest rate forecast is provided for the next 3½ years. In this case, the current rate of 13.50 percent is forecast to increase to 14.00 percent in six months, 14.50 percent in 12 months, 15.00 percent in 18 months, 15.25 percent in 24 months, 15.75 percent in 30 months, and 16.00 percent for the next six months. Any interest rate forecast will be used by the computer; this one is purely illustrative of the use of the template and Lotus 1-2-3.

By examining the output, we see that the limits are not violated by the set of inputs used. In addition, the table shows an initial monthly debt service of $874.23. Every six months, a new debt service (or mortgage payment) is provided since the interest rate forecast was always increasing. In this case, the monthly payments jump to $902.62, $931.04, $959.46, $973.65, and $1,001.98.

At the bottom of the schedule, the new outstanding balance is provided, after the appropriate month and the remaining term of the loan is shown. At this point, the user may wish to generate another 36 months of results. The custom-designed menu will lead you to the solution. This procedure may be repeated until the outstanding balance of the loan is zero. Note also that if additional calculations are needed, the interest rate forecast must be changed as well. The template permits an unlimited number of interest rate level changes, although most instruments used in practice tend to limit these changes to the first few years of the loan.

Graphics.   The graph is very illustrative. Each six-month set of payments is provided and compared in size to the previous and subsequent payments. In this manner, the analyst can identify the impact of the interest rate forecast on the size of the debt service. Note in particular that the outstanding balance owed on the loan is also a function of the rate at which the loan is repaid.

Possible Modifications.   The most important modification of this template is probably to create a horizontal window in order to better facilitate the insertions of data for additional calculations. This can easily be done, as in earlier templates, by placing the input lines in the top window and the amortization schedule in the bottom. Other possible changes include the addition of other mortgage provisions, the analysis of tax effects, and the outputting of annual interest payments for assistance in the calculation of tax returns.

EXAMPLE TEMPLATE 7.3
Adjustable Rate Mortgage (ARM).

```
lot703x                                      Real Estate Diskette #2
==================================================================
ADJUSTABLE RATE MORTGAGE (ARM)      Copyright (C) Reston Pub. Co., 1985
==================================================================

~~~~~~~~~~~~~~~~~~~~~~~~~~~~~~~~~~~~~~~~~~~~~~~~~~~~~~~~~~~~~~~~~~~~~~


                  ***  TABLE OF CONTENTS  ***
                  ===========================
              Table                            Page
              -----                            ----

     I.   INPUT ASSUMPTIONS                       1

    II.   SOLUTIONS                                2

   III.   RECALCULATION                            3


~~~~~~~~~~~~~~~~~~~~~~~~~~~~~~~~~~~~~~~~~~~~~~~~~~~~~~~~~~~~~~~~~~~~~~

                      I. INPUT ASSUMPTIONS
                      ====================

   Enter the following assumptions:


       Basic Requirements:
       -------------------
         Initial Mortgage Amount (Mort)  >>>     $  75,000

         Initial Interest Rate (i')      >>>        13.50   %

         Term of Loan (n')               >>>           25   years
          \

       Rate Changes (After each 6 months):
       -----------------------------------
         Maximum Rate Increase Per Period >>>       1.00  % pts

         Maximum Rate Increase Over Life  >>>       5.00  % pts

       Interest Rate Forecast:
       -----------------------
         After  6 months                 >>>       14.00   %
         After 12 months                 >>>       14.50   %
         After 18 months                 >>>       15.00   %
         After 24 months                 >>>       15.25   %
         After 30 months                 >>>       15.75   %
         After 36 months                 >>>       16.00   %


   Press  [Alt] M  for MENU        Press  [Ctrl] [Break]  for READY

~~~~~~~~~~~~~~~~~~~~~~~~~~~~~~~~~~~~~~~~~~~~~~~~~~~~~~~~~~~~~~~~~~~~~~
```

II. SOLUTIONS

The proposed interest rate forecast does not exceed the maximum
   increase per period DURING the first 3 years: 1 !

The proposed interest rate forecast does not exceed the maximum
   increase OVER the life of the loan: 1 !

       -----(Computer returns 0 if FALSE, 1 if TRUE)-----

(If either of these statements are FALSE, redo assumptions.)

For any fully-amortized, level-payment, ordinary annuity loan,

            if Mort is: $ 75,000 ,

            if i' is: 13.50 percent,

            if n' is: 25 years,

$$

the Monthly Debt Service is: $ 874.23

and

the Adjustable Rate Mortgage is amortized as follows:

Month	Beg Bal	Mort Pay	Interest	Amort	End Bal	New MP
1	75,000	874.23	843.75	30.48	74,970	874.23
2	74,970	874.23	843.41	30.83	74,939	
3	74,939	874.23	843.06	31.17	74,908	
4	74,908	874.23	842.71	31.52	74,876	
5	74,876	874.23	842.35	31.88	74,844	
6	74,844	874.23	842.00	32.24	74,812	
7	74,812	902.62	872.81	29.82	74,782	902.62
8	74,782	902.62	872.46	30.17	74,752	
9	74,752	902.62	872.11	30.52	74,721	
10	74,721	902.62	871.75	30.88	74,690	
11	74,690	902.62	871.39	31.24	74,659	
12	74,659	902.62	871.02	31.60	74,628	
13	74,628	931.04	901.75	29.29	74,598	931.04
14	74,598	931.04	901.40	29.64	74,569	
15	74,569	931.04	901.04	30.00	74,539	
16	74,539	931.04	900.68	30.36	74,508	
17	74,508	931.04	900.31	30.73	74,478	
18	74,478	931.04	899.94	31.10	74,447	
19	74,447	959.46	930.58	28.88	74,418	959.46
20	74,418	959.46	930.22	29.24	74,388	
21	74,388	959.46	929.86	29.61	74,359	
22	74,359	959.46	929.49	29.98	74,329	
23	74,329	959.46	929.11	30.35	74,298	
24	74,298	959.46	928.73	30.73	74,268	
25	74,268	973.65	943.82	29.83	74,238	973.65
26	74,238	973.65	943.44	30.21	74,208	
27	74,208	973.65	943.06	30.60	74,177	
28	74,177	973.65	942.67	30.99	74,146	
29	74,146	973.65	942.27	31.38	74,115	
30	74,115	973.65	941.87	31.78	74,083	
31	74,083	1001.98	972.34	29.64	74,053	1001.98
32	74,053	1001.98	971.95	30.03	74,023	
33	74,023	1001.98	971.56	30.42	73,993	
34	73,993	1001.98	971.16	30.82	73,962	
35	73,962	1001.98	970.75	31.22	73,931	
36	73,931	1001.98	970.34	31.63	73,899	

The outstanding balance is $ 73899.18   after month: 36

The remaining term of the loan will be   22 years.

$$

Press [Alt] M for MENU   Press [Ctrl] [Break] for READY

~~~~~~

GROWING EQUITY MORTGAGE (GEM)
(Template: lot704)

This is another new form of long-term mortgage financing. The *growing equity mortgage*, or *GEM*, is a mortgage where the payment grows at a specified percentage rate each year. Therefore, the loan is amortized more quickly than with a traditional fixed rate mortgage since each higher debt service payment repays the amount borrowed faster. This results in a rapidly falling outstanding balance and a shorter effective term of the loan.

Principles. The GEM permits a borrower to begin the repayment with regular payments. Over time, as the borrower's income may be rising, the mortgage payment increases at a prescribed rate. The borrower then makes the larger payment, although over time, the amount of interest owed each period continues to fall. The effect of the larger payment is to rapidly reduce the outstanding balance of the loan since any payment left over after the payment of interest reduces the amount owed on the loan. Thus, with each increase in the debt service payment, the rate at which the loan is repaid increases and the outstanding balance falls quicker and quicker. Soon the loan is repaid, the lender has earned a competitive rate on his or her funds, and the investment has been successfully financed! For borrowers who expect their incomes to be rising in the future, it is not surprising that GEMs have become a popular vehicle.

Using the Template. The set-up of this template is similar to the previous one: inputs are required for the initial mortgage amount, the interest rate on the loan, and the term of the loan. However, unlike an ARM, the GEM does not require an interest rate level forecast. Instead, the GEM requires a rate of increase per year percentage. This will determine how fast the monthly payments will rise. In actual practice, there frequently is a limit as to how much the debt service can rise. When using this template, there is no implicit limit; the desired limit may be imposed by the user.

An Example. In the example, the same $75,000 loan is used, with an interest rate of 13.50 percent for 25 years (300 payments). The mortgage payments are scheduled to increase by 3.50 percent each year (12 months). That's it . . . Lotus 1-2-3 does the rest!

Note that the amortization schedule shows that the monthly payment is $874.23 for the first 12 months of the loan. In the thirteenth month, the payment rises to $904.83, which is precisely 3.50 percent higher than $874.23. Thereafter, the payments increase by 3.50 percent each year.

If additional amortization periods are desired, the user should point to the recalculation option and the next series of payments will automatically be inserted. Note also that if, as in some instruments in practice, the percentage increase in the payments stops after the first few years, the user can change the rate of index increase per year to "0.00" and the loan will be amortized without difficulty.

Graphics.   The GEM graph is large and colorful. Each payment is shown for each month. Notice as per the definition of the mortgage, the GEM grows at the given rate, in this case, every six months. Note also that the graph may be generated after subsequent months' data has replaced the data for the initial 36 months. Lotus 1-2-3 will take care of the updates, including the graph!

Possible Modifications.   This template will also benefit from the use of a window for inputting changes in the Table I. Also, the user might want to investigate various types of changes in percentage increases within the same mortgage. Finally, tax effects have been ignored in this template, although the GEM has important tax differences from other mortgages. (Since there is less interest paid with a GEM, the tax shelter aspects of this mortgage are lower than many other types of instruments. This may be an important aspect for some users.)

EXAMPLE TEMPLATE 7.4
Growing Equity Mortgage (GEM).

```
lot704x                                  Real Estate Diskette #2
================================================================
GROWING EQUITY MORTGAGE (GEM)      Copyright (C) Reston Pub. Co., 1985
================================================================

~~~~~~~~~~~~~~~~~~~~~~~~~~~~~~~~~~~~~~~~~~~~~~~~~~~~~~~~~~~~~~~~~~~~~~

                   ***  TABLE OF CONTENTS  ***
                   ==================
                Table                              Page
                -----                              ----

      I.  INPUT ASSUMPTIONS                          1

     II.  SOLUTIONS                                  2

    III.  RECALCULATION                              3


~~~~~~~~~~~~~~~~~~~~~~~~~~~~~~~~~~~~~~~~~~~~~~~~~~~~~~~~~~~~~~~~~~~~~~

                      I. INPUT ASSUMPTIONS
                      ====================

      Enter the following assumptions:


         Mortgage Amount (Mort)        >>>     $  75,000

         Interest Rate (i)             >>>        13.50   %

         Term of Loan (n)              >>>           25   years

         Rate of Index Increase/Year (r)  >>>      3.50   %


   Press  [Alt] M  for MENU        Press  [Ctrl] [Break]  for READY


~~~~~~~~~~~~~~~~~~~~~~~~~~~~~~~~~~~~~~~~~~~~~~~~~~~~~~~~~~~~~~~~~~~~~~

                         II. SOLUTIONS
                         =============

     For any fully-amortized, level-payment, ordinary annuity loan,


              if Mort is:          $   75,000  ,

              if i is:                 13.50  percent,

              if n is:                    25  years,

              and if r is:              3.50  percent,
```

```
$$$$$$$$$$$$$$$$$$$$$$$$$$$$$$$$$$$$$$$$$$$$$$$$$$$$$$$$$$$$$$$$$$$$$$$

              the Initial Debt Service is:    $    874.23

                  and

      the Growing Equity Mortgage is amortized as follows:
```

Month	Beg Bal	Mort Pay	Interest	Amort	End Bal	New MP
1	75,000	874.23	843.75	30.48	74,970	874.23
2	74,970	874.23	843.41	30.83	74,939	
3	74,939	874.23	843.06	31.17	74,908	
4	74,908	874.23	842.71	31.52	74,876	
5	74,876	874.23	842.35	31.88	74,844	
6	74,844	874.23	842.00	32.24	74,812	
7	74,812	874.23	841.63	32.60	74,779	
8	74,779	874.23	841.27	32.97	74,746	
9	74,746	874.23	840.90	33.34	74,713	
10	74,713	874.23	840.52	33.71	74,679	
11	74,679	874.23	840.14	34.09	74,645	
12	74,645	874.23	839.76	34.48	74,611	
13	74,611	904.83	839.37	65.46	74,545	904.83
14	74,545	904.83	838.63	66.20	74,479	
15	74,479	904.83	837.89	66.94	74,412	
16	74,412	904.83	837.14	67.70	74,344	
17	74,344	904.83	836.37	68.46	74,276	
18	74,276	904.83	835.60	69.23	74,207	
19	74,207	904.83	834.83	70.01	74,137	
20	74,137	904.83	834.04	70.79	74,066	
21	74,066	904.83	833.24	71.59	73,994	
22	73,994	904.83	832.44	72.40	73,922	
23	73,922	904.83	831.62	73.21	73,849	
24	73,849	904.83	830.80	74.03	73,775	
25	73,775	936.50	829.97	106.54	73,668	936.50
26	73,668	936.50	828.77	107.73	73,560	
27	73,560	936.50	827.55	108.95	73,451	
28	73,451	936.50	826.33	110.17	73,341	
29	73,341	936.50	825.09	111.41	73,230	
30	73,230	936.50	823.84	112.66	73,117	
31	73,117	936.50	822.57	113.93	73,003	
32	73,003	936.50	821.29	115.21	72,888	
33	72,888	936.50	819.99	116.51	72,772	
34	72,772	936.50	818.68	117.82	72,654	
35	72,654	936.50	817.35	119.15	72,535	
36	72,535	936.50	816.01	120.49	72,414	

```
   The outstanding balance is:   $72414.10    after period:       36


$$$$$$$$$$$$$$$$$$$$$$$$$$$$$$$$$$$$$$$$$$$$$$$$$$$$$$$$$$$$$$$$$$$$$$$

Press   [Alt] M  for MENU            Press   [Ctrl] [Break]  for READY
```

WRAPAROUND MORTGAGE FINANCING
(Template: lot705)

The final type of financing strategy is also very popular, but differs from the previous two methods in that this method has enjoyed a long following for several years in commercial and industrial markets. Wraparound mortgage financing has been a mainstay in these markets for 50 years. It is one of the essential methods of real estate finance in use by professional investors and modern corporate real estate users.

Principles. The idea of wraparound mortgage financing is not as complicated as some believe. Imagine a property which has an existing mortgage securing the property. The original mortgage has a remaining life and balance which are lower than new mortgages on the property would be. In addition, a necessary ingredient in this story is that the existing interest rate on the loan is considerably lower than current rates.

The owner seeks some of the equity which has built-up through amortization of the original loan and/or appreciation in the value of the property. One option is to sell the property outright, get the value of the property in the market, pay off the remaining balance of the loan, and get the equity. Another method is to refinance the loan at the current market rate, retain ownership, and free up some of the cash in the project. However, another option, and one which is preferred in many cases, is to use a wraparound mortgage.

The borrower proposes to obtain additional funds from either the same lender who holds the initial loan or a new lender (it does not make any difference), and agrees to pay a single mortgage payment, which will include the payment for the initial loan and the payment for the new funds. The new lender promises to "pass along" the funds to the original lender (if it differs) so that the original loan is not impaired, and the new lender retains the difference as payment for the new money.

The rate charged on the new loan is higher than the rate charged on the old loan, *but the borrower pays this rate on both loans* (since the new loan is now "wrapped around" the old one), so the lender earns a higher rate of return on the new money. If the lender is the same person for both loans, the use of a wraparound mortgage is a method where the lender can increase the rate of return on the old loan as well. As long as the rate of interest charged for the wraparound mortgage is lower than the rate charged for second mortgages, all else constant, the borrower will be better off as well. Thus, both parties benefit from the creation of this instrument.

The underlying factor that provides opportunities for wraparound mortgage financing is the inability of a lender to insert and exercise a "due-on-sale clause" in the mortgage. Thus, if a subsequent purchaser of property can "assume" the existing mortgage financing, a sale can take place with wraparound mortgage financing supplying additional mortgage financing, without disturbing the existing financing. If an "acceleration clause" is enforced in the mortgage (this means that upon any conveyance or transaction, the remaining number of payments are accelerated from the future to the present), wrap-around mortgage financing will be precluded. The reader is invited to investigate wraparound mortgage financing and other creative financing methods in one or more of several real estate finance or investment texts. For example, clear definitional and numerical presentations are provided in Tom Morton, *Real Estate Finance: A Practical Approach* (Glenview, IL: Scott, Foresman and Company, 1983).

Using the Template. This template requires three sets of inputs. First, the information about the original financing is required. This includes the original mortgage balance, the interest rate on the existing mortgage and the initial term of the loan. The second set of inputs consists of the new financing information. Specifically, the additional amount of mortgage financing and the new interest rate for the wraparound financing are required. Finally, the user is required to input some other information: the remaining life of the initial mortgage, and the rate of payment and compounding. After this information has been provided, return to the menu and evaluate the solutions. Then, sit back and watch Lotus 1-2-3 do the work.

A word of caution. There are two hidden formulas in this template. These are stored in cells in Columns K and L. Do not alter these formulas. They are required to calculate the outstanding balance of the loan.

An Example. Note that in this example, the $75,000 mortgage with an interest rate of 13.50 percent, compounded monthly over 30 years, requires a mortgage payment of $859.06 per month. At year 18, the remaining balance of the loan should be $61,111.80 assuming all payments have been made on time. If the borrower obtains an additional $30,000 and agrees to a wraparound mortgage interest rate of 15.00 percent, the new mortgage payment will be $1,367.48 for a new mortgage balance of $91,111.80.

The rate of return to the lender on the new money (in this case, $30,000), will always be higher than the rate on the wraparound loan *if* the wraparound interest rate is greater than the interest rate on the original loan. The lender is very interested in how high this rate is since the new $30,000 is what the lender is concerned with at the time the wraparound mortgage is made. The borrower is also pleased since new funds are made available (this is the objective, of course) without a sale or refinancing. In effect, this instrument permits the borrower to take advantage of the "financing gain" earned by holding a fixed rate mortgage in an era when mortgage rates have increased over time.

Graphics.   The graph compares the original and new financing sources regarding the mortgage balances and their respective debt services. Since an infinite number of financing arrangements are possible, this type of comparison may be helpful.

Possible Modifications.   Taxes have not been considered in this template. In addition, the summary states that the yield to the lender will be greater than the wraparound mortgage interest rate. However, it is often useful, especially for lenders, to know how high the yield will be. This would be an excellent modification to the template. Also, the template has restricted the remaining life of the old mortgage and the new life of the wraparound mortgage to be the same. This is only one possibility, since the new mortgage can be adopted with any life agreed upon by the borrower, lender, and the government regulators. Finally, other twists can be introduced to the calculation of wraparound mortgage financing. Practitioners can introduce their own ideas and favorite provisions as they become useful.

EXAMPLE TEMPLATE 7.5
Wraparound mortgage financing.

```
lot705x                                   Real Estate Diskette #2
================================================================
WRAPAROUND MORTGAGE FINANCING     Copyright (C) Reston Pub. Co., 1985
================================================================

~~~~~~~~~~~~~~~~~~~~~~~~~~~~~~~~~~~~~~~~~~~~~~~~~~~~~~~~~~~~~~~~~~~~

                   ***  TABLE OF CONTENTS  ***
                   =================

             Table                              Page
             -----                              ----

     I.  INPUT ASSUMPTIONS                        1

    II.  SOLUTIONS                                 2


~~~~~~~~~~~~~~~~~~~~~~~~~~~~~~~~~~~~~~~~~~~~~~~~~~~~~~~~~~~~~~~~~~~~


                    I. INPUT ASSUMPTIONS
                    ====================

     Enter the following assumptions:


          Original Financing
          ------------------
             Mortgage Amount (Exist)      >>>    $  75,000

             Interest Rate (i')           >>>       13.50   %

             Term of Loan (n')            >>>          30   years


          New Financing
          -------------
             Additional Mortgage Funds (Add)  >>>  $  30,000

             New Interest Rate (i")       >>>       15.00   %


          Other Information
          -----------------
             Remaining Life of First Mortgage  >>>     12   years

             Rate of Compounding/
               Payments per Annum (m)     >>>       12.00   times/yr

 Press  [Alt] M  for MENU          Press  [Ctrl] [Break]  for READY


~~~~~~~~~~~~~~~~~~~~~~~~~~~~~~~~~~~~~~~~~~~~~~~~~~~~~~~~~~~~~~~~~~~~
```

```
                         II. SOLUTIONS
                         =============

For any fully-amortized, level-payment, ordinary annuity loan,


            if Exist is:                 $  75,000  ,

            if i' is:                    13.50  percent,

            if n' is:                       30  years,

            and if m is:                 12.00  times per year,
   _____

            the Debt Service will be:                $  859.06

            at Year      18 , the Remaining Balance will be:   $61111.81

   _____



            For any wraparound mortgage, with level-payments,


            if Add is:                   $  30,000  ,

            if i" is:                    15.00  percent,
   _____

            the New Mortgage Balance will be:            $  91,112

            the New Debt Service will be:                $ 1367.48

   _____


   $$$$$$$$$$$$$$$$$$$$$$$$$$$$$$$$$$$$$$$$$$$$$$$$$$$$$$$$$$$$$$$$$$$$$$

        Therefore, for an additional amount of  $  30,000  , the
   borrower (lender) pays (receives)  $  508.42  each period.
   This amount represents the difference between the New Debt
   Service $ 1367.48 , and the original Debt Service,  $  859.06

        The yield to the lender on the additional mortgage funds
   is greater than      15.00  percent.

   $$$$$$$$$$$$$$$$$$$$$$$$$$$$$$$$$$$$$$$$$$$$$$$$$$$$$$$$$$$$$$$$$$$$$$

Press  [Alt] M  for MENU            Press  [Ctrl] [Break]  for READY

   ~~~~~~~~~~~~~~~~~~~~~~~~~~~~~~~~~~~~~~~~~~~~~~~~~~~~~~~~~~~~~~~~~~~~~~
```

8 Forecasting Income from Real Estate Investments

Overview

One of the most important tasks for real estate investors is the forecasting of income. This is essential to making effective decisions about potential projects for sale and for ensuring that rent levels are set at their optimal levels for projects in the investor's portfolio. In addition, careful consideration must be paid to the estimation and management of operating expenses. This area is also a critical concern; poor management techniques can result in considerable waste of resources, or worse, a decline in property values due to under-maintained premises. Operating expense analysis is frequently overlooked by some real estate investors. They seem to act as if "properties manage themselves."

After the estimation of income (including vacancies and bad debts) and expenses, the investor arrives at net operating income. This is a well-known measure and serves as a fundamental measure of income for many investors. However, when debt service is deducted, the result is called *before-tax cash flow*. (It is also referred to as *cash throw-off*.) This is a very useful measure of cash available from the investment each period. (In Chapter 9, the analysis continues to consider depreciation and taxes and permits the analysis of *after-tax cash flow*.) Finally, since income and expenses are not constant over time, the analyst typically is concerned with growth in net operating income. A changing income stream can have a dramatic impact on the value of the property and the rate of return to the investor.

All of these considerations are treated in the four templates developed in this chapter. Many investors regard this area of analysis as one of the most critical and yet it is one of the most overlooked in real estate investment analysis.

CALCULATING THE RENT ROLL
(Template: lot801)

For a property manager, the calculation of the rent roll is the beginning of an analysis of monthly or annual income. For an investor with several properties in an investment portfolio, the measurement of gross or net income is the first step toward identifying the investment attractiveness of certain properties or all properties over time in the investor's portfolio. For a real estate appraiser, the estimation of income levels serves as the initial element from which value is derived. Therefore, the calculation of the rent roll is an important activity for many real estate participants.

Principles. Different investors measure the rental income from a series of projects differently. It is generally agreed that an effective analysis of income includes individual projects, with attention paid to each type of unit within the project, the number of units in each project, the current rent level, and perhaps special characteristics such as size or neighborhood. In addition, a record of vacancies is needed, since vacancies constitute the inventory of a real estate owner. Also, attention should probably be paid toward expectations about rental growth in the future.

The results of a rent roll analysis should provide information about current rents and vacancies and expected changes in the future. The measure called *effective gross income* comes from this analysis and is generally "the top line" in the analysis.

Using the Template. In this template, the user can enter up to ten different properties or complexes. Each complex can have up to four different types of units. They have been named "efficiency," "one-bedroom," "two-bedroom," and "three-bedroom" units. (Note that these names may be changed to suit specific purposes; in fact, data may be entered for, say three-bedroom units which differ from other types of units even though the complex does not have any three-bedroom configurations. For example, consider other income from laundry and vending machines.)

The user can provide a number for each property and a name, if desired. There is space to indicate the number of each type of unit, the monthly rent by type of unit and the number currently vacant. In addition, the template is designed to include expected growth in income so rental growth rates may be input, if desired. Note that different growth rates may be applied to each and every type of unit in each complex.

The results of these inputs are shown in Table II. Each property is shown and their gross possible rent is calculated by Lotus 1-2-3. If the size of the units are input, the rent per square feet is shown. In addition, any vacancy losses are included. The results indicate the effective gross income (on an annual basis) for each complex.

Two other outputs are available. Growth rates are applied to each source of income and expected rents are shown after a five-year period. Also, the percentage of income by type of unit per project is calculated. This is useful to identify for each complex which unit contributes the most to effective gross income from the project.

In the summary, the income analysis is aggregated and each property's income and vacancies are shown for comparison purposes. Totals of each column are also produced with overall percentage changes for each individual property. In this manner, the analyst can monitor which properties are likely to increase (or decrease) in value as a result of changes in effective gross income.

An Example. Note that this example consists of ten projects having a current gross possible income of nearly $318,000. Each property is analyzed individually. In this case, there are small complexes (such as Number 101– Heaven's Gate with 32 units) and large ones (such as Number 104–Twin Towers with 169 units). Also note that each property generates its income and vacancy data. For example, Number 110–Royal Palace has 65 units with a gross possible rental income of $44,200, a vacancy loss of $3,400, leaving an effective gross income of $40,800 for the current year. The analyst expects that rents at this complex will grow relatively rapidly at 8 percent for the efficiency and one-bedroom units and 7.5 percent for the two- and three-bedroom units. This results in an overall growth rate over the five-year period of 7.75 percent, or an effective gross income of $64,196.19 in five years. In this manner, the analyst can carefully dissect and monitor changes in market conditions and expectations which are likely to affect the rents of the investor's properties.

Graphics. The graph of this template is very helpful. It is a line graph which compares the gross possible rent, vacancy losses and therefore, the effective gross income by project. In this way, the user can center in on properties with high vacancies and test the sensitivity of these vacancies on rents. Note that each line contains its own symbols and legend. Also, each line is a different color if you have a color monitor.

Possible Modifications. There are a number of changes or additions which can be made to this template. Certainly the number of complexes can be raised for large investment portfolios or large property management firms. However, this template is relatively large now and increasing the size may result in slower processing time by Lotus. (However, this may be the most important template for some users such as property managers in which case, the added time to process is a small price to pay for the development of a computerized inventory of properties.) Also, the growth rates are available for one period: annually for five years. In some cases, it might be advantageous to analyze more than one growth rate over a period. Also, the investor might wish to estimate growth in rents over several periods. Finally, there may be other types of output of interest to some investors. For example, it might be useful to know the percentages of each property in the investment portfolio. Or, how growth in one property's income will impact the rent roll of the entire portfolio. These and other changes can easily be made to this template once the user becomes familiar with Lotus and with this specific template.

EXAMPLE TEMPLATE 8.1
Calculating the rent roll.

```
lot801x                                    Real Estate Diskette #2
========================================================================
CALCULATING THE RENT ROLL           Copyright (C) Reston Pub. Co., 1985
========================================================================

~~~~~~~~~~~~~~~~~~~~~~~~~~~~~~~~~~~~~~~~~~~~~~~~~~~~~~~~~~~~~~~~~~~~~~~~~~~~

                   ***   TABLE OF CONTENTS   ***
                         ==================
            Table                                        Page
            -----                                        ----

    I.   INPUTS FOR RENT ROLL                              1

    II.  OUTPUT FOR RENT ROLL                              2

    III. SUMMARY OF INCOME ANALYSIS                        3


~~~~~~~~~~~~~~~~~~~~~~~~~~~~~~~~~~~~~~~~~~~~~~~~~~~~~~~~~~~~~~~~~~~~~~~~~~~~

                      I. INPUTS FOR RENT ROLL
                      =======================
```

Property #	Name of Property	Type of Property	No. of Units	Monthly Rent ($)	Square Feet	Annual Growth % (%)	Vacant Units
101	Heaven's Gate	Luxury					
		Effic	5	300.00	500	3.50	0
		1 Bed	15	475.00	655	4.00	1
		2 Bed	12	595.00	710	4.00	0
		3 Bed	-----	-----	-----	-----	-----
102	ABC Apts	Student					
		Effic	-----	-----	-----	-----	-----
		1 Bed	25	400.00	600	5.50	0
		2 Bed	49	475.00	680	5.50	5
		3 Bed	10	600.00	758	4.50	1
103	Swan's Way	Garden-Type					
		Effic	7	190.00	465	3.00	0
		1 Bed	20	255.00	525	3.50	1
		2 Bed	30	310.00	680	3.50	2
		3 Bed	12	385.00	775	3.00	0
104	Twin Towers	High Rise					
		Effic	35	275.00	500	6.00	7
		1 Bed	59	325.00	635	5.50	12
		2 Bed	75	400.00	710	5.50	12
		3 Bed	-----	-----	-----	-----	-----

105	College	Townhouses					
	Town	Effic	-----	-----	-----	-----	-----
		1 Bed	26	295.00	590	2.00	6
		2 Bed	28	400.00	740	5.00	3
		3 Bed	16	550.00	830	5.00	2
106	Treetop	Low Density					
	Village	Effic	-----	-----	-----	-----	-----
		1 Bed	14	330.00	600	4.00	0
		2 Bed	30	465.00	795	4.00	2
		3 Bed	-----	-----	-----	-----	-----
107	The	Adults-Only					
	Cascades	Effic	36	290.00	500	5.00	3
		1 Bed	55	360.00	645	5.00	2
		2 Bed	32	460.00	728	4.00	4
		3 Bed	-----	-----	-----	-----	-----
108	Western	Garden-Type					
	Hamlet	Effic	15	205.00	530	7.00	1
		1 Bed	22	310.00	700	6.00	0
		2 Bed	35	425.00	750	6.00	5
		3 Bed	-----	-----	-----	-----	-----
109	The Park	Low Income					
	West	Effic	-----	-----	-----	-----	-----
		1 Bed	44	195.00	550	3.00	12
		2 Bed	38	230.00	650	3.00	9
		3 Bed	21	280.00	800	3.00	5
110	Royal	Luxury					
	Place	Effic	18	500.00	450	8.00	1
		1 Bed	20	650.00	604	8.00	2
		2 Bed	24	800.00	735	7.50	2
		3 Bed	3	1000.00	846	7.50	0

Press [Alt] M for MENU   Press [Ctrl] [Break] for READY

~~~~~~

II. OUTPUT FOR RENT ROLL
==========================

Property #	No. of Units	Gross Pos Rent ($)	Rent/ SF ($)	Vacancy Losses ($)	Effect Gr Inc ($)	Rent in Yr 5 ($)	% Income Tot Prop (%)
101	5	1500.00	0.60	0.00	1500.00	1781.53	0.095
	15	7125.00	0.73	475.00	6650.00	8668.65	0.452
	12	7140.00	0.84	0.00	7140.00	8686.90	0.453
	0	0.00	ERR	0.00	0.00	0.00	0.000
Totals	32	15765.00		475.00	15290.00	19137.08	1.00
						3.95	% Change
102	0	0.00	ERR	0.00	0.00	0.00	0.000
	25	10000.00	0.67	0.00	10000.00	13069.60	0.255
	49	23275.00	0.70	2375.00	20900.00	30419.49	0.593
	10	6000.00	0.79	600.00	5400.00	7477.09	0.153
Totals	84	39275.00		2975.00	36300.00	50966.19	1.00
						5.35	% Change
103	7	1330.00	0.41	0.00	1330.00	1541.83	0.065
	20	5100.00	0.49	255.00	4845.00	6057.20	0.251
	30	9300.00	0.46	620.00	8680.00	11045.48	0.457
	12	4620.00	0.50	0.00	4620.00	5355.85	0.227
Totals	69	20350.00		875.00	19475.00	24000.36	1.00
						3.35	% Change
104	35	9625.00	0.55	1925.00	7700.00	12880.42	0.164
	59	19175.00	0.51	3900.00	15275.00	25060.96	0.326
	75	30000.00	0.56	4800.00	25200.00	39208.80	0.510
	0	0.00	ERR	0.00	0.00	0.00	0.000
Totals	169	58800.00		10625.00	48175.00	77150.18	1.00
						5.58	% Change
105	0	0.00	ERR	0.00	0.00	0.00	0.000
	26	7670.00	0.50	1770.00	5900.00	8468.30	0.277
	28	11200.00	0.54	1200.00	10000.00	14294.35	0.405
	16	8800.00	0.66	1100.00	7700.00	11231.28	0.318
Totals	70	27670.00		4070.00	23600.00	33993.93	1.00
						4.20	% Change
106	0	0.00	ERR	0.00	0.00	0.00	0.000
	14	4620.00	0.55	0.00	4620.00	5620.94	0.249
	30	13950.00	0.58	930.00	13020.00	16972.31	0.751
	0	0.00	ERR	0.00	0.00	0.00	0.000
Totals	44	18570.00		930.00	17640.00	22593.24	1.00
						4.00	% Change

```
 107       36 10440.00    0.58    870.00  9570.00 13324.38   0.232
           55 19800.00    0.56    720.00 19080.00 25270.37   0.440
           32 14720.00    0.63   1840.00 12880.00 17909.13   0.327
            0     0.00    ERR      0.00     0.00     0.00     0.000
          _____ _____  _____  _____ _____ _____   _____
 Totals   123 44960.00            3430.00 41530.00 56503.89   1.00
                                                     4.68  % Change

 108       15  3075.00    0.39    205.00  2870.00  4312.85   0.124
           22  6820.00    0.44      0.00  6820.00  9126.70   0.275
           35 14875.00    0.57   2125.00 12750.00 19906.11   0.601
            0     0.00    ERR      0.00     0.00     0.00     0.000
          _____ _____  _____  _____ _____ _____   _____
 Totals    72 24770.00            2330.00 22440.00 33345.65   1.00
                                                     6.13  % Change

 109        0     0.00    ERR      0.00     0.00     0.00     0.000
           44  8580.00    0.35   2340.00  6240.00  9946.57   0.370
           38  8740.00    0.35   2070.00  6670.00 10132.06   0.377
           21  5880.00    0.35   1400.00  4480.00  6816.53   0.253
          _____ _____  _____  _____ _____ _____   _____
 Totals   103 23200.00            5810.00 17390.00 26895.16   1.00
                                                     3.00  % Change

 110       18  9000.00    1.11    500.00  8500.00 13223.95   0.204
           20 13000.00    1.08   1300.00 11700.00 19101.26   0.294
           24 19200.00    1.09   1600.00 17600.00 27564.08   0.434
            3  3000.00    1.18      0.00  3000.00  4306.89   0.068
          _____ _____  _____  _____ _____ _____   _____
 Totals    65 44200.00            3400.00 40800.00 64196.19   1.00
                                                     7.75  % Change


 Press  [Alt] M  for MENU            Press  [Ctrl] [Break]  for READY
```

~~~~~~

```
              III. SUMMARY OF INCOME ANALYSIS
              ==================================

    The summary of income analysis for these investments is:


$$$$$$$$$$$$$$$$$$$$$$$$$$$$$$$$$$$$$$$$$$$$$$$$$$$$$$$$$$$$$$$$$$$$$$

  # of    Property  No. of   Gross Pos Vacancy   Effect   % Change
Projects     #      Units      Rent    Losses    Gr Inc   Over 5 Yr
                               ($)       ($)       ($)       (%)
-------------------------------------------------------------------

       1      101       32 15765.00    475.00 15290.00      3.95
       2      102       84 39275.00   2975.00 36300.00      5.35
       3      103       69 20350.00    875.00 19475.00      3.35
       4      104      169 58800.00  10625.00 48175.00      5.58
       5      105       70 27670.00   4070.00 23600.00      4.20
       6      106       44 18570.00    930.00 17640.00      4.00
       7      107      123 44960.00   3430.00 41530.00      4.68
       8      108       72 24770.00   2330.00 22440.00      6.13
       9      109      103 23200.00   5810.00 17390.00      3.00
      10      110       65 44200.00   3400.00 40800.00      7.75
                    -------  ------- -------  -------  -------
TOTALS       10      831  317,560   34,920  282,640



$$$$$$$$$$$$$$$$$$$$$$$$$$$$$$$$$$$$$$$$$$$$$$$$$$$$$$$$$$$$$$$$$$$$$$


Press  [Alt] M  for MENU          Press  [Ctrl] [Break]  for READY


~~~~~~~~~~~~~~~~~~~~~~~~~~~~~~~~~~~~~~~~~~~~~~~~~~~~~~~~~~~~~~~~~~~~~~
```

OPERATING EXPENSE ANALYSIS
(Template: lot802)

The complementary part of income analysis is operating expense analysis. This is equally important for managers, investors, appraisers, and others. Operating expense analysis is frequently the difference between a below market return and the highest possible return to an investor.

Principles.   There are many different types of operating expenses that a real estate owner must pay. Although few properties have all of the expenses listed in the template, many have several of them. Some smaller properties have only a few items but nearly every real estate investment has items including electricity, advertising, some management, property taxes, property insurance, repairs, supplies, and others. This template provides the opportunity to list and monitor these expenses before the owner loses control and wastes a lot of money.

Using the Template.   This template is very large because it enables up to 74 different types of expenses. As a result, although Lotus operates as fast as it can, this template is still a bit slower than some others. Be patient—if you have a lot of expense items for a property, this can be a very valuable template. *Remember Lotus has a large number of calculations to make if you enter a lot of data.*

The user is asked to enter the monthly expenses (since most services and fees are paid on a monthly basis) and the expected annual growth rate (if any) for each item. If the expenses are not expected to grow, the user can enter "0.00" percent or simply leave it blank. For this expense item, Lotus 1-2-3 will understand that you expect the price to be the same in the future as it is today. In addition, if the item does not apply to the property under analysis, leave the item blank.

Note that there are eleven categories of expenses. In the summary of the template, the category totals are reported. This template enables the user to review both items within categories and the totals of categories compared to each other. For additional discussion of operating expense analysis, the reader is invited to review one of several property management books which deal with the subject such as Sidney Glassman, *Tools for Creative Property Management* (Chicago, IL: Institute of Real Estate Management, 1974).

An Example.   In this case, several expenses have been entered for a hypothetical property. Note that in each category, some of the items apply. Note also that the growth rates for the items are indicated from 2.5 to 9 percent. In the summary, each result is added and reported by category. Note that both monthly and annual sums are reported. The percentage of the total of each category is also shown. In this case, the property's expenses are mostly utilities (22.21 percent), administrative (20.36 percent), and redecoration (17.63 percent). The final two columns report expense projections for three and five years using the growth rates by item as input by the analyst.

Totals are also included for each column in the summary. The annual total of operating expenses may be used as an input for other templates used in real estate investment analysis. In this case, the total operating expenses is $52,740. It is expected to increase to $64,765 in three years (a 7.09 percent increase per year), and to $74,341 in five years (a 7.11 percent increase per year).

Graphics.   A pie chart was selected from the available graphics options. This is because the user can monitor changes in types of operating expenses over time easily with a series of pie charts. Also, the relative importance of each expense category is shown by the percentage of the total expenses for the project.

Possible Modifications.   It is rather unlikely that many investors will have properties with several expenses not built into the template. However, it is possible to add some additional items to the list. It is important, of course, to be very careful when adding such items, especially with this template which makes use of numerous calculations in Table II, which can be found in the second set of columns.

Certain other outputs may be of interest. Percentages can be added at several places in the template, especially during the calculation of Table II. In addition, investors may wish to concentrate on other years of forecasting besides three and five years from the time the analysis is done. Although this type of analysis is done in a later template in this chapter, this feature might be useful for some investors or property managers.

EXAMPLE TEMPLATE 8.2
Operating expense analysis.

```
lot802x                                        Real Estate Diskette #2
=====================================================================
OPERATING EXPENSE ANALYSIS            Copyright (C) Reston Pub. Co., 1985
=====================================================================

~~~~~~~~~~~~~~~~~~~~~~~~~~~~~~~~~~~~~~~~~~~~~~~~~~~~~~~~~~~~~~~~~~~~~~~~~

                   ***   TABLE OF CONTENTS   ***
                   ==================
              Table                                    Page
              -----                                    ----

      I.   INPUTS FOR OPERATING EXPENSE STATEMENT        1

     II.   OUTPUT FOR OPERATING EXPENSE STATEMENT         2

    III.   SUMMARY OF OPERATING EXPENSE ANALYSIS          3


~~~~~~~~~~~~~~~~~~~~~~~~~~~~~~~~~~~~~~~~~~~~~~~~~~~~~~~~~~~~~~~~~~~~~~~~~
```

```
                I. INPUTS FOR OPERATING EXPENSE STATEMENT
                ==============================================

        Enter the following assumptions:

                                                        Expected
                                               Monthly  Growth %

        PAYROLL EXPENSES

            Assistant Manager      >>>    $    40.00     5.00  %
            Clerical               >>>    $    25.00     5.00  %
            Doorman                >>>    $   100.00     5.00  %
            Garagemen              >>>    $   _____      _____  %
            Groundskeepers         >>>    $    25.00     4.00  %
            Group Hospitalization  >>>    $   _____      _____  %
            Maids                  >>>    $   _____      _____  %
            Maintenance            >>>    $    75.00     5.00  %
            Painters               >>>    $    10.00     7.00  %
            Payroll Taxes          >>>    $    27.00     6.00  %
            Porters                >>>    $   _____      _____  %
            Resident Manager       >>>    $   175.00     5.00  %
            Security               >>>    $    23.00     4.00  %
            Telephone Operators    >>>    $   _____      _____  %
            Vacations and Bonuses  >>>    $   _____      _____  %

        ADMINISTRATIVE EXPENSES

            Audit Fee              >>>    $    10.00     6.00  %
            Credit Reports         >>>    $    25.00     4.50  %
            Donations              >>>    $   _____      _____  %
            Legal Expenses         >>>    $     5.00     5.00  %
            Licenses and Permits   >>>    $     5.00     3.00  %
            Management Fee         >>>    $   800.00     8.00  %
            Miscellaneous Admin    >>>    $    25.00     5.00  %
            Postage                >>>    $    10.00     4.00  %
            Stationary and Printing >>>   $    15.00     4.00  %

        UTILITIES

            Electricity            >>>    $   355.00     8.50  %
            Fuel                   >>>    $   280.00     9.00  %
            Gas                    >>>    $   _____      _____  %
            Telephone              >>>    $    82.00     4.00  %
            Sewer                  >>>    $   100.00     7.00  %
            Water                  >>>    $   159.00     7.00  %

        REPAIRS AND MAINTENANCE

            Appliances             >>>    $    15.00     5.00  %
            Building and Bldg Equip >>>   $   _____      _____  %
            Electrical             >>>    $    25.00     6.00  %
            Elevator               >>>    $   _____      _____  %
            Grounds                >>>    $    22.00     5.00  %
            Heat and Air Cond      >>>    $    40.00     7.00  %
            Plumbing               >>>    $    30.00     7.00  %
            Television             >>>    $     5.00     6.00  %
```

```
SUPPLIES

    Electrical                 >>>   $    10.00    7.50  %
    Hardware                   >>>   $    15.00    7.00  %
    Janitor                    >>>   $    39.00    8.00  %
    Miscellaneous              >>>   $     5.00    5.00  %
    Paper Products             >>>   $   _____    _____  %
    Plumbing                   >>>   $    25.00    9.00  %

REDECORATION

    Contractor Interior Paint  >>>   $    50.00    7.50  %
    Paint - Interior           >>>   $    25.00    5.00  %
    Painters - Interior        >>>   $   100.00    8.00  %
    Contractor Exterior Paint  >>>   $   200.00    7.50  %
    Paint - Exterior           >>>   $   100.00    5.00  %
    Painters - Exterior        >>>   $   300.00    8.00  %

SERVICES

    Building Cleaning          >>>   $    99.00    6.00  %
    Extermination              >>>   $    30.00    5.00  %
    Music                      >>>   $   _____    _____  %
    Security                   >>>   $    10.00    3.00  %
    Service Contracts          >>>   $     7.00    2.50  %
    Snow Removal               >>>   $   _____    _____  %
    Trash Removal              >>>   $    57.00    6.00  %
    Uniforms                   >>>   $   _____    _____  %
    Window Cleaning            >>>   $   _____    _____  %

SWIMMING POOL

    Contract                   >>>   $   100.00    5.00  %
    Repairs                    >>>   $   _____    _____  %
    Supplies                   >>>   $    10.00    4.00  %

ADVERTISING

    Brochures                  >>>   $    23.00    3.00  %
    Newspaper                  >>>   $    10.00    3.00  %
    Other                      >>>   $   _____    _____  %

GENERAL OPERATING EXPENSES

    Equipment Rental           >>>   $   100.00    5.00  %
    Furniture Rental           >>>   $    55.00    6.00  %
    Miscellaneous              >>>   $   _____    _____  %
    Motor Vehicle              >>>   $   _____    _____  %

TAXES AND OTHER EXPENSES

    Franchise Tax              >>>   $   _____    _____  %
    Insurance                  >>>   $   355.00    8.00  %
    Personal Property Tax      >>>   $   _____    _____  %
    Real Property Tax          >>>   $   162.00    8.00  %
    Other                      >>>   $   _____    _____  %

Press  [Alt] M  for MENU         Press  [Ctrl] [Break]  for READY
```

II. OUTPUT FOR OPERATING EXPENSE STATEMENT
===

	Monthly	Annually	3 Yr Growth %	5 Yr Growth %
	($)	($)	($)	($)
PAYROLL EXPENSES				
Assistant Manager	40.00	480.00	555.66	612.62
Clerical	25.00	300.00	347.29	382.88
Doorman	100.00	1200.00	1389.15	1531.54
Garagemen	0.00	0.00	0.00	0.00
Groundskeepers	25.00	300.00	337.46	365.00
Group Hospitalization	0.00	0.00	0.00	0.00
Maids	0.00	0.00	0.00	0.00
Maintenance	75.00	900.00	1041.86	1148.65
Painters	10.00	120.00	147.01	168.31
Payroll Taxes	27.00	324.00	385.89	433.59
Porters	0.00	0.00	0.00	0.00
Resident Manager	175.00	2100.00	2431.01	2680.19
Security	23.00	276.00	310.46	335.80
Telephone Operators	0.00	0.00	0.00	0.00
Vacations and Bonuses	0.00	0.00	0.00	0.00
ADMINISTRATIVE EXPENSES				
Audit Fee	10.00	120.00	142.92	160.59
Credit Reports	25.00	300.00	342.35	373.85
Donations	0.00	0.00	0.00	0.00
Legal Expenses	5.00	60.00	69.46	76.58
Licenses and permits	5.00	60.00	65.56	69.56
Management Fee	800.00	9600.00	12093.24	14105.55
Miscellaneous Admin	25.00	300.00	347.29	382.88
Postage	10.00	120.00	134.98	146.00
Stationary and Printing	15.00	180.00	202.48	219.00
UTILITIES				
Electricity	355.00	4260.00	5441.25	6405.58
Fuel	280.00	3360.00	4351.30	5169.78
Gas	0.00	0.00	0.00	0.00
Telephone	82.00	984.00	1106.87	1197.19
Sewer	100.00	1200.00	1470.05	1683.06
Water	159.00	1908.00	2337.38	2676.07
REPAIRS AND MAINTENANCE				
Appliances	15.00	180.00	208.37	229.73
Building and Bldg Equip	0.00	0.00	0.00	0.00
Electrical	25.00	300.00	357.30	401.47
Elevator	0.00	0.00	0.00	0.00
Grounds	22.00	264.00	305.61	336.94
Heat and Air Cond	40.00	480.00	588.02	673.22
Plumbing	30.00	360.00	441.02	504.92
Television	5.00	60.00	71.46	80.29

SUPPLIES

Electrical	10.00	120.00	149.08	172.28
Hardware	15.00	180.00	220.51	252.46
Janitor	39.00	468.00	589.55	687.65
Miscellaneous	5.00	60.00	69.46	76.58
Paper Products	0.00	0.00	0.00	0.00
Plumbing	25.00	300.00	388.51	461.59

REDECORATION

Contractor Interior Paint	50.00	600.00	745.38	861.38
Paint − Interior	25.00	300.00	347.29	382.88
Painters − Interior	100.00	1200.00	1511.65	1763.19
Contractor Exterior Paint	200.00	2400.00	2981.51	3445.51
Paint − Exterior	100.00	1200.00	1389.15	1531.54
Painters − Exterior	300.00	3600.00	4534.96	5289.58

SERVICES

Building Cleaning	99.00	1188.00	1414.93	1589.81
Extermination	30.00	360.00	416.75	459.46
Music	0.00	0.00	0.00	0.00
Security	10.00	120.00	131.13	139.11
Service Contracts	7.00	84.00	90.46	95.04
Snow Removal	0.00	0.00	0.00	0.00
Trash Removal	57.00	684.00	814.65	915.35
Uniforms	0.00	0.00	0.00	0.00
Window Cleaning	0.00	0.00	0.00	0.00

SWIMMING POOL

Contract	100.00	1200.00	1389.15	1531.54
Repairs	0.00	0.00	0.00	0.00
Supplies	10.00	120.00	134.98	146.00

ADVERTISING

Brochures	23.00	276.00	301.59	319.96
Newspaper	10.00	120.00	131.13	139.11
Other	0.00	0.00	0.00	0.00

GENERAL OPERATING EXPENSES

Equipment Rental	100.00	1200.00	1389.15	1531.54
Furniture Rental	55.00	660.00	786.07	883.23
Miscellaneous	0.00	0.00	0.00	0.00
Motor Vehicle	0.00	0.00	0.00	0.00

TAXES AND OTHER EXPENSES

Franchise Tax	0.00	0.00	0.00	0.00
Insurance	355.00	4260.00	5366.37	6259.34
Personal Property Tax	0.00	0.00	0.00	0.00
Real Property Tax	162.00	1944.00	2448.88	2856.37
Other	0.00	0.00	0.00	0.00

~~~~~~

III. SUMMARY OF OPERATING EXPENSE ANALYSIS
==

Category	Monthly	Annually	% of Total	Expected In 3 Yrs	Expected In 5 Yrs
	($)	($)	(%)	($)	($)
PAYROLL EXPENSES	500.00	6000.00	11.38	6945.79	7658.57
ADMINISTRATIVE EXPENSES	895.00	10740.00	20.36	13398.27	15534.00
UTILITIES	976.00	11712.00	22.21	14706.85	17131.67
REPAIRS AND MAINTENANCE	137.00	1644.00	3.12	1971.79	2226.57
SUPPLIES	94.00	1128.00	2.14	1417.09	1650.54
REDECORATION	775.00	9300.00	17.63	11509.95	13274.09
SERVICES	203.00	2436.00	4.62	2867.91	3198.77
SWIMMING POOL	110.00	1320.00	2.50	1524.13	1677.54
ADVERTISING	33.00	396.00	0.75	432.72	459.07
GENERAL OPER EXPENSES	155.00	1860.00	3.53	2175.22	2414.77
TAXES AND OTHER EXPENSES	517.00	6204.00	11.76	7815.25	9115.71
TOTALS	4,395	52,740	100.00	64,765	74,341

~~~~~~

CALCULATION OF BEFORE-TAX CASH FLOW
(Template: lot803)

This is one of the most important and useful templates in real estate investment analysis for several reasons. The format has been adopted for many of the remaining templates in this book. A lot of data is required, most of which can be calculated separately using one or more of the earlier templates. This template uses data on income, expenses, vacancies, bad debts, growth rates in income and operating expenses, financing inputs, and the expected holding period. With this type of data, an investor can analyze gross possible income, effective gross income, operating expenses, and debt service. The result is called *before-tax cash flow* and is a major measure of investment benefits.

Principles.   Since debt service is regarded as a cash outflow from the investor, the subtraction of debt service from net operating income provides a measure of cash flow rather than income. Although the IRS emphasizes the measurement of income, real estate investors are concerned with cash flow. The measurement of taxable income is important for identifying tax liability, but cash flow is important for measuring performance.

Using the Template.   The template requires a number of important inputs. This template can accommodate up to four different types of units for an investment. For each rental type, the number of units must be entered, with their monthly rents, expected vacancies, and bad debt allowances. The initial operating expense ratio is entered. Growth rates are entered for both income and expenses.

Financing is a major part of real estate investing. In this template, there are three types of debt financing possible as well as equity financing (downpayment). The template can accommodate a first mortgage, a second mortgage, and any interest-only financing. For each type of financing, the user must input the appropriate amounts borrowed, the interest rate on the mortgage (only fixed-rate mortgages are allowed here) and the term of the loan. Finally, the expected holding period must be entered. The template indicates that the maximum allowable is 20 years.

There are two parts to the output table. The first provides a summary of the financing calculations. Each mortgage is shown and a typical payment is calculated. Then for all debt financing, a schedule of mortgage payments is provided. Note that when one loan has been repaid, zeros are reported after that date. Note also that at the conclusion of the term of the interest-only loan, the principal is assumed to be repaid in full.

The second part of the output table calculates the cash flows from the investment by year. Items reported include gross possible income, vacancies and bad debts, effective gross income, operating expenses, net operating income, financing expenses, and finally, before-tax cash flow. Note that the growth rates are automatically applied by Lotus 1-2-3 and that the cash flows are calculated for the specified expected holding period.

In the summary, three items are reported per year of the holding period: net operating income, before-tax cash flow, and return on equity. The latter is defined as each year's before-tax cash flow divided by the downpayment. (This rate of return measure and others are discussed at length in Chapter 10.)

An Example.   The example shows a project with several types of units and monthly rents from $175.00 per month to $400.00 per month. The initial operating expense ratio is 45.00 percent, but operating expenses are expected to grow at a rate of 4.00 percent per year. Rents are forecast to grow at 5.50 percent per year. There are three mortgages: a first mortgage for $425,000 at 13.25 percent (compounded annually), for 30 years; a second mortgage for $75,000 at 15.00 percent (compounded annually), for 10 years; and interest-only financing for $50,000 at 18.50 percent (compounded annually), with the principal due in five years. The equity downpayment is $40,000 and the expected holding period is 12 years.

Note that the financing expenses are $81,887 each year for the first four years. In year five, the interest-only principal is due. After that, the financing expenses are lower. The cash flow calculations show that before-tax cash flow increases each year (except in year five) throughout the expected holding period. The expected returns on equity become very high as a result of the repaying of the mortgages and the relatively high growth rates in income. By year 6, the expected return on equity is over 100 percent!

Graphics.   The "XY" graph compares growth in net operating income with growth in before-tax cash flow. Note that net operating income grows at a constant percentage rate since there is a constant growth rate assumed for income and a separate constant rate for expenses. However, changes in before-tax cash flow which are expected over time are more irregular. Note also that the effect of paying off the interest-only loan is substantial in terms of its impact on cash flow and in the summary, the return on equity (ROE).

Possible Modifications.   The user may wish to include some other items in this analysis. Several other items have been included in subsequent templates. These include depreciation and tax liability, growth in sales prices, and other rate of return measures. The reader is referred to the templates in Chapters 9 and 10 for these additions. As before, the user may also wish to increase the number of financing options or other types of inputs. This can be done in this template.

It is also highly recommended that the user test the sensitivity of several of the inputs on before-tax cash flow and the return on equity. This can be done quite effectively using a horizontal window and Lotus 1-2-3. Note also that the analyst can show the impact of changing rents, operating expenses, and growth rates on cash flow in this manner.

EXAMPLE TEMPLATE 8.3
Calculation of before-tax cash flow.

```
lot803x                                    Real Estate Diskette #3
==================================================================
CALCULATION OF BEFORE-TAX CASH FLOW  Copyright (C) Reston Pub. Co., 1985
==================================================================

~~~~~~~~~~~~~~~~~~~~~~~~~~~~~~~~~~~~~~~~~~~~~~~~~~~~~~~~~~~~~~~~~~~~


                    ***   TABLE OF CONTENTS   ***
                          ==================
                Table                               Page
                -----                               ----

       I.   INPUTS FOR BEFORE-TAX CASH FLOW           1

      II.   OUTPUT TABLES FOR BEFORE-TAX CASH FLOW     2

     III.   SUMMARY OF BEFORE-TAX CASH FLOW            3


~~~~~~~~~~~~~~~~~~~~~~~~~~~~~~~~~~~~~~~~~~~~~~~~~~~~~~~~~~~~~~~~~~~~
```

```
                    I. INPUTS FOR BEFORE-TAX CASH FLOW
                    ===================================

        Enter the following assumptions:


            Number of Unit Types (max.=4)...........>>>         4   types

            Number of Rental Units by Type:
                Type # 1..............................>>>         5
                Type # 2..............................>>>        20
                Type # 3..............................>>>        15
                Type # 4..............................>>>         8

            Expected Monthly Rents by Type:
                Type # 1..............................>>> $    175.00
                Type # 2..............................>>> $    225.00
                Type # 3..............................>>> $    300.00
                Type # 4..............................>>> $    400.00

            Vacancy and Bad Debt Allowances:
                Type # 1..............................>>>         5.00   %
                Type # 2..............................>>>         5.00   %
                Type # 3..............................>>>         2.50   %
                Type # 4..............................>>>         2.50   %

            Initial Operating Expense Ratio........>>>         45.00   %

            Annual Growth Rates:
                Rental Growth Rate....................>>>         5.50   %
                Operating Expenses....................>>>         4.00   %

            Financing Inputs:
                First Mortgage Amount.................>>> $ 425,000
                    Interest Rate on Mortgage.........>>>        13.25   %
                    Mortgage Term (max.=30)...........>>>        30   years
                Second Mortgage Amount................>>> $  75,000
                    Interest Rate on Mortgage.........>>>        15.00   %
                    Mortgage Term (max.=30)...........>>>        10   years
                Interest-Only Financing...............>>> $  50,000
                    Interest Rate on Mortgage.........>>>        18.50   %
                    Mortgage Term (max.=30)...........>>>         5   years

            Equity Investment (Downpayment)........>>> $  40,000

            Expected Holding Period (max.=20).......>>>        12   years


    Press  [Alt] M  for MENU           Press  [Ctrl] [Break]  for READY


    ~~~~~~~~~~~~~~~~~~~~~~~~~~~~~~~~~~~~~~~~~~~~~~~~~~~~~~~~~~~~~~~~~~~~~~~~~~~~~
```

II. OUTPUT TABLES FOR BEFORE-TAX CASH FLOW
===

Financing Calculations:

	Amount	Int Rate	Mort Term	Fin Exp
	($)	(%)	(yrs)	($)
First Mortgage:	425,000	13.25	30	57,693
Second Mortgage:	75,000	15.00	10	14,944
Interest-Only Financing:	50,000	18.50	5	9,250

Year	1st Mort	2nd Mort	Int-Only	Total Fin Exp
1	57,693	14,944	9,250	81,887
2	57,693	14,944	9,250	81,887
3	57,693	14,944	9,250	81,887
4	57,693	14,944	9,250	81,887
5	57,693	14,944	59,250	131,887
6	57,693	14,944	0	72,637
7	57,693	14,944	0	72,637
8	57,693	14,944	0	72,637
9	57,693	14,944	0	72,637
10	57,693	14,944	0	72,637
11	57,693	0	0	57,693
12	57,693	0	0	57,693
NA	NA	NA	NA	NA
NA	NA	NA	NA	NA
NA	NA	NA	NA	NA
NA	NA	NA	NA	NA
NA	NA	NA	NA	NA
NA	NA	NA	NA	NA
NA	NA	NA	NA	NA
NA	NA	NA	NA	NA

```
Cash Flow Calculations:
-----------------------

Year    GPI    Vac & BD    EGI       OE       NOI     Fin Exp    BTCF
-------------------------------------------------------------------------
        ($)      ($)       ($)       ($)      ($)       ($)        ($)

  1   156,900   5,535    151,365   68,114   83,251    81,887      1,364
  2   165,530   5,839    159,690   70,839   88,851    81,887      6,965
  3   174,634   6,161    168,473   73,672   94,801    81,887     12,914
  4   184,238   6,499    177,739   76,619  101,120    81,887     19,233
  5   194,372   6,857    187,515   79,684  107,831   131,887   (24,056)

  6   205,062   7,234    197,828   82,871  114,957    72,637     42,320
  7   216,340   7,632    208,709   86,186  122,522    72,637     49,886
  8   228,239   8,052    220,188   89,634  130,554    72,637     57,917
  9   240,792   8,494    232,298   93,219  139,079    72,637     66,442
 10   254,036   8,962    245,074   96,948  148,126    72,637     75,490

 11   268,008   9,455    258,553  100,826  157,728    57,693    100,035
 12   282,748   9,975    272,774  104,859  167,915    57,693    110,222
 NA      NA       NA        NA       NA       NA        NA         NA
 NA      NA       NA        NA       NA       NA        NA         NA
 NA      NA       NA        NA       NA       NA        NA         NA

 NA      NA       NA        NA       NA       NA        NA         NA
 NA      NA       NA        NA       NA       NA        NA         NA
 NA      NA       NA        NA       NA       NA        NA         NA
 NA      NA       NA        NA       NA       NA        NA         NA
 NA      NA       NA        NA       NA       NA        NA         NA

-------------------------------------------------------------------------


Press  [Alt] M  for MENU          Press  [Ctrl] [Break]  for READY

~~~~~~~~~~~~~~~~~~~~~~~~~~~~~~~~~~~~~~~~~~~~~~~~~~~~~~~~~~~~~~~~~~~~~~~~~~
```

III. SUMMARY OF BEFORE-TAX CASH FLOW
=====================================

For any real estate investment,

$$$$$$$$$$$$$$$$$$$$$$$$$$$$$$$$$$$$$$$

Year	NOI	BTCF	ROE
	($)	($)	(%)
1	83,251	1,364	3.41
2	88,851	6,965	17.41
3	94,801	12,914	32.28
4	101,120	19,233	48.08
5	107,831	(24,056)	(60.14)
6	114,957	42,320	105.80
7	122,522	49,886	124.71
8	130,554	57,917	144.79
9	139,079	66,442	166.11
10	148,126	75,490	188.72
11	157,728	100,035	250.09
12	167,915	110,222	275.56
NA	NA	NA	NA
NA	NA	NA	NA
NA	NA	NA	NA
NA	NA	NA	NA
NA	NA	NA	NA
NA	NA	NA	NA
NA	NA	NA	NA
NA	NA	NA	NA

$$

Press [Alt] M for MENU   Press [Ctrl] [Break] for READY

~~~~~~

FORECASTING GROWTH IN NET OPERATING INCOME
(Template: lot804)

The final template in this chapter deals exclusively with the forecasting of income and expenses. In this template, various growth rates are compared over time. This template proves how important forecasting can be and how difficult it is to do an effective analysis without carefully examining the numbers of a financial analysis. Luckily, spreadsheets such as Lotus 1-2-3 can be an important aid in the development of forecasts of income and expenses.

Principles. If income and/or expenses are expected to vary in future years, it is essential that this information be taken into account by investors, appraisers, and other real estate professionals. With the power of compound interest, a relatively small growth rate will result, over a long period of time in a large sum. Instead of approximating future values, the power of Lotus 1-2-3 can be used to assist users in evaluating future estimates of income, expenses, and thus, net operating income.

Using the Template. This template enables up to three types of units to be analyzed. Each of these rental types can have an unlimited number of units as far as the computer is concerned. The monthly rent of each type of unit is required for calculation of the current effective gross income. The initial operating expense ratio is also input. With this information, the current net operating income may be calculated.

Since the primary focus of this template is on forecasting income and expenses, the estimated future growth rates for each of the unit types and for operating expenses take on special meaning. The user can test the sensitivity in estimating rental or operating growth rates in this analysis. Finally, the expected holding period must be input. The template allows for up to 20 years, a long enough period for most real estate forecasts.

An Example. In the example, three types of units are analyzed. Each has its own rent level and number of units. In this case, the total effective gross income for the first year is $28,200. Given the initial operating expenses ratio of 47.00 percent, the first year's net operating income is $14,946.

The example shows the impact of various growth rates. In this case, 3.00 percent, 4.00 percent, and 5.00 percent annual growth rates are tested. The operating expense growth rate is 1.50 percent per year. Finally, the analyst can observe percentage changes from year to year as a result of the interaction between the various growth rates in types of rental unit and the operating expense growth rates. In this case, the growth in net operating income increases at a steadily decreasing rate.

The summary provides a sample of the results of each rental unit and a few of the years of net operating income.

Graphics. Note that the extensive graph is a different type. It is called a "stacked bar" graph since each data series per year is shown "stacked" on top of each other. In this manner, the analyst can see the relative impacts of each type of rental unit and their respective growth rates.

Possible Modifications. This is a relatively small template, given all of the data input by the user. Other parameters can be included such as debt service payments or more detailed analysis of operating expenses. In addition, the user could develop additional space for other growth rates. In that way, the analysis of the effects of growth rates could be carefully and systematically evaluated.

EXAMPLE TEMPLATE 8.4
Forecasting growth in net operating income.

```
lot804x                                          Real Estate Diskette #3
=========================================================================
FORECASTING GROWTH IN NET OPERATING INCOME
                                   Copyright (C) Reston Pub. Co., 1985
=========================================================================


~~~~~~~~~~~~~~~~~~~~~~~~~~~~~~~~~~~~~~~~~~~~~~~~~~~~~~~~~~~~~~~~~~~~~~~~~~~~

                   ***  TABLE OF CONTENTS  ***
                       =================
            Table                                        Page
            -----                                        ----

     I.   INPUTS FOR FORECASTING NET OPERATING
          INCOME                                           1

    II.   OUTPUT FOR FORECASTING NET OPERATING
          INCOME                                           2

   III.   SUMMARY OF FORECASTING NET OPERATING
          INCOME                                           3



~~~~~~~~~~~~~~~~~~~~~~~~~~~~~~~~~~~~~~~~~~~~~~~~~~~~~~~~~~~~~~~~~~~~~~~~~~~~

           I. INPUTS FOR FORECASTING NET OPERATING INCOME
           ==============================================

    Enter the following assumptions:

        Number of Unit Types (max.=3)..........>>>       3  types

        Number of Rental Units by Type:
          Type # 1..............................>>>       2
          Type # 2..............................>>>       5
          Type # 3..............................>>>       7

        Expected Monthly Rents by Type:
          Type # 1..............................>>>  $  100.00
          Type # 2..............................>>>  $  150.00
          Type # 3..............................>>>  $  200.00

        Initial Operating Expense Ratio........>>>     47.00  %

        Annual Growth Rates:
          Type # 1 Rental Growth Rate..........>>>      3.00  %
          Type # 2 Rental Growth Rate..........>>>      4.00  %
          Type # 3 Rental Growth Rate..........>>>      5.00  %
          Operating Expense Growth Rate........>>>      1.50  %

        Expected Holding Period (max.=20)......>>>      20  years


  Press  [Alt] M  for MENU          Press  [Ctrl] [Break]  for READY
~~~~~~~~~~~~~~~~~~~~~~~~~~~~~~~~~~~~~~~~~~~~~~~~~~~~~~~~~~~~~~~~~~~~~~~~~~~~
```

II. OUTPUT FOR FORECASTING NET OPERATING INCOME
==

*** Rental Units ***

Year	#1	#2	#3	EGI	OE	NOI	% Change
Growth Rates (%)	3.00	4.00	5.00		1.50		
1	2400.00	9000.00	16800.00	28,200	13,254	14,946	NA
2	2472.00	9360.00	17640.00	29,472	13,453	16,019	7.18
3	2546.16	9734.40	18522.00	30,803	13,655	17,148	7.05
4	2622.54	10123.78	19448.10	32,194	13,859	18,335	6.92
5	2701.22	10528.73	20420.51	33,650	14,067	19,583	6.81
6	2782.26	10949.88	21441.53	35,174	14,278	20,895	6.70
7	2865.73	11387.87	22513.61	36,767	14,492	22,275	6.60
8	2951.70	11843.39	23639.29	38,434	14,710	23,724	6.51
9	3040.25	12317.12	24821.25	40,179	14,931	25,248	6.42
10	3131.46	12809.81	26062.31	42,004	15,154	26,849	6.34
11	3225.40	13322.20	27365.43	43,913	15,382	28,531	6.27
12	3322.16	13855.09	28733.70	45,911	15,613	30,298	6.19
13	3421.83	14409.29	30170.39	48,002	15,847	32,155	6.13
14	3524.48	14985.66	31678.91	50,189	16,084	34,105	6.06
15	3630.22	15585.09	33262.85	52,478	16,326	36,152	6.00
16	3739.12	16208.49	34925.99	54,874	16,571	38,303	5.95
17	3851.30	16856.83	36672.29	57,380	16,819	40,561	5.90
18	3966.83	17531.10	38505.91	60,004	17,071	42,932	5.85
19	4085.84	18232.35	40431.20	62,749	17,327	45,422	5.80
20	4208.41	18961.64	42452.76	65,623	17,587	48,035	5.75

Press [Alt] M for MENU   Press [Ctrl] [Break] for READY

~~~~~~

```
        III. SUMMARY OF FORECASTING NET OPERATING INCOME
        ==================================================

             The results of this analysis are as follows:


$$$$$$$$$$$$$$$$$$$$$$$$$$$$$$$$$$$$$$$$$$$$$$$$$$$$$$$$$$$$$$$$$$


        Rental Unit # 1 has a first year total of:        $ 2400.00
        Rental Unit # 1 has a fifth year total of:        $ 2701.22
        Rental Unit # 1 has a tenth year total of:        $ 3131.46
        Rental Unit # 1 has a fifteenth year total of:    $ 3630.22
        Rental Unit # 1 has a twentieth year total of:    $ 4208.41

        Rental Unit # 2 has a first year total of:        $ 9000.00
        Rental Unit # 2 has a fifth year total of:        $10528.73
        Rental Unit # 2 has a tenth year total of:        $12809.81
        Rental Unit # 2 has a fifteenth year total of:    $15585.09
        Rental Unit # 2 has a twentieth year total of:    $18961.64

        Rental Unit # 3 has a first year total of:        $16800.00
        Rental Unit # 3 has a fifth year total of:        $20420.51
        Rental Unit # 3 has a tenth year total of:        $26062.31
        Rental Unit # 3 has a fifteenth year total of:    $33262.85
        Rental Unit # 3 has a twentieth year total of:    $42452.76

        At the end of year one, net operating income is:   $14946.00
        At the end of year five, net operating income is:  $19583.14
        At the end of year ten, net operating income is:   $26849.09
        At the end of year fifteen, net operating income is: $36152.46
        At the end of year twenty, net operating income is:  $48035.42


$$$$$$$$$$$$$$$$$$$$$$$$$$$$$$$$$$$$$$$$$$$$$$$$$$$$$$$$$$$$$$$$$$


Press  [Alt] M  for MENU          Press  [Ctrl] [Break]  for READY


~~~~~~~~~~~~~~~~~~~~~~~~~~~~~~~~~~~~~~~~~~~~~~~~~~~~~~~~~~~~~~~~~~~~~
```

9 Real Estate Tax Analysis

Overview

Tax planning is a fundamental part of many real estate transactions. The federal tax law has always treated investments in real estate a bit differently than investments in other long-term durable goods. In previous times, the calculation of depreciation, tax shelter benefits, taxable income, taxes, and after-tax cash flows remained tedious tasks. Now, with Lotus 1-2-3 and microcomputers, these calculations are fairly routine.

While the calculation of the numbers has become routine, the importance of tax planning remains in the foreground. The three templates in this chapter help real estate investors evaluate the tax consequences associated with buying and selling real property. For many users, these templates will be the most time-saving and therefore, the most valuable.

ANALYSIS OF DEPRECIATION
(Template: lot901)

Prior to the Economic Recovery Tax Act of 1981 (or ERTA), the calculation of depreciation allowances involved several choices for investors. The decision was not which one was preferred by individuals but rather which one resulted in the greatest present value of tax savings. Thus, the decision was largely made by examining the specific numbers involved in each case.

Consultants used to earn fortunes generating depreciation schedules for clients and showing them the advantages of one depreciation method over another. In this case, the same schedules were reproduced over and over again with little difficulty (but with high consulting fees).

With changes in the new tax law in 1981, the number of depreciation choices were streamlined. A new system was introduced called the *Accelerated Cost Recovery System (ACRS)* and with the exception of the old standby method of straight line depreciation, all of the other methods were made obsolete overnight. This included sum of the year's digits, double declining balance, 150% declining balance, 125% declining balance, and component depreciation. (Note that low-income housing retained more accelerated depreciation as evidenced by a special ACRS table.) In addition, switching from accelerated methods to straight-line depreciation had all but been eliminated. (If such a switch was desired under ERTA, it became much simpler than previously.) If you are one of those millions who learned these methods, don't fret—as this book goes to press, Congress has just changed the rules once again!

The new tax law is called *The Deficit Reduction Act of 1984*. It is extensive but results in only a limited number of substantive changes affecting real estate. The most well-known change is the extension of the shortest depreciable life from 15 to 18 years. In addition, separate tables have been prepared for each election. Therefore, unlike previous tax law changes, straight-line depreciation does not exist anymore; it, too, has become part of the ACRS system.

Principles.   The ACRS system is really quite simple and convenient to use, especially with this template and Lotus 1-2-3. For each depreciation allowance, a table provides the appropriate percentage. Each percentage is then multiplied by the depreciable amount of the property. While there are distinctions in the law for low income and non-low income, the 1984 Act led to the development of seven ACRS tables for low and non-low income real estate. Hence, with depreciable lives of 18, 35, and 45 years, and either an accelerated election (about 175% declining balance) or a flat election (about straight line), four of the tables have been incorporated into this template.

If the accelerated election is made, the depreciable period is 18 years. If the flat election is made, the investor can choose between 18, 35, and 45 years. Using Lotus 1-2-3 and this template, all of the allowances are calculated each time. In subsequent templates, the user must elect the specific table to be used in the analysis.

The new tables became available from the Treasury Department on October 22, 1984. As this manuscript goes to press, the tables are only now being widely circulated. However, until the next law change, the tables are likely to become one of the tools for calculating tax liabilities by hand throughout the real estate community. As always, the use of tables and hand calculations are inconvenient to use. With this template, these tables are automatically produced and the appropriate factors are applied as needed.

Note also that even with the 1984 Act, the investor has the option of electing straight-line depreciation. In this template, the straight-line method of depreciation is approximated by the ACRS SL% columns. Note also that only three depreciable lives are permitted: 18, 35, or 45 years. This is considerably different than not so many years ago.

Using the Template.   The template requires some fundamental depreciation inputs. These include the total cost of the property, the land-to-value ratio, the elected useful life, and the month when the property was put into service (this determines which column in the preprinted ACRS tables should be used by the template).

The IRS says that only the improvements to the property may be depreciated. Hence, the product of the land-to-value ratio times the total cost of the property provides an estimate of the value of the land. The difference between the total cost of the property and the value of the land is the depreciable basis (i.e., an estimate for tax purposes of the value of the improvements).

The elected useful life is constrained by the current tax rules. As indicated, if the accelerated ACRS system is elected, there is no choice: 18 years must be elected. Otherwise, the investor may choose any of the three permitted lives.

The output table automatically computes the appropriate ACRS percentages. The correct percentages are determined by the input of which month the investment was begun. (Note that in most books, the entire tables are produced. With Lotus 1-2-3, the percentages are applied as needed.) The first four columns provide the ACRS percentages for each year for each election. The ACRS percentages are multiplied by the depreciable basis to obtain the yearly allowances. The investor no longer has to worry about accumulated depreciation accounts. Also, the computer applies the proper "SL Deduct" according to the useful life input on the initial page.

The results are shown for the ACRS accelerated and elected straight-line schedules, given the depreciable basis. The final column provides the excess depreciation amounts per year. The excess depreciation is defined as the difference between the ACRS deduction and the elected straight-line deduction. It is used at the time of sale under some conditions.

An Example.   The illustration shows a $2 million property which is 75% depreciable. Note that it will result in a total amount of depreciation of $1.5 million. Over an 18-year period, the ACRS percentages are given for the project which was begun in March (hence the "3" for the third month).

Note that there is depreciation left over for year 19 since the property is not put into service until the third month. Note also that the sum of all of the ACRS percentages is equal to 100 percent. (Change the month from 3 to some other month, and watch the percentages change, but the sum will always equal 100%.) Finally, note that the ACRS 175% declining balance always provides higher deductions in the earlier years and lower deductions in the later years of the useful life. A summary in Table III provides a survey of some of the ACRS deductions for the property.

Graphics.   The graph is a plot of the depreciation allowances permitted under the current law, given the inputs. In addition, the excess depreciation per year is indicated. By definition, the excess depreciation is the difference between the accelerated ACRS allowances and the straight-line ACRS allowance. Note also that the 175% declining balance results decline in steps as per the Treasury Department's schedule. Because of rounding, so, too, does the SL calculation.

Possible Modifications.   The calculation of depreciation deductions is straightforward, constrained by the current federal tax law, and not subject to modification. However, the analyst can make use of this template in two additional ways. First, the investor can integrate this template into others where other types of output are required. (This is done in the next two templates as well.) Second, the investor can carefully examine the choices of either the accelerated ACRS method or straight-line ACRS method when making investment decisions. If neither of these are attractive, the investor can be assured that this template and Lotus 1-2-3 will always calculate their depreciation deductions from now on without error!

The Deficit Reduction Act of 1984 altered the ACRS life from 15 to 18 years. The expectation is that more changes are in store for real estate investors. The user should modify this template to keep current with the law. Good luck—you will probably change this template every year!

EXAMPLE TEMPLATE 9.1
Analysis of depreciation.

```
lot901x                                    Real Estate Diskette #3
=================================================================
ANALYSIS OF DEPRECIATION          Copyright (C) Reston Pub. Co., 1985
=================================================================

~~~~~~~~~~~~~~~~~~~~~~~~~~~~~~~~~~~~~~~~~~~~~~~~~~~~~~~~~~~~~~~~~~~~~~


                  ***   TABLE OF CONTENTS   ***
                        ==================

                Table                               Page
                -----                               ----


     I.   INPUTS FOR DEPRECIATION METHODS             1

    II.   OUTPUT FOR DEPRECIATION METHODS             2

   III.   SUMMARY OF ANALYSIS OF DEPRECIATION         3



~~~~~~~~~~~~~~~~~~~~~~~~~~~~~~~~~~~~~~~~~~~~~~~~~~~~~~~~~~~~~~~~~~~~~~


                  I. INPUTS FOR DEPRECIATION METHODS
                  ==================================


     Enter the following assumptions:


        Total Cost of Property            >>>    $ 2000000

        Land-to-Value Ratio              >>>       25.00  %

        Useful Life (18, 35 or 45 years)  >>>          18  years
          (If 175%DB, you must elect 18 yrs)

        Month When Investment Begins      >>>           3
          (Enter the number which matches
          the calendar month, ie, Jan = 1)


  Press  [Alt] M  for MENU          Press  [Ctrl] [Break]  for READY


~~~~~~~~~~~~~~~~~~~~~~~~~~~~~~~~~~~~~~~~~~~~~~~~~~~~~~~~~~~~~~~~~~~~~~
```

II. OUTPUT FOR DEPRECIATION METHODS
==

Year	ACRS 175% DB% (18 Yr)	ACRS SL % (18 Yr)	ACRS SL % (35 Yr)	ACRS SL % (45 Yr)	175% DB Deduct	SL Deduct	Excess Dep
	(%)	(%)	(%)	(%)	($)	($)	($)
1	8.00	4.00	2.00	1.80	120000	60000	60000
2	9.00	6.00	3.00	2.30	135000	90000	45000
3	8.00	6.00	3.00	2.30	120000	90000	30000
4	7.00	6.00	3.00	2.30	105000	90000	15000
5	7.00	6.00	3.00	2.30	105000	90000	15000
6	6.00	6.00	3.00	2.30	90000	90000	NA
7	5.00	6.00	3.00	2.30	75000	90000	NA
8	5.00	6.00	3.00	2.30	75000	90000	NA
9	5.00	6.00	3.00	2.30	75000	90000	NA
10	5.00	6.00	3.00	2.30	75000	90000	NA
11	5.00	5.00	3.00	2.30	75000	75000	NA
12	5.00	5.00	3.00	2.20	75000	75000	NA
13	4.00	5.00	3.00	2.20	60000	75000	NA
14	4.00	5.00	3.00	2.20	60000	75000	NA
15	4.00	5.00	3.00	2.20	60000	75000	NA
16	4.00	5.00	3.00	2.20	60000	75000	NA
17	4.00	5.00	3.00	2.20	60000	75000	NA
18	4.00	5.00	3.00	2.20	60000	75000	NA
19	1.00	2.00	3.00	2.20	15000	30000	NA
20			3.00	2.20		0	
21			3.00	2.20		0	
22			3.00	2.20		0	
23			3.00	2.20		0	
24			3.00	2.20		0	
25			3.00	2.20		0	
26			3.00	2.20		0	
27			3.00	2.20		0	
28			3.00	2.20		0	
29			3.00	2.20		0	
30			3.00	2.20		0	
31			2.00	2.20		0	
32			2.00	2.20		0	
33			2.00	2.20		0	
34			2.00	2.20		0	
35			2.00	2.20		0	
36			1.00	2.20		0	
37				2.20		0	
38				2.20		0	
39				2.20		0	
40				2.20		0	

```
      41                           2.20              0
      42                           2.20              0
      43                           2.20              0
      44                           2.20              0
      45                           2.20              0

      46                           0.40              0
           _____  _____  _____  _____  _____  _____
    Totals 100.00   100.00   100.00   100.00  1500000  1500000

Press  [Alt] M  for MENU          Press  [Ctrl] [Break]  for READY


~~~~~~~~~~~~~~~~~~~~~~~~~~~~~~~~~~~~~~~~~~~~~~~~~~~~~~~~~~~~~~~~~~~~~~~~~~~~~~~
```

```
            III. SUMMARY OF ANALYSIS OF DEPRECIATION
            ==========================================

        For any real estate investment project,


            if the total cost of the property is:  $ 2000000  ,

            if the land-to-value ratio is:            25.00  percent,

            if the useful life is:                       18  years,

            and if the beginning service month is:        3  ,


    $$$$$$$$$$$$$$$$$$$$$$$$$$$$$$$$$$$$$$$$$$$$$$$$$$$$$$$$$$


        the ACRS 175% Deduction in Year  1 is:     $   120000
        the ACRS 175% Deduction in Year  5 is:     $   105000
        the ACRS 175% Deduction in Year 10 is:     $    75000
        the ACRS 175% Deduction in Year 15 is:     $    60000

        the ACRS SL Deduction in Year  1 is:       $    60000
        the ACRS SL Deduction in Year  5 is:       $    90000
        the ACRS SL Deduction in Year 10 is:       $    90000
        the ACRS SL Deduction in Year 15 is:       $    75000
        the ACRS SL Deduction in Year 20 is:       $        0

        the ACRS SL Deduction in Year 25 is:       $        0
        the ACRS SL Deduction in Year 30 is:       $        0
        the ACRS SL Deduction in Year 35 is:       $        0
        the ACRS SL Deduction in Year 40 is:       $        0
        the ACRS SL Deduction in Year 45 is:       $        0


    $$$$$$$$$$$$$$$$$$$$$$$$$$$$$$$$$$$$$$$$$$$$$$$$$$$$$$$$$$$$


    Press  [Alt] M  for MENU           Press   [Ctrl] [Break]  for READY


~~~~~~~~~~~~~~~~~~~~~~~~~~~~~~~~~~~~~~~~~~~~~~~~~~~~~~~~~~~~~~~~~~~~~~~~~~~
```

CALCULATION OF TAXABLE INCOME
(Template: lot902)

The next two templates are among the largest templates in the system. In addition, they build directly upon the previous depreciation template as well as the income, expense, financing, and cash flow templates in Chapter 8. The first calculates taxable income and the second uses the measure of taxable income to obtain tax liability and ultimately, calculate after-tax cash flow.

Principles. The definition of taxable income is net operating income minus financing expenses plus principal (amortization) minus depreciation allowance. (Alternatively, the same answer is obtained by deducting interest and depreciation from net operating income.) Therefore, in order to calculate taxable income, net operating income is presumed to be known or estimated, financing expenses are required and depreciation is needed. In the standard format used in previous templates, the user must input several of these items and Lotus 1-2-3 and the template will do the rest.

However, in this case, and in several of the templates which follow, the user has the choice of entering either a single year's net operating income and an annual growth rate or up to 20 years' net operating income. In either case, the template presumes that these estimates were derived previously, perhaps using one or more of the templates in Chapter 8. After net operating income estimates are input, the user can add up to three types of mortgages. As before, both a first and second mortgage are provided for, with separate interest rates and terms. Also, interest-only financing can be used in the template. The equity downpayment is required in order to calculate the total cost of the property when the depreciable basis is needed for depreciation.

The depreciation inputs are the same as in the previous template, except that the user must indicate which ACRS table should be applied. Indeed, the previous template has been merged into this one. (The careful reader will note that one of the templates from Chapter 8 has also been merged into this template as well. This was purposely done so that the templates can build upon each other.) Finally, the expected holding period is required to tell the computer how many years for which to present the results.

Using the Template. The output of this template is large because some of the earlier templates are used implicitly to calculate parts of this template. For example, the financing portions are taken from Template lot803 and the depreciation portion is taken from Template lot901. Note that in Table II (Part I), the final output page is the calculation of taxable income. This is the primary function and objective of this template.

In Table IV, the results are summarized. The table includes net operating income, taxable income, and before-tax cash flow. Notice also that the final two columns are two similar rates of return on equity. The first is the "IRS" return on equity because taxable income is the measure of benefit. The second uses before-tax cash flow as the benefit measure. Notice how much different the results are in these two columns.

An Example.   In this example, the project has negative taxable income for the first five years although before-tax cash flow is positive throughout the period. Should the investor be alarmed? Should this project be passed over for more "profitable" ventures?

Based upon the investment analysis possible to this point in the development of the template system, this is a *very attractive* project! This may surprise readers who view the negative taxable income figures for the first five years. Remember, taxable income is a definition of the IRS; the investor needs to know taxable income to figure out how much to pay the IRS, as required by law. In this case, it is a time to rejoice, at least during the first five years: taxable income is very negative! This means that not only does the investor not have to pay any taxes from the annual income but if there is other ordinary income from other sources, the investor can "offset" this other income with these "losses."

Note that I said "losses" in quotation marks. They are not really losses in an economic sense. Why not? Because if you look at the results under the better measure of performance each year: the before-tax cash flow; it is greater than zero in all but the fifth year. (That is because of the large outlay required to pay off the interest-only loan.) The point is that *cash flow tells the investor if he has any money left over after paying all of the bills, not taxable income.* If the investor viewed taxable income as a measure of performance, this would be a terrible project. However, look at the cash flows expected by investing in this project!

Graphics.   The graph shows the relationship between several measures taken from the calculations. The graph compares net operating income, taxable income, and before-tax cash flow for all of the years in the expected holding period. Notice that net operating income grows at a constant rate. On the other hand, there is a close but not constant relationship between changes in taxable income and changes in cash flow. This is because tax shelter is an important part of cash flow. Note as indicated above that while taxable income is negative for the first five years, only in the fifth year is before-tax cash flow negative. The graph is very helpful in this type of analysis.

Possible Modifications.   It is possible to custom tailor this and other templates to suit personal needs. A major deficiency of this template is its inability to perform the analysis of taxes on an after- rather than before-tax basis. This is corrected in full in the next template.

EXAMPLE TEMPLATE 9.2
Calculation of taxable income.

```
lot902x                                    Real Estate Diskette #3
=================================================================
CALCULATION OF TAXABLE INCOME      Copyright (C) Reston Pub. Co., 1985
=================================================================

~~~~~~~~~~~~~~~~~~~~~~~~~~~~~~~~~~~~~~~~~~~~~~~~~~~~~~~~~~~~~~~~~~~~~


                    ***   TABLE OF CONTENTS   ***
                    ==================

              Table                                   Page
              -----                                   ----

     I.   INPUTS FOR TAXABLE INCOME                    1

    II.   OUTPUT TABLES FOR TAXABLE INCOME
                    (PART I)                           2

   III.   OUTPUT TABLES FOR TAXABLE INCOME
                    (PART II)                          3

    IV.   SUMMARY OF TAXABLE INCOME                    4


~~~~~~~~~~~~~~~~~~~~~~~~~~~~~~~~~~~~~~~~~~~~~~~~~~~~~~~~~~~~~~~~~~~~~








                    I. INPUTS FOR TAXABLE INCOME
                    ============================

   Enter the following assumptions:


     Net Operating Income Estimates:

     EITHER:

        Net Operating Income for Year One.....>>> $  _____
        Annual Rental Growth Rate.............>>>     _____   %
```

OR:

```
            Year One...............................>>> $      83251
            Year Two...............................>>> $      88851
            Year Three.............................>>> $      94801
            Year Four..............................>>> $     101120
            Year Five..............................>>> $     107831

            Year Six...............................>>> $     114957
            Year Seven.............................>>> $     122522
            Year Eight.............................>>> $     130554
            Year Nine..............................>>> $     139079
            Year Ten...............................>>> $     148126

            Year Eleven............................>>> $     157728
            Year Twelve............................>>> $     167915
            Year Thirteen..........................>>> $     _____
            Year Fourteen..........................>>> $     _____

            Year Fifteen...........................>>> $     _____

            Year Sixteen...........................>>> $     _____
            Year Seventeen.........................>>> $     _____
            Year Eighteen..........................>>> $     _____
            Year Nineteen..........................>>> $     _____
            Year Twenty............................>>> $     _____

        Financing Inputs:
            First Mortgage Amount..................>>> $     425000
                Interest Rate on Mortgage..........>>>          13.25  %
                Mortgage Term (max.=30).............>>>             30  years
            Second Mortgage Amount.................>>> $      75000
                Interest Rate on Mortgage..........>>>          15.00  %
                Mortgage Term (max.=30).............>>>             10  years
            Interest-Only Financing................>>> $      50000
                Interest Rate on Mortgage..........>>>          18.50  %
                Mortgage Term (max.=30).............>>>              5  years

        Equity Investment (Downpayment)........>>> $       40000

        Depreciation Inputs:
            Land-to-Value Ratio....................>>>          25.00  %
            Depreciation Method:
                If ACRS SL is used, input 1.00......>>>         _____
                If ACRS 175% DB is used, input 1.75.>>>          1.75
            Useful Life (18, 35, or 45 years).....>>>             18  years
                (If ACRS 175% DB, you must elect 18 yrs)
            Month When Investment Begins...........>>>              7
                (Enter the number which matches
                the calendar month, ie, Jan = 1)

        Expected Holding Period (max.=20).......>>>             12  years


    Press  [Alt] M  for MENU              Press  [Ctrl] [Break]  for READY

    ~~~~~~~~~~~~~~~~~~~~~~~~~~~~~~~~~~~~~~~~~~~~~~~~~~~~~~~~~~~~~~~~~~~~~~~~~
```

II. OUTPUT TABLES FOR TAXABLE INCOME
=======================================
(PART I)

Financing Calculations:

	Amount ($)	Int Rate (%)	Mor Term (yrs)	Fin Exp ($)
First Mortgage:	425000	13.25	30	57693
Second Mortgage:	75000	15.00	10	14944
Interest-Only Financing:	50000	18.50	5	9250

Year	1st Mort	2nd Mort	Int-Only	Total Fin Exp
1	57693	14944	9250	81887
2	57693	14944	9250	81887
3	57693	14944	9250	81887
4	57693	14944	9250	81887
5	57693	14944	59250	131887
6	57693	14944	0	72637
7	57693	14944	0	72637
8	57693	14944	0	72637
9	57693	14944	0	72637
10	57693	14944	0	72637
11	57693	0	0	57693
12	57693	0	0	57693
NA	NA	NA	NA	NA
NA	NA	NA	NA	NA
NA	NA	NA	NA	NA
NA	NA	NA	NA	NA
NA	NA	NA	NA	NA
NA	NA	NA	NA	NA
NA	NA	NA	NA	NA
NA	NA	NA	NA	NA

Depreciation Calculations:

Year	ACRS 175% DB% (%)	ACRS SL % (%)	175% DB Deduct ($)	SL Deduct ($)
1	4.00	NA	17700	NA
2	9.00	NA	39825	NA
3	8.00	NA	35400	NA
4	8.00	NA	35400	NA
5	7.00	NA	30975	NA
6	6.00	NA	26550	NA
7	6.00	NA	26550	NA
8	5.00	NA	22125	NA
9	5.00	NA	22125	NA
10	5.00	NA	22125	NA
11	5.00	NA	22125	NA
12	5.00	NA	22125	NA
13	5.00	NA	22125	NA
14	4.00	NA	17700	NA
15	4.00	NA	17700	NA
16	4.00	NA	17700	NA
17	4.00	NA	17700	NA
18	4.00	NA	17700	NA
19	2.00	NA	8850	NA
20		NA		NA

Taxable Income Calculations:

Year	NOI	Fin Exp	BTCF	Amort	Dep All	TI
	($)	($)	($)	($)	($)	($)
1	83,251	81,887	1,364	5,074	17,700	(11,262)
2	88,851	81,887	6,964	5,811	39,825	(27,050)
3	94,801	81,887	12,914	6,656	35,400	(15,830)
4	101,120	81,887	19,233	7,623	35,400	(8,544)
5	107,831	131,887	(24,056)	8,731	30,975	(46,300)
6	114,957	72,637	42,320	10,001	26,550	25,771
7	122,522	72,637	49,885	11,456	26,550	34,792
8	130,554	72,637	57,917	13,124	22,125	48,916
9	139,079	72,637	66,442	15,035	22,125	59,352
10	148,126	72,637	75,489	17,224	22,125	70,589
11	157,728	57,693	100,035	4,790	22,125	82,700
12	167,915	57,693	110,222	5,425	22,125	93,522
NA	NA	NA	NA	NA	NA	NA
NA	NA	NA	NA	NA	NA	NA
NA	NA	NA	NA	NA	NA	NA
NA	NA	NA	NA	NA	NA	NA
NA	NA	NA	NA	NA	NA	NA
NA	NA	NA	NA	NA	NA	NA
NA	NA	NA	NA	NA	NA	NA
NA	NA	NA	NA	NA	NA	NA

Press [Alt] M for MENU   Press [Ctrl] [Break] for READY

~~~~~~

III. OUTPUT TABLES FOR TAXABLE INCOME
======================================
(PART II)

Additional Financing Considerations:

	Amount ($)	Int Rate (%)	Mor Term (yrs)	Fin Exp ($)
First Mortgage:	425000	13.25	30	57693
Second Mortgage:	75000	15	10	14944
Interest-Only Financing:	50000	18.5	5	9250

---First Mortgage---			---Second Mortgage---			---Int-Only---	
Beg Bal	Interest	End Bal	Beg Bal	Interest	End Bal	Interest	End Bal
425000	56313	423620	75000	11250	71306	9250	50000
423620	56130	422056	71306	10696	67058	9250	50000
422056	55922	420286	67058	10059	62173	9250	50000
420286	55688	418281	62173	9326	56555	9250	50000
418281	55422	416011	56555	8483	50094	0	0
416011	55121	413439	50094	7514	42665	0	0
413439	54781	410527	42665	6400	34120	0	0
410527	54395	407229	34120	5118	24294	0	0
407229	53958	403494	24294	3644	12995	0	0
403494	53463	399265	12995	1949	0	0	0
399265	52903	394474	0	0	0	0	0
394474	52268	389049	0	0	0	0	0
NA	NA	NA	NA	NA	NA	NA	NA
NA	NA	NA	NA	NA	NA	NA	NA
NA	NA	NA	NA	NA	NA	NA	NA
NA	NA	NA	NA	NA	NA	NA	NA
NA	NA	NA	NA	NA	NA	NA	NA
NA	NA	NA	NA	NA	NA	NA	NA
NA	NA	NA	NA	NA	NA	NA	NA
NA	NA	NA	NA	NA	NA	NA	NA

Press [Alt] M for MENU   Press [Ctrl] [Break] for READY

~~~~~~

```
            IV. SUMMARY OF TAXABLE INCOME
            ===============================

            For any real estate investment,

        $$$$$$$$$$$$$$$$$$$$$$$$$$$$$$$$$$$$$$$$$$$$$$$$$$$$$


                                      "IRS"
        Year    NOI      TI      BTCF    ROE      ROE
        ---------------------------------------------------

                ($)      ($)      ($)     (%)      (%)

          1    83,251  (11,262)   1,364  (28.15)   3.41
          2    88,851  (27,050)   6,964  (67.62)  17.41
          3    94,801  (15,830)  12,914  (39.58)  32.29
          4   101,120   (8,544)  19,233  (21.36)  48.08
          5   107,831  (46,300) (24,056) (115.75) (60.14)

          6   114,957   25,771   42,320   64.43  105.80
          7   122,522   34,792   49,885   86.98  124.71
          8   130,554   48,916   57,917  122.29  144.79
          9   139,079   59,352   66,442  148.38  166.11
         10   148,126   70,589   75,489  176.47  188.72
         11   157,728   82,700  100,035  206.75  250.09
         12   167,915   93,522  110,222  233.81  275.56
         NA       NA       NA       NA       NA       NA
         NA       NA       NA       NA       NA       NA
         NA       NA       NA       NA       NA       NA

         NA       NA       NA       NA       NA       NA
         NA       NA       NA       NA       NA       NA
         NA       NA       NA       NA       NA       NA
         NA       NA       NA       NA       NA       NA
         NA       NA       NA       NA       NA       NA


        $$$$$$$$$$$$$$$$$$$$$$$$$$$$$$$$$$$$$$$$$$$$$$$$$$$$$


   Press  [Alt] M  for MENU        Press  [Ctrl] [Break]  for READY
```

~~~~~~

CALCULATION OF AFTER-TAX CASH FLOW
(Template: lot903)

If you have bought the idea of the importance of cash flow for the investor and the importance of taxable income for the IRS, as an investor you will most likely make your investment decisions based upon cash flows. In the previous template, only before-tax cash flows were calculated. In this template, tax liability is added to the analysis and the magical item is finally reached: *after-tax cash flow*.

Principles.   After-tax cash flow is defined as before-tax cash flow minus income taxes. (Are you surprised?) The important point, however, is that the investor's tax rate is *not* multiplied by before-tax cash flow to get after-tax cash flow. The tax rate is multiplied by taxable income to get taxes. Therefore, it is important to calculate both before-tax cash flow and taxable income in order to get after-tax cash flow.

Using the Template.   This template is very similar to the previous one which calculated taxable income except for two factors. First, since after-tax cash flow is desired, the investor's tax rate is required. This must be input into Table I in the template. Second, the final output portion of Table II (Page 2) calculated after-tax cash flow (this is an additional table from the previous template). In this table, net operating income minus financing expenses equals before-tax cash flow. This figure minus taxes equals after-tax cash flow.

If you compare this template with the previous one, the only difference in the inputs is the tax rate. Note that the template says the "*marginal* income tax rate"; the same rate we used in an earlier template. Many new investment analysts are puzzled by the use of the marginal (or rate on the last dollar's worth of income) tax rate. In a progressive tax system, such as the federal income tax, the more money an individual (or couple who file jointly) make, the higher the *rate* of tax is on the last levels of income. This is what is meant by the term "progressive." Note that the marginal tax rate suggests that the investor is required to input in the tax rate on the *last* dollar's worth of income.

If the investor's income extends over more than one tax bracket, the *average* or effective tax rate will always be less than the marginal tax rate. (Test this for yourself!) The question is should you use the effective tax rate or the marginal tax rate for real estate investment purposes?

The position adopted in this book is that the investor should use the *marginal* tax rate since the investor wants to account for the tax effects of adding this investment to his/her investment portfolio. As a result, an attempt to use the effective tax rate is equivalent to analyzing this project in isolation of the other income the investor might have. In effect, failure to use the marginal tax rate will understate the effect of the tax law on the investor's balance sheet. Therefore, the marginal tax rate should be used in any form of investment analysis.

An Example.   The example uses the same data as previous templates. In this case, note that after-tax cash flow is expected to be *greater* than before-tax cash flow during the first five years. Why? The federal tax law permits the offsetting of other income against current (and past) tax losses. In this case, taxable income is negative during those years so this amounts to a "tax savings." (The reader is referred to one of several books for additional discussion of this point.)

Note also that the template computes before- and after-tax returns on equity for each year. See how the tax savings results in higher after-tax than before-tax returns for the first five years. After five years, when taxable income is greater than zero and taxes must be paid, then the after-tax returns are lower than the before-tax returns.

Graphics.   A similar graph to the one in Template lot902 is shown for this template. However, in this case, the comparison is between before- and after-tax cash flows. Observe that after-tax cash flow is greater than before-tax cash flow when taxable income is less than zero. With tax liability, after-tax cash flow falls below before-tax cash flow. In this example, the switch takes place after five years.

Possible Modifications.   Since this template is relatively large, it is generally not a wise idea to further enlarge it dramatically. As before, experienced users may be interested in custom modifying it to suit their needs. Some users may wish to include various investment criteria and methods of investment analysis to be used with after-tax cash flow. Don't despair—these topics are the subjects of Chapters 10 and 11.

EXAMPLE TEMPLATE 9.3
Calculation of after-tax cash flow.

```
lot903x                                      Real Estate Diskette #3
===================================================================
CALCULATION OF AFTER-TAX CASH FLOW   Copyright (C) Reston Pub. Co., 1985
===================================================================

~~~~~~~~~~~~~~~~~~~~~~~~~~~~~~~~~~~~~~~~~~~~~~~~~~~~~~~~~~~~~~~~~~~~~~

              ***   TABLE OF CONTENTS   ***
                    ==================

              Table                              Page
              -----                              ----

    I.   INPUTS FOR AFTER-TAX CASH FLOW            1

   II.   OUTPUT TABLES FOR AFTER-TAX CASH FLOW
                   (PART I)                        2

  III.   OUTPUT TABLES FOR AFTER-TAX CASH FLOW
                   (PART II)                       3

   IV.   SUMMARY OF AFTER-TAX CASH FLOW            4


~~~~~~~~~~~~~~~~~~~~~~~~~~~~~~~~~~~~~~~~~~~~~~~~~~~~~~~~~~~~~~~~~~~~~~

              I. INPUTS FOR AFTER-TAX CASH FLOW
              ================================

   Enter the following assumptions:


      Net Operating Income Estimates:

      EITHER:

         Net Operating Income for Year One.....>>> $  _____
         Annual Rental Growth Rate.............>>>    _____   %

      OR:

         Year One..............................>>> $   83251
         Year Two..............................>>> $   88851
         Year Three............................>>> $   94801
         Year Four.............................>>> $  101120
         Year Five.............................>>> $  107831

         Year Six..............................>>> $  114957
         Year Seven............................>>> $  122522
         Year Eight............................>>> $  130554
         Year Nine.............................>>> $  139079
         Year Ten..............................>>> $  148126
```

```
          Year Eleven.........................>>> $   157728
          Year Twelve.........................>>> $   167915
          Year Thirteen.......................>>> $   _____
          Year Fourteen.......................>>> $   _____
          Year Fifteen........................>>> $   _____

          Year Sixteen........................>>> $   _____
          Year Seventeen......................>>> $   _____
          Year Eighteen.......................>>> $   _____
          Year Nineteen.......................>>> $   _____
          Year Twenty.........................>>> $   _____

      Financing Inputs:
          First Mortgage Amount...............>>> $   425000
             Interest Rate on Mortgage........>>>      13.25   %
             Mortgage Term (max.=30)..........>>>         30   years
          Second Mortgage Amount..............>>> $    75000
             Interest Rate on Mortgage........>>>      15.00   %
             Mortgage Term (max.=30)..........>>>         10   years
          Interest-Only Financing.............>>> $    50000
             Interest Rate on Mortgage........>>>      18.50   %
             Mortgage Term (max.=30)..........>>>          5   years

      Equity Investment (Downpayment)........>>> $    40000

      Depreciation Inputs:
          Land-to-Value Ratio.................>>>      25.00   %
          Depreciation Method:
             If ACRS SL is used, input 1.00...>>>      _____
             If ACRS 175% DB is used, input 1.75.>>>   1.75
          Useful Life (18, 35, or 45 years)...>>>         18   years
             (If ACRS 175% DB, you must elect 18 yrs)
          Month When Investment Begins........>>>          7
             (Enter the number which matches
             the calendar month, ie, Jan = 1)

      Marginal Income Tax Rate...............>>>      40.00   %

      Expected Holding Period (max.=20)......>>>         12   years


 Press   [Alt] M  for MENU          Press   [Ctrl] [Break]  for READY


~~~~~~~~~~~~~~~~~~~~~~~~~~~~~~~~~~~~~~~~~~~~~~~~~~~~~~~~~~~~~~~~~~~~~~~~~~~
```

II. OUTPUT TABLES FOR AFTER-TAX CASH FLOW
===
(PART I)

Financing Calculations:

	Amount ($)	Int Rate (%)	Mor Term (yrs)	Fin Exp ($)
First Mortgage:	425000	13.25	30	57693
Second Mortgage:	75000	15.00	10	14944
Interest-Only Financing:	50000	18.50	5	9250

Year	1st Mort	2nd Mort	Int-Only	Total Fin Exp
1	57693	14944	9250	81887
2	57693	14944	9250	81887
3	57693	14944	9250	81887
4	57693	14944	9250	81887
5	57693	14944	59250	131887
6	57693	14944	0	72637
7	57693	14944	0	72637
8	57693	14944	0	72637
9	57693	14944	0	72637
10	57693	14944	0	72637
11	57693	0	0	57693
12	57693	0	0	57693
NA	NA	NA	NA	NA
NA	NA	NA	NA	NA
NA	NA	NA	NA	NA
NA	NA	NA	NA	NA
NA	NA	NA	NA	NA
NA	NA	NA	NA	NA
NA	NA	NA	NA	NA
NA	NA	NA	NA	NA

Depreciation Calculations:

Year	ACRS 175% DB%	ACRS SL %	175% DB Deduct	SL Deduct
	(%)	(%)	($)	($)
1	4.00	NA	17700	NA
2	9.00	NA	39825	NA
3	8.00	NA	35400	NA
4	8.00	NA	35400	NA
5	7.00	NA	30975	NA
6	6.00	NA	26550	NA
7	6.00	NA	26550	NA
8	5.00	NA	22125	NA
9	5.00	NA	22125	NA
10	5.00	NA	22125	NA
11	5.00	NA	22125	NA
12	5.00	NA	22125	NA
13	5.00	NA	22125	NA
14	4.00	NA	17700	NA
15	4.00	NA	17700	NA
16	4.00	NA	17700	NA
17	4.00	NA	17700	NA
18	4.00	NA	17700	NA
19	2.00	NA	8850	NA
20		NA		NA

```
Taxable Income Calculations:
----------------------------

Year              NOI     Fin Exp      BTCF     Amort    Dep All        TI

                  ($)        ($)        ($)       ($)       ($)        ($)

   1           83,251     81,887      1,364     5,074    17,700    (11,262)
   2           88,851     81,887      6,964     5,811    39,825    (27,050)
   3           94,801     81,887     12,914     6,656    35,400    (15,830)
   4          101,120     81,887     19,233     7,623    35,400     (8,544)
   5          107,831    131,887    (24,056)    8,731    30,975    (46,300)

   6          114,957     72,637     42,320    10,001    26,550     25,771
   7          122,522     72,637     49,885    11,456    26,550     34,792
   8          130,554     72,637     57,917    13,124    22,125     48,916
   9          139,079     72,637     66,442    15,035    22,125     59,352
  10          148,126     72,637     75,489    17,224    22,125     70,589

  11          157,728     57,693    100,035     4,790    22,125     82,700
  12          167,915     57,693    110,222     5,425    22,125     93,522
  NA               NA         NA         NA        NA        NA         NA
  NA               NA         NA         NA        NA        NA         NA
  NA               NA         NA         NA        NA        NA         NA

  NA               NA         NA         NA        NA        NA         NA
  NA               NA         NA         NA        NA        NA         NA
  NA               NA         NA         NA        NA        NA         NA
  NA               NA         NA         NA        NA        NA         NA
  NA               NA         NA         NA        NA        NA         NA


Press  [Alt] M  for MENU            Press  [Ctrl] [Break]  for READY

~~~~~~~~~~~~~~~~~~~~~~~~~~~~~~~~~~~~~~~~~~~~~~~~~~~~~~~~~~~~~~~~~~~~~~~~~~~
```

```
          III. OUTPUT TABLES FOR AFTER-TAX CASH FLOW
          ==========================================
                        (PART II)

   Additional Financing Considerations:
   ------------------------------------

                              Amount   Int Rate Mor Term Fin Exp
                               ($)       (%)     (yrs)    ($)

          First Mortgage:      425000   13.25      30     57693
          Second Mortgage:      75000   15.00      10     14944
          Interest-Only Financing: 50000 18.50      5      9250


      ---First Mortgage---      ---Second Mortgage---    ---Int-Only---
   ---------------------------  ---------------------------  ------------------
   Beg Bal Interest  End Bal   Beg Bal Interest  End Bal Interest  End Bal
   ---------------------------------------------------------------------------
    425000   56313   423620     75000   11250    71306    9250     50000
    423620   56130   422056     71306   10696    67058    9250     50000
    422056   55922   420286     67058   10059    62173    9250     50000
    420286   55688   418281     62173    9326    56555    9250     50000
    418281   55422   416011     56555    8483    50094       0         0

    416011   55121   413439     50094    7514    42665       0         0
    413439   54781   410527     42665    6400    34120       0         0
    410527   54395   407229     34120    5118    24294       0         0
    407229   53958   403494     24294    3644    12995       0         0
    403494   53463   399265     12995    1949       0       0         0

    399265   52903   394474         0       0       0       0         0
    394474   52268   389049         0       0       0       0         0
       NA      NA      NA         NA      NA      NA      NA        NA
       NA      NA      NA         NA      NA      NA      NA        NA
       NA      NA      NA         NA      NA      NA      NA        NA

       NA      NA      NA         NA      NA      NA      NA        NA
       NA      NA      NA         NA      NA      NA      NA        NA
       NA      NA      NA         NA      NA      NA      NA        NA
       NA      NA      NA         NA      NA      NA      NA        NA
       NA      NA      NA         NA      NA      NA      NA        NA
```

Cash Flow Calculations:

Year	NOI	Fin Exp	BTCF	Taxes	ATCF
	($)	($)	($)	($)	($)
1	83,251	81,887	1,364	(4,505)	5,869
2	88,851	81,887	6,964	(10,820)	17,784
3	94,801	81,887	12,914	(6,332)	19,246
4	101,120	81,887	19,233	(3,418)	22,651
5	107,831	131,887	(24,056)	(18,520)	(5,536)
6	114,957	72,637	42,320	10,309	32,012
7	122,522	72,637	49,885	13,917	35,969
8	130,554	72,637	57,917	19,566	38,351
9	139,079	72,637	66,442	23,741	42,702
10	148,126	72,637	75,489	28,236	47,254
11	157,728	57,693	100,035	33,080	66,955
12	167,915	57,693	110,222	37,409	72,813
NA	NA	NA	NA	NA	NA
NA	NA	NA	NA	NA	NA
NA	NA	NA	NA	NA	NA
NA	NA	NA	NA	NA	NA
NA	NA	NA	NA	NA	NA
NA	NA	NA	NA	NA	NA
NA	NA	NA	NA	NA	NA
NA	NA	NA	NA	NA	NA

Press [Alt] M for MENU   Press [Ctrl] [Break] for READY

```
         IV. SUMMARY OF AFTER-TAX CASH FLOW
         ====================================

          For any real estate investment,

$$$$$$$$$$$$$$$$$$$$$$$$$$$$$$$$$$$$$$$$$$$$$$$$$$$$$$$


                                    BT        AT
     Year    NOI      BTCF    ATCF    ROE       ROE
    -----------------------------------------------------

             ($)       ($)    ($)     (%)       (%)

       1   83,251    1,364   5,869    3.41     14.67
       2   88,851    6,964  17,784   17.41     44.46
       3   94,801   12,914  19,246   32.29     48.12
       4  101,120   19,233  22,651   48.08     56.63
       5  107,831  (24,056) (5,536) (60.14)   (13.84)

       6  114,957   42,320  32,012  105.80     80.03
       7  122,522   49,885  35,969  124.71     89.92
       8  130,554   57,917  38,351  144.79     95.88
       9  139,079   66,442  42,702  166.11    106.75
      10  148,126   75,489  47,254  188.72    118.13

      11  157,728  100,035  66,955  250.09    167.39
      12  167,915  110,222  72,813  275.56    182.03
      NA       NA       NA      NA      NA        NA
      NA       NA       NA      NA      NA        NA
      NA       NA       NA      NA      NA        NA

      NA       NA       NA      NA      NA        NA
      NA       NA       NA      NA      NA        NA
      NA       NA       NA      NA      NA        NA
      NA       NA       NA      NA      NA        NA
      NA       NA       NA      NA      NA        NA


$$$$$$$$$$$$$$$$$$$$$$$$$$$$$$$$$$$$$$$$$$$$$$$$$$$$$$$


Press  [Alt] M  for MENU          Press  [Ctrl] [Break]  for READY
```

10 Ratio Analysis

Overview

In the previous two chapters, templates were developed that provided information for real estate investors. This information assisted the investor in making decisions about income, expenses, financing, and taxes. The "bottom line" is known as *after-tax cash flow*. In this and the next chapter, the cash flow statement serves as input for a variety of investment criteria. These measures are essential for investors, lenders, and appraisers. Investment criteria provide measures of what to expect from the investment when looking ahead, and when looking back, how well the investor actually performed. These results can then be compared to comparable returns in the market.

This chapter contains three templates. All deal with various types of ratios. The first centers on a variety of simple rates of return. Most of these measures are well-known to seasoned investors. The second template is devoted to ratios from financial statements, which are perhaps more familiar to lenders and institutional investors. Finally, the third template provides an easy method of calculating the effective rate of return. More sophisticated rate of return calculations and other criteria are discussed in detail in Chapter 11.

CALCULATING SIMPLE RATES OF RETURN
(Template: lot1001)

Real estate investors have always favored using several, rather than a few, rate of return calculations. With Lotus 1-2-3, this is no problem at all. The user must enter the appropriate data and the returns can easily be calculated. This template uses four measures of benefit (effective gross income, net operating income, before-tax cash flow, and after-tax cash flow) and debt and equity financing amounts for developing most of the well-known single-period rates of return.

Principles. A rate of return is a measure of a "bang for your buck." In most cases, the calculation compares the expected benefit with the expected cost. This ratio may then be compared with other measures at the time. It is also frequently compared across time to spot any trends in the market.

Rate of return calculations are important because investors use these measures to judge how well or poorly an investment will or has been performing. Therefore, it is important to try to understand the meaning and interpretation of these ratios.

Using the Template. The user may input up to ten years' worth of data in this template. The four types of income mentioned above may be used. In addition, the template continues the convention of permitting a first and second mortgage as well as interest-only financing. By inputting the downpayment, the computer can also calculate the total cost of the investment. The expected holding period instructs the computer how long to generate the results.

There are two pages of output. The first shows the total cost and breakdown of debt and equity financing. In addition, the income inputs are summarized in table form. The second page of output shows six important rates of return. These are discussed individually as follows:

- **Gross Income Multiplier (GIM).** This measure is defined as the ratio of total cost of the property to the effective gross income. It is frequently used by real estate appraisers as a measure of the market's attention to the relationship between the value of the property and its income. Real estate appraisers tend to use this measure as a guideline or "rule of thumb."

- **Overall Cap(italization) Rate (R).** This is a very well-known measure and is defined as the ratio of net operating income to the total cost of the property. This ratio measures the return on and of the investment. The "cap" rate is regarded as an important measure of financial return by many investors.

- **Before-Tax Return on Equity (BT ROE).** This ratio has been introduced in earlier templates. It is defined as the ratio of before-tax cash flow to the equity downpayment. This term is also called the "cash-on-cash" return since both the numerator and the denominator represent cash flow to or from the equity investor.

- **Before-Tax Return on Investment (BT ROI).** This ratio is similar to the previous one except the denominator is the total cost of the investment instead of the equity downpayment. Some investors feel this measure is also useful since it provides information about the cash flow in relation to the entire project.

- **After-Tax Return on Equity (AT ROE).** This ratio is defined as the ratio of after-tax cash flow to the equity downpayment. It is a version of the "cash-on-cash" return except after-tax considerations are emphasized.

- **After-Tax Return on Investment (AT ROI).** This ratio relates after-tax cash flow to the total cost of the investment. It is, therefore, similar to BT ROI except it uses after-tax cash flow as a measure of benefits.

Note that in each case, the template calculates the ratio for each year and then provides an average for the entire series of ratios. The investor can then compare these results with expected results from other projects.

An Example. Note that the example uses ten years of data. If the data looks familiar, you are correct. The data in this template has been taken directly from the data used in the previous templates. In this manner, the investor can apply several of the templates to one set of data and fully evaluate the investment.

In this case, the project consists of debt financing of $550,000 and an equity downpayment of $40,000. As before, with the exception of the fifth year, all cash flows are positive and rising. (Recall that taxable income was negative in several years.)

The summary provides the output with the six rates of return defined above. This table provides a convenient way of consolidating a large amount of information into rate of return statistics.

Graphics. The bar graph shows the five rates of return for each year (the GIM is omitted). If you have a color monitor, you already know that this is a very colorful picture. If not, Lotus 1-2-3 distinguishes between each data set with different symbols. Notice that the rates of return fall dramatically in the fifth year due to the expiration and cash requirements of the interest-only financing. The graphics capability of Lotus 1-2-3 also adjusts the Y axis for each specific set of data.

Possible Modifications. One important change which could be made to this template would be to introduce trend analysis into the output. Then the user could identify any trends in the rates of return over time. In addition, there are other criteria which might be of interest to the investor. Many of these are developed in the next template and in Chapter 11.

EXAMPLE TEMPLATE 10.1
Calculating simple rates of return.

```
lot1001x                                    Real Estate Diskette #3
==================================================================
CALCULATING SIMPLE RATES OF RETURN   Copyright (C) Reston Pub. Co., 1985
==================================================================


~~~~~~~~~~~~~~~~~~~~~~~~~~~~~~~~~~~~~~~~~~~~~~~~~~~~~~~~~~~~~~~~~~~~~

                  ***  TABLE OF CONTENTS  ***
                      ==================
          Table                                        Page
          -----                                        ----


    I.   INPUTS FOR SIMPLE RATES OF RETURN                1

   II.   OUTPUT FOR SIMPLE RATES OF RETURN                2

  III.   SUMMARY OF SIMPLE RATES OF RETURN                3



~~~~~~~~~~~~~~~~~~~~~~~~~~~~~~~~~~~~~~~~~~~~~~~~~~~~~~~~~~~~~~~~~~~~~



              I. INPUTS FOR SIMPLE RATES OF RETURN
              ====================================

     Enter the following assumptions:


        INCOME AND CASH FLOWS PER YEAR (max.=10):

           Year One:
              Effective Gross Income...............>>> $ 151,365
              Net Operating Income.................>>> $  83,251
              Before-Tax Cash Flow.................>>> $   1,364
              After-Tax Cash Flow..................>>> $  11,179

           Year Two:
              Effective Gross Income...............>>> $ 159,690
              Net Operating Income.................>>> $  88,851
              Before-Tax Cash Flow.................>>> $   6,965
              After-Tax Cash Flow..................>>> $  21,324

           Year Three:
              Effective Gross Income...............>>> $ 168,473
              Net Operating Income.................>>> $  94,801
              Before-Tax Cash Flow.................>>> $  12,914
              After-Tax Cash Flow..................>>> $  22,786

           Year Four:
              Effective Gross Income...............>>> $ 177,739
              Net Operating Income.................>>> $ 101,120
              Before-Tax Cash Flow.................>>> $  19,233
              After-Tax Cash Flow..................>>> $  22,651
```

```
    Year Five:
        Effective Gross Income..............>>> $ 187,515
        Net Operating Income................>>> $ 107,831
        Before-Tax Cash Flow................>>> $ (24,056)
        After-Tax Cash Flow.................>>> $  (5,536)

    Year Six:
        Effective Gross Income..............>>> $ 197,828
        Net Operating Income................>>> $ 114,957
        Before-Tax Cash Flow................>>> $  42,320
        After-Tax Cash Flow.................>>> $  33,782

    Year Seven:
        Effective Gross Income..............>>> $ 208,709
        Net Operating Income................>>> $ 122,522
        Before-Tax Cash Flow................>>> $  49,886
        After-Tax Cash Flow.................>>> $  35,969

    Year Eight:
        Effective Gross Income..............>>> $ 220,188
        Net Operating Income................>>> $ 130,554
        Before-Tax Cash Flow................>>> $  57,917
        After-Tax Cash Flow.................>>> $  40,121

    Year Nine:
        Effective Gross Income..............>>> $ 232,298
        Net Operating Income................>>> $ 139,079
        Before-Tax Cash Flow................>>> $  66,442
        After-Tax Cash Flow.................>>> $  44,472

    Year Ten:
        Effective Gross Income..............>>> $ 245,074
        Net Operating Income................>>> $ 148,126
        Before-Tax Cash Flow................>>> $  75,490
        After-Tax Cash Flow.................>>> $  47,254

FINANCING INPUTS:

    First Mortgage Amount...................>>> $ 425,000
    Second Mortgage Amount..................>>> $  75,000
    Interest-Only Financing.................>>> $  50,000

EQUITY INVESTMENT:

    Downpayment.............................>>> $  40,000

EXPECTED HOLDING PERIOD (max.=10):

    ......................................>>>        10  years


Press  [Alt] M  for MENU          Press  [Ctrl] [Break]  for READY
```

```
            II. OUTPUT FOR SIMPLE RATES OF RETURN
            ========================================

            For  an  investment  of  $ 590,000

                         consisting  of

       $ 550,000    debt    and     $   40,000    equity,


           Year            EGI      NOI      BTCF     ATCF
       ------------------------------------------------------
                           ($)      ($)      ($)      ($)

            1            151,365   83,251    1,364    11,179
            2            159,690   88,851    6,965    21,324
            3            168,473   94,801   12,914    22,786
            4            177,739  101,120   19,233    22,651
            5            187,515  107,831  (24,056)   (5,536)

            6            197,828  114,957   42,320    33,782
            7            208,709  122,522   49,886    35,969
            8            220,188  130,554   57,917    40,121
            9            232,298  139,079   66,442    44,472
           10            245,074  148,126   75,490    47,254


  Press  [Alt] M  for MENU           Press  [Ctrl] [Break]  for READY
```

```
          III. SUMMARY OF SIMPLE RATES OF RETURN
          ==========================================


               For any real estate investment,

$$$$$$$$$$$$$$$$$$$$$$$$$$$$$$$$$$$$$$$$$$$$$$$$$$$$$$$$$$$$$$$$$$$$$$$$$


                    Overall      BT       BT       AT       AT
   Year        GIM  Cap Rate    ROE      ROI      ROE      ROI
--------------------------------------------------------------------

             (times)   (%)       (%)      (%)      (%)      (%)

      1       3.90    14.11     3.41     0.23    27.95     1.89
      2       3.69    15.06    17.41     1.18    53.31     3.61
      3       3.50    16.07    32.29     2.19    56.97     3.86
      4       3.32    17.14    48.08     3.26    56.63     3.84
      5       3.15    18.28   (60.14)   (4.08)  (13.84)   (0.94)

      6       2.98    19.48   105.80     7.17    84.46     5.73
      7       2.83    20.77   124.72     8.46    89.92     6.10
      8       2.68    22.13   144.79     9.82   100.30     6.80
      9       2.54    23.57   166.11    11.26   111.18     7.54
     10       2.41    25.11   188.73    12.79   118.14     8.01
             ------   ------   ------   ------   ------   ------

   AVERAGES   3.10    19.17    77.12     5.23    68.50     4.64


$$$$$$$$$$$$$$$$$$$$$$$$$$$$$$$$$$$$$$$$$$$$$$$$$$$$$$$$$$$$$$$$$$$$$$$$$


Press  [Alt] M  for MENU         Press  [Ctrl] [Break]  for READY


~~~~~~~~~~~~~~~~~~~~~~~~~~~~~~~~~~~~~~~~~~~~~~~~~~~~~~~~~~~~~~~~~~~~~~~~~~
```

CALCULATING FINANCIAL RATIOS
(Template: lot1002)

Bankers, accountants, and corporate executives have long relied upon financial statements for economic evaluation of firms, clients, and investment opportunities. It is fitting then that a template be developed to permit the financial evaluation of real estate projects using financial ratios.

Principles. Financial ratio analysis has a long tradition in accounting and finance. In real estate, the analysis is less formal, but nonetheless important and widely practiced. The main idea is to be able to disassemble income and balance sheet items and detect important relationships. These relationships are of two types: comparative with other investors or investments and performance over time. The analyst might like to know the trends that are occurring or those that are expected to take place.

Using the Template. There are some basic inputs to be made by the user. These include an initial estimate of effective gross income for the project and the initial operating expense ratio; the amount, cost, and term of the mortgage financing; the equity downpayment; some basic depreciation (ACRS straight-line only here, for simplification purposes); the investor's income tax rate; and annual growth rates in income and expenses. These basic inputs provide the necessary information for any financial statement analysis.

There are two output tables in this template. Each is provided for ten years. The first calculates the financing and depreciation measures including a number of items which have become standard fare for readers who are proceeding through this book from the start: an amortization schedule with financing expenses, interest, amortization, and beginning and ending balances of the mortgage, depreciation allowances, and remaining book values (the amount of depreciable basis which remains available). The second table provides the income and cash flow calculations. These, too, are familiar to the reader: effective gross income, operating expenses, net operating income, financing expenses, before-tax cash flow, taxes, and after-tax cash flow. This table presents the results of a number of templates up to this point. (It should be apparent where all of these numbers come from. If these figures are not so apparent, it is suggested that the reader return to earlier templates for more review before proceeding.)

The financial ratios are provided in Table III. Each is defined and briefly discussed below:

- **Loan/Value.** The loan-to-value ratio relates the amount of debt financing employed by the investor to the current, or more typically, the historic cost of the property. This ratio is used by lenders as a borrowing constraint and by investors as a measure of leverage. The higher the ratio, the greater the use of leverage.

- **Debt Coverage Ratio.** This is a very important measure and is defined as the ratio of net operating income to financing expenses (debt service). It is a measure of risk for the lender. The measure is used by lenders to evaluate the extent to which the income from the property is expected to be able to cover the fixed, financial obligations of the borrower. The higher the ratio, the better the prospect for loan approval. However, the higher the ratio, the less the available loan amount!

- **Default Ratio.** This is another well-known ratio. It is defined as the ratio of operating expenses and financing expenses to effective gross income. The default ratio tests how well the income from the investment is expected to meet any of its likely expenditures. The lower this ratio becomes, the safer the investment appears.

- **Total Asset Turnover.** This ratio is defined as the ratio of effective gross income to the total cost (or value) of the property. Turnover ratios are used to measure the efficiency of obtaining income from properties. The greater this ratio, the more income is being generated from the investment.

- **Profit Margin.** This is one of the most well-known profitability ratios used in financial analysis of firms. It is defined as the ratio of after-tax cash flow to effective gross income. This is a slightly different ratio than several others in that it measures two types of income in the same ratio. This ratio provides a measure of profit per dollar of gross income. The higher the value, the more profitable the investment.

- **Return on Investment (ROI).** This ratio has been used in some of the earlier templates. It is defined as the ratio of after-tax cash flow to the total cost of the investment. The higher this ratio, the greater the return to the investor.

- **Return on Equity (ROE).** This is the final ratio in the template and one which has also been used previously in earlier templates. This measure is defined as the ratio of after-tax cash flow to the equity investment. As above, the higher the ratio, the greater the return to the investor. Note that ROE will exceed ROI whenever favorable leverage exists for the investment.

The reader who is interested in additional discussion of these and other measures of return should seek other material in this area. For example, see Austin J. Jaffe and C. F. Sirmans, *Real Estate Investment Decision Making*. (Englewood Cliffs, NJ: Prentice-Hall, Inc., 1982).

An Example.   In this example, a project costing $225,000 is considered. The interest deductions are sizable and the depreciation allowance (even using ACRS SL) is relatively large. Thus, taxes for the first three years are negative;

tax savings are available. This results in large after-tax cash flows throughout the ten years ($2,307 in year one to $23,499 in year ten).

The ratios provide a similar favorable picture. The leverage and financial risk ratios (loan-to-value ratio and debt coverage ratio) are both acceptable by most standards and become even better after the first few years. The profit margin is very high. The rates of return, especially on equity (as a result of the tax savings) are very favorable. As a result, this project looks like an excellent choice for an investor. (The only real problem is trying to find a project this favorable in many real-world markets!)

Graphics.   The line graph shows trends in the ratios over time. This is very useful information both in terms of analyzing past performance and in cases where the analyst is interested in what is expected to happen. Also note that some of the ratios do not change materially as forecasts are made over the expected planning horizon of ten years.

Possible Modifications.   This template has been streamlined. Investors could expand the template to include detailed analysis of several other considerations. This is also an excellent template to employ a window for quick sensitivity testing of the results of changes in inputs.

EXAMPLE TEMPLATE 10.2
Calculating financial ratios.

```
lot1002x                                    Real Estate Diskette #4
=================================================================
CALCULATING FINANCIAL RATIOS        Copyright (C) Reston Pub. Co., 1985
=================================================================


~~~~~~~~~~~~~~~~~~~~~~~~~~~~~~~~~~~~~~~~~~~~~~~~~~~~~~~~~~~~~~~~~~~~~~~

                    ***  TABLE OF CONTENTS  ***
                    ==================

            Table                                       Page
            -----                                       ----


    I.   INPUTS FOR FINANCIAL RATIOS                      1

   II.   OUTPUT TABLES FOR FINANCIAL RATIOS               2

  III.   SUMMARY OF FINANCIAL RATIOS                      3



~~~~~~~~~~~~~~~~~~~~~~~~~~~~~~~~~~~~~~~~~~~~~~~~~~~~~~~~~~~~~~~~~~~~~~~

                   I. INPUTS FOR FINANCIAL RATIOS
                   ==============================

    Enter the following assumptions:


        Income and Expense Estimates:
          Initial Effective Gross Income........>>> $  50,000
          Initial Operating Expense Ratio.......>>>    43.00  %

        Financing Inputs:
          Mortgage Amount.......................>>> $ 200,000
          Interest Rate on Mortgage.............>>>    13.50  %
          Mortgage Term.........................>>>    30     years

        Equity Investment:
          Downpayment...........................>>> $  25,000

        Depreciation Inputs (ACRS SL Only):
          Land-to-Value Ratio...................>>>    25.00  %
          Useful Life (18, 35, or 45 years).....>>>    18     years
          Month When Investment Begins..........>>>    7

        Marginal Income Tax Rate.................>>>    40.00  %

        Annual Growth Rates:
          Income................................>>>    7.00   %
          Expenses..............................>>>    4.00   %


  Press  [Alt] M  for MENU       Press  [Ctrl] [Break]  for READY


~~~~~~~~~~~~~~~~~~~~~~~~~~~~~~~~~~~~~~~~~~~~~~~~~~~~~~~~~~~~~~~~~~~~~~~
```

II. OUTPUT TABLES FOR FINANCIAL RATIOS
==

Financing and Depreciation Calculations:

Year	Beg Bal	Fin Exp	Interest	Amort	End Bal	Dep All	End BV
	($)	($)	($)	($)	($)	($)	($)
1	200,000	27,618	27,000	618	199,382	5,063	163,688
2	199,382	27,618	26,917	702	198,680	10,125	153,563
3	198,680	27,618	26,822	797	197,883	10,125	143,438
4	197,883	27,618	26,714	904	196,979	10,125	133,313
5	196,979	27,618	26,592	1,026	195,952	10,125	123,188
6	195,952	27,618	26,454	1,165	194,787	10,125	113,063
7	194,787	27,618	26,296	1,322	193,465	10,125	102,938
8	193,465	27,618	26,118	1,501	191,964	10,125	92,813
9	191,964	27,618	25,915	1,703	190,261	10,125	82,688
10	190,261	27,618	25,685	1,933	188,328	10,125	72,563

Income and Cash Flow Calculations:

Year	EGI	OE	NOI	Fin Exp	BTCF	Taxes	ATCF
	($)	($)	($)	($)	($)	($)	($)
1	50,000	21,500	28,500	27,618	882	(1,425)	2,307
2	53,500	22,360	31,140	27,618	3,522	(2,361)	5,882
3	57,245	23,254	33,991	27,618	6,372	(1,182)	7,555
4	61,252	24,185	37,068	27,618	9,449	91	9,358
5	65,540	25,152	40,388	27,618	12,769	1,468	11,301
6	70,128	26,158	43,970	27,618	16,351	2,956	13,395
7	75,037	27,204	47,832	27,618	20,214	4,564	15,649
8	80,289	28,293	51,997	27,618	24,378	6,302	18,077
9	85,909	29,424	56,485	27,618	28,867	8,178	20,689
10	91,923	30,601	61,322	27,618	33,703	10,205	23,499

Press [Alt] M for MENU   Press [Ctrl] [Break] for READY

~~~~~~

III. SUMMARY OF FINANCIAL RATIOS
=================================

For any real estate investment,

$$$

Year	Loan/ Value (%)	Debt Cov Ratio (%)	Default Ratio (%)	Tot Asst Turnover (%)	Profit Margin (%)	Ret on Invest (%)	Ret on Equity (%)
1	88.61	103.19	98.24	22.22	4.61	1.03	9.23
2	88.30	112.75	93.42	23.78	10.99	2.61	23.53
3	87.95	123.07	88.87	25.44	13.20	3.36	30.22
4	87.55	134.21	84.57	27.22	15.28	4.16	37.43
5	87.09	146.23	80.52	29.13	17.24	5.02	45.20
6	86.57	159.20	76.68	31.17	19.10	5.95	53.58
7	85.98	173.19	73.06	33.35	20.86	6.96	62.60
8	85.32	188.27	69.64	35.68	22.51	8.03	72.31
9	84.56	204.52	66.40	38.18	24.08	9.19	82.75
10	83.70	222.03	63.34	40.85	25.56	10.44	93.99
AVERAGES	86.56	156.67	79.47	30.70	17.34	5.68	51.08

$$$

Press [Alt] M for MENU   Press [Ctrl] [Break] for READY

~~~~~~

CALCULATING THE EFFECTIVE RATE OF INTEREST
(Template: lot1003)

The final template in this chapter is relatively short and simple, but is very useful. The measurement of the effective rate of interest is important but many investors have difficulty doing the proper calculation by hand. Frequently, approximations are relied upon. With Lotus 1-2-3, the effective rate of interest can be calculated precisely, quickly, and perhaps most importantly, repeatedly.

Principles. Suppose an investor had some money now and wanted to know what the rate of return would be on an investment over a period of time if the future value of the investment could be estimated. In effect, what would the actual rate of return be on an annual basis by buying a piece of land now and selling it for five times the purchase price in 20 years?

This is the model which answers this question. It is important to recognize that many investors use very rough (and often inaccurate) "rules of thumb" to answer this question. The inaccuracy really becomes critical when the number of years is relatively long (such as 15, 20, or more years). The method in this template is to calculate the ratio of future value to present value and take the nth root of the ratio and subtract one. This calculation provides the effective rate of return on the investment.

Using the Template. As always, Lotus does the number crunching; you put in the appropriate inputs. In this template, you must put in the present value of the investment, the expected (or past) future value, and the range of time periods you wish to examine. (As earlier, if you are interested in only one time period, enter the single period as the entire range. In this case, however, you can feel free to enter a wide range since the template is small and Lotus will perform quickly.)

Note that the maximum range of time periods is automatically set at 95 years, with five year increments. Note also that in every case, the longer it takes for the future value to reach its future sum, the lower the effective rate of interest (return) will be.

An Example. The example chosen here is deliberate. Suppose you are the heir to a small inheritance of $10,000. (It is also possible for some people to save $10,000 in a relatively short time, too!) In any event, assume the sum of $10,000 is available today. The question is how long and at what interest rates will it take before you become a millionaire? Do you think this is impossible or crazy or unheard of? Let's look at the results.

Certainly if you begin with $10,000, it will be difficult for you to become a millionaire overnight. Note that if your plan is to do it in five years, you must earn 151.19 percent per year (not 200 percent per year, however). So you will not achieve this milestone by 1990.

On the other hand, look at the rest of the table. For example, over a period of 35 years, you would have to earn slightly more than 14 percent per year. If you are younger than me and if you could earn at the rate of 9.65 percent for fifty years, you can still achieve your goal—it is not so impossible. Lotus 1-2-3 can show you how much and how long you need to invest. Do not overlook this template. Although it is simpler than several of the others, it can be eye opening and very useful.

Graphics.   The graph is also simple. It shows the percent to be earned given various holding periods in order to result in your initial sum to be transformed into your future sum. Notice that after several years, the rate of return differences narrow to a very small amount.

Possible Modifications.   One of the likely modifications to this template is to introduce taxes into the analysis. Since income is taxable each year, the returns shown in the table are taxable (unless, of course, they are tax-exempt such as certain state and local bonds, special annuities or Individual Retirement Accounts). In addition, the investor might like to be able to calculate this type of return for investments with cash flows throughout the investment period. This is coming up in the next chapter.

EXAMPLE TEMPLATE 10.3
Calculating the effective rate of interest.

```
lot1003x                                    Real Estate Diskette #4
==================================================================
CALCULATING THE EFFECTIVE RATE OF INTEREST
                               Copyright (C) Reston Pub. Co., 1985
==================================================================

~~~~~~~~~~~~~~~~~~~~~~~~~~~~~~~~~~~~~~~~~~~~~~~~~~~~~~~~~~~~~~~~~~~~~

                    ***  TABLE OF CONTENTS  ***
                    ==================
           Table                                   Page
           -----                                   ----

     I.   INPUTS FOR EFFECTIVE RATES OF INTEREST      1

     II.  OUTPUT TABLE FOR EFFECTIVE RATES
          OF INTEREST                                 2


~~~~~~~~~~~~~~~~~~~~~~~~~~~~~~~~~~~~~~~~~~~~~~~~~~~~~~~~~~~~~~~~~~~~~

           I.  INPUTS FOR EFFECTIVE RATES OF INTEREST
           =========================================

     Enter the following assumptions:

        Initial Sum (PV)              >>>    $   10000

        Future Sum (FV)               >>>    $ 1000000

        Time Period Range [t(1)...t(n)]

              From t(1)               >>>          5   years
                To t(n)               >>>        100   years


Press  [Alt] M  for MENU        Press  [Ctrl] [Break]  for READY


~~~~~~~~~~~~~~~~~~~~~~~~~~~~~~~~~~~~~~~~~~~~~~~~~~~~~~~~~~~~~~~~~~~~~
```

II. OUTPUT TABLE FOR EFFECTIVE RATES OF INTEREST
==

For any single sum,

if the PV is: $ 10000   ,

if the FV is: $ 1000000   ,

if the [t(1)...t(n)] is: 5   yrs to   100   yrs ,

the Effective Rate of Interest Table is as follows:

$$

Years	Effective Rate of Interest
(t)	(%)
5	151.19
10	58.49
15	35.94
20	25.89
25	20.23
30	16.59
35	14.06
40	12.20
45	10.78
50	9.65
55	8.73
60	7.98
65	7.34
70	6.80
75	6.33
80	5.93
85	5.57
90	5.25
95	4.97
100	4.71

$$

Press [Alt] M for MENU   Press [Ctrl] [Break] for READY

~~~~~~

11 Discounted Cash Flow Criteria

Overview

In the previous chapter, the templates presented criteria using income and expense statements. Financial ratios and measures of return require only the first year's data estimates. However, a major drawback of these approaches is that the time value of money is neglected in the analysis. This means that the benefits and costs are not adjusted for *when* they are expected to occur. As a result, investors who use only these measures are constrained by the limitations of the methods.

In this chapter, the next generation of models are introduced and demonstrated. These models are called *discounted cash flow models* and for the last few years, they have been heralded as the most sophisticated and most useful real estate investment analysis techniques.

This chapter presents five complete templates, each with a different, but related investment criterion. The first four templates enable the Lotus 1-2-3 user to perform a series of financial calculations which only a few years ago were reserved for mainframe users with expensive real estate software. The models in these templates are *net present value (NPV)*, *internal rate of return*

(IRR), profitability index (PI), and *net terminal value (NTV).* The final template introduces risk analysis to the template system by measuring *variance* and *standard deviation.* These templates provide powerful tools for Lotus users interested in making real estate decisions.

NET PRESENT VALUE (NPV)
(Template: lot1101)

This model is called *net present value (NPV)* because the present value of the benefits (after-tax cash flows) are netted out against the present value of the costs (equity investment). In this manner, the investor performs his/her own form of cost-benefit analysis when deciding whether or not to purchase (or sell) a real estate project. This model is particularly useful in practice since it provides a clear and consistent decision rule and is very useful for comparing a variety of projects. For some investors, it is the only criterion used in making investment decisions.

Principles.   The NPV of a real estate investment is defined as the difference between the present value of all (after-tax) benefits (cash flows and the equity reversion at the time of sale or other disposition) and the present value of the costs (equity investment, or downpayment). If the NPV is greater than zero, this means that the expected (after-tax) benefits are greater than the expected equity costs, using a given discount rate. The discount rate should be chosen based upon the required return to the equity investor for projects of this "risk class." If NPV is calculated to be less than zero, this says that the expected benefits are not high enough to offset the costs and the project should not be pursued.

The interpretation of the NPV approach is also straightforward, although some investors seem to have difficulty in understanding what an NPV of, say, $20,000 means. Consider a project with an estimated NPV of $20,000. Assuming the estimates were made as bias free as possible, this result says that on a present value basis (i.e., after discounting future flows to the present), the benefits exceed the costs of the project by $20,000. Thus, by investing in the project, the investor can expect to become $20,000 richer by purchasing than by avoiding the project.

Another way of saying the same thing is with the given investment of $20,000, the investor would earn the required yield (at the discount rate) and $20,000 extra. In effect, the investor gets a higher yield than the discount rate as long as the NPV is positive.

If a project is rejected with an NPV of $20,000, on an expected basis, the opportunity cost associated with rejecting the project is $20,000; the investor is $20,000 poorer than if the project was chosen. As a result, projects which are estimated to have positive NPVs are projects which make investors wealthier. If the financial objective as an investor is to become as wealthy as possible, the investor should choose to invest in all projects with NPVs greater than zero and the investor should choose those with the largest NPVs first.

Using the Template.   The NPV template allows inputs for up to 20 years. For each year, the user can enter the cash flows (generally after-tax, but some users also calculate before-tax NPVs) and/or the expected sales proceeds at the time of sale. The sales proceeds are generally the gross sales price minus sales commissions and other expenses minus the outstanding balance(s) of the debt financing minus any capital gains taxes if the NPV is after tax and to the equity investor. The figure is also called the "after-tax equity reversion" or sometimes just "reversion." Note that the reversion occurs by definition in the last year of the holding period for any fee estate. The last year of the holding period may also have a cash flow as well.

The user is also requested to input a discount range of values which are used to generate a table of NPV values. This is because NPVs are an inverse function of the discount rate. This will be made clearer by examining the results of the example below. Each discount rate varies within the range by 2.5 percentage points. Finally, the remaining input is the investment outlay. In most cases, for example, when after-tax cash flows are used, the investment outlay is the equity contribution or downpayment used by the investor.

The output table consists of a reproduction of the inputs in a consolidated form as well as the Net Present Value Table. This table shows the estimates of NPV for each discount rate. The user must choose the appropriate discount rate from the table and check the decision rule in the summary in Table III. Note that when NPV is greater than (or equal) to zero, the summary states that the investor should invest. When NPV is less than zero, the investor should not invest. This template employs Lotus's "TRUE" and "FALSE" logical functions to display the decision rules.

An Example.   In this example, for an investment of $185,000, a set of cash flows are estimated with an expected sale to take place such that the investor expects to receive $300,000 at the end of five years. Using a discount range from 5 to 25 percent, the NPVs are shown for each discount rate. For example, at 12.50 percent, the NPV is $79,958. Note also in the summary, at 12.50 percent, the investor should invest in the project.

The estimation of the discount rate using the NPV approach is critical to making the investment decision. There has been much discussion and analysis of how the discount rate should be chosen. The reader is referred to real estate investment texts for additional discussion of this point. However, the investor can solve this problem by answering the following question: which rate is the minimum required (after-tax) rate of return the investor would accept in order to invest in a project with these risk characteristics? If 5 percent is too low and 25 percent is too high, continue to ask the question until a rate is chosen. This is the investor's discount rate for this project.

Graphics.   There is a standard graph to illustrate net present value as a function of the discount rate. With this graph the investor locates the appropriate discount rate and checks to see if the NPV at that point is greater than or less than zero. This is the decision rule for the investor. The graph illustrates this function and shows where the NPV is positive and at which discount rates the NPV is negative. In this case, the NPV is positive unless the discount rate is greater than about 22 percent.

Possible Modifications.   The NPV template like those which follow has been designed with a maximum amount of flexibility built in. It was already noted that either before-tax or after-tax flows could be used. The cash flows could be from the project as a whole or after the lender has been paid. The cash flows can even be for non-real estate projects as well as real estate investments. The important point is that the investor must be consistent with any data used. This means if after-tax cash flows are used, an after-tax discount rate must be used. It means if financing expenses are deducted from the cash flow each year, at the time of sale, the outstanding mortgage balance must be deducted before measuring the sales proceeds to the equity investor.

Lotus 1-2-3 contains a function for NPV. Experienced users may find this key useful in other applications as well. This template has used this function in developing this and other templates.

EXAMPLE TEMPLATE 11.1
Net present value (NPV).

```
lot1101x                                        Real Estate Diskette #4
=======================================================================
NET PRESENT VALUE (NPV)               Copyright (C) Reston Pub. Co., 1985
=======================================================================

~~~~~~~~~~~~~~~~~~~~~~~~~~~~~~~~~~~~~~~~~~~~~~~~~~~~~~~~~~~~~~~~~~~~~~~~~~~

                     ***   TABLE OF CONTENTS   ***
                         ==================
            Table                                        Page
            -----                                        ----

     I.   INPUTS FOR NET PRESENT VALUE
          CALCULATIONS                                      1

     II.  OUTPUT TABLE OF NET PRESENT VALUES                2

    III.  SUMMARY OF NET PRESENT VALUES                     3


~~~~~~~~~~~~~~~~~~~~~~~~~~~~~~~~~~~~~~~~~~~~~~~~~~~~~~~~~~~~~~~~~~~~~~~~~~~
```

```
          I. INPUTS FOR NET PRESENT VALUE CALCULATIONS
          ================================================

     Enter the following assumptions:


          Investment Outlay........................>>> $   185000

          Cash Flows and/or Sales Proceeds (Reversion):


                                                    CF                    SP
                                                 _____             _____

               Year One.....................>>> $   10000    >>> $    _____
               Year Two.....................>>> $   20000    >>> $    _____
               Year Three...................>>> $   30000    >>> $    _____
               Year Four....................>>> $   40000    >>> $    _____
               Year Five....................>>> $   50000    >>> $   300000

               Year Six.....................>>> $    _____    >>> $    _____
               Year Seven...................>>> $    _____    >>> $    _____
               Year Eight...................>>> $    _____    >>> $    _____
               Year Nine....................>>> $    _____    >>> $    _____
               Year Ten.....................>>> $    _____    >>> $    _____

               Year Eleven..................>>> $    _____    >>> $    _____
               Year Twelve..................>>> $    _____    >>> $    _____
               Year Thirteen................>>> $    _____    >>> $    _____
               Year Fourteen................>>> $    _____    >>> $    _____
               Year Fifteen.................>>> $    _____    >>> $    _____

               Year Sixteen.................>>> $    _____    >>> $    _____
               Year Seventeen...............>>> $    _____    >>> $    _____
               Year Eighteen................>>> $    _____    >>> $    _____
               Year Nineteen................>>> $    _____    >>> $    _____
               Year Twenty..................>>> $    _____    >>> $    _____


          Discount Rate Range [k(1)...k(m)]

               From k(1).........................>>>     5.00   %
               To  k(m)..........................>>>    25.00   %


     Press  [Alt] M  for MENU          Press  [Ctrl] [Break]  for READY
```

$$\sim\sim\sim\sim\sim\sim\sim\sim\sim\sim\sim\sim\sim\sim\sim\sim\sim\sim\sim\sim\sim\sim\sim\sim\sim\sim\sim\sim\sim\sim\sim\sim\sim\sim\sim\sim\sim\sim\sim\sim$$

```
        II. OUTPUT TABLE OF NET PRESENT VALUES
        ======================================

        For any real estate investment,

   if the investment outlay is:   $    185000   , and

if the sum of the cash flows and the sales proceeds is:


            $    10000    in Year       1
            $    20000    in Year       2
            $    30000    in Year       3
            $    40000    in Year       4
            $   350000    in Year       5

            $       0     in Year      NA
            $       0     in Year      NA
            $       0     in Year      NA
            $       0     in Year      NA
            $       0     in Year      NA

            $       0     in Year      NA
            $       0     in Year      NA
            $       0     in Year      NA
            $       0     in Year      NA
            $       0     in Year      NA

            $       0     in Year      NA
            $       0     in Year      NA
            $       0     in Year      NA
            $       0     in Year      NA
            $       0     in Year      NA
```

the Net Present Value Table is provided as follows:

$$

Discount Rate	Net Present Value
(%)	($)
5.00	175,722
7.50	139,505
10.00	107,802
12.50	79,958
15.00	55,426
17.50	33,746
20.00	14,531
22.50	(2,548)
25.00	(17,768)
NA	NA

$$$

Press [Alt] M for MENU   Press [Ctrl] [Break] for READ

~~~~~~

```
            III. SUMMARY OF NET PRESENT VALUES
            ===================================

    Therefore, the investor can use the following decision rules:

$$$$$$$$$$$$$$$$$$$$$$$$$$$$$$$$$$$$$$$$$$$$$$$$$$$$$$$$$$$$$$$$$$$


    At     5.00   percent, the investor should invest     1  !
    At     7.50   percent, the investor should invest     1  !
    At    10.00   percent, the investor should invest     1  !
    At    12.50   percent, the investor should invest     1  !
    At    15.00   percent, the investor should invest     1  !

    At    17.50   percent, the investor should invest     1  !
    At    20.00   percent, the investor should invest     1  !
    At    22.50   percent, the investor should invest     0  !
    At    25.00   percent, the investor should invest     0  !
    At      NA    percent, the investor should invest    NA  !

        -----(Computer returns 0 if FALSE, 1 if TRUE)-----


$$$$$$$$$$$$$$$$$$$$$$$$$$$$$$$$$$$$$$$$$$$$$$$$$$$$$$$$$$$$$$$$$$$


Press  [Alt] M  for MENU          Press  [Ctrl] [Break]  for READY


~~~~~~~~~~~~~~~~~~~~~~~~~~~~~~~~~~~~~~~~~~~~~~~~~~~~~~~~~~~~~~~~~~~~~~~
```

INTERNAL RATE OF RETURN (IRR)
(Template: lot1102)

An equally important model is the *internal rate of return (IRR)* template. This is an even more widely used investment model in real estate and is generally discussed and understood by investors who are familiar with NPV. In some cases, investors prefer IRR for one of several reasons, although there are numerous drawbacks to its use as an investment criterion. While this is not the appropriate place to discuss a complete comparison between the two methods, there are some instances when the NPV and IRR indicate different projects to buy. Thus, they can provide conflicts when more than one acceptable project is available.

Principles. The IRR suffers from a type of mysticism in some circles regarding its definition, meaning, and interpretation. This is unfortunate and rather unwarranted since it is closely related to NPV; the ability to grasp the definition, calculation, and interpretation of NPV qualifies the investor to automatically understand the IRR.

The IRR is defined as the rate of return which makes the present value of the benefits (typically after-tax cash flows and reversion) equal to the present value of the costs (typically the equity contribution). That's it—clean and simple! The rate of return which equates the inflows to the outflows is called the IRR. It is generally calculated on an expected basis, either before or after taxes have been evaluated. The IRR is in the form of a rate of return percentage and higher is preferred to lower from the investor's point of view.

Another way of saying the same thing is to find the discount rate using the NPV approach which makes the estimate of NPV equal to zero. At that point, stop! You have solved for the IRR! This is really two sides of the same coin!

Finally, the decision rule for the IRR is equally clear: if the IRR is greater than (or equal to) the investor's chosen discount rate, the project should be acquired. If the IRR is less than the discount rate, the project should not be acquired.

Using the Template. The format of the template is identical to the NPV template with a small exception. (You are probably not surprised since the above definition shows how closely related the two models are.) In the IRR template a space is left for the "IRR Estimate and Tester." This is the place to estimate what the IRR is for the project.

Unlike the NPV calculation, the IRR method is difficult for the computer to calculate. (In fact, if the holding period is longer than two years, it is *impossible* for even the best computer to solve for the IRR directly; it must then be estimated by one of several "trial-and-error" procedures.) A trial-and-error procedure has been developed for use with this template using the Lotus

1-2-3 @IRR Function. On the last line of the input page, notice the "IRR Estimate." This is where the best guess is inserted and Lotus uses this estimate to begin the calculation process.

In addition, the template shows where net present value approaches zero, (one of the definitions of the IRR). This is the same approach used with two of the templates in Chapter 6 dealing with the effective cost of borrowing and the lender's yield. Due to the conceptual difficulty associated with understanding the IRR, the standard approach has also been retained.

Note that the IRR results are shown between the double-dashed line. However, note if it takes a long time (more than 20 calculations) to approximate the answer to at least two decimal points, Lotus 1-2-3 stops and returns an "ERR" message. For most real estate investments, however, an answer will be obtained without difficulty.

Are you confused? Let's look at the example.

An Example. In this case, the same data as in the previous template has been entered. Suppose the user inserted 7.50 percent as the IRR Estimate for the IRR. The output table shows that using 7.50 percent as a discount rate results in a value of NPV equal to $139,505. Since one of the definitions of IRR is the rate which makes NPV equal to zero, we know that the estimate of 7.50 percent is too *low*. (This is also implied in the output table where, on the 7.50 percent line, the template reports that it is "1" (or True) that the IRR is greater than 7.50 percent.)

Suppose further that the investor chose to test a higher value for IRR. Suppose that 15.00 percent was tested. The NPV of $55,426 is calculated using 15.00 percent as a discount rate. Clearly, the true IRR is still higher yet since the NPV is still greater than zero. By testing 25.00 percent, the NPV becomes negative (−$17,768). The investor thus knows that the true IRR is greater than 15.00 percent but less than 25.00 percent.

How much greater than 15.00 percent and how much less than 25.00 percent is this rate? By trial-and-error, the @IRR Function shows that at 22.1081 percent, the NPV is near zero. *This is the true IRR!!*

Graphics. This is precisely the same graph as in the previous template with one major exception: the internal rate of return is now plotted onto the NPV function. Since the IRR is defined at that point on the graph where NPV equals zero, the intersection of the function and zero is the IRR Solution. On this graph, it is represented with the "x" symbol, at the approximate point.

Possible Modifications. Lotus 1-2-3 can very quickly test various rates and estimate different IRRs. This may effectively be done by establishing a small window at the top of the screen for the IRR estimate cell and centering the output portion of the template at the bottom of the screen. By moving back and forth (using the Function Key F6 convention with a Lotus window), the proper rate may be centered in on in a matter of minutes. Remember however, that the menus must be disabled in order to do this procedure.

It is important to point out that in recent years, numerous modifications have been made to the IRR calculation. Many of the modifications have attempted to deal with several of the technical shortcomings of the calculation. Among the most well-known and widely heralded is the *Financial Management Rate of Return* (or *FMRR*). (The inquisitive reader is encouraged to read the following for more discussion of this and other models of this type: Stephen D. Messner and M. Chapman Findlay, III, "Real Estate Investment Analysis: IRR Versus FMRR," *The Real Estate Appraiser*, 41 (July–August 1975), 5–20, or Austin J. Jaffe and C. F. Sirmans, *Real Estate Investment Decision Making* (Englewood Cliffs, NJ: Prentice-Hall, Inc., 1982), pp. 461–70.)

EXAMPLE TEMPLATE 11.2
Internal rate of return (IRR).

```
lot1102x                                  Real Estate Diskette #4
================================================================
INTERNAL RATE OF RETURN (IRR)      Copyright (C) Reston Pub. Co., 1985
================================================================

~~~~~~~~~~~~~~~~~~~~~~~~~~~~~~~~~~~~~~~~~~~~~~~~~~~~~~~~~~~~~~~~~~~~

                   ***   TABLE OF CONTENTS   ***
                       =================
                Table                              Page
                -----                              ----

     I.   INPUTS FOR INTERNAL RATE OF
          RETURN CALCULATION                         1

    II.   OUTPUT TABLE OF INTERNAL RATE OF
          RETURN                                      2

   III.   SUMMARY OF INTERNAL RATE OF RETURN          3


~~~~~~~~~~~~~~~~~~~~~~~~~~~~~~~~~~~~~~~~~~~~~~~~~~~~~~~~~~~~~~~~~~~~
```

```
    I.  INPUTS FOR INTERNAL RATE OF RETURN CALCULATION
    ================================================

  Enter the following assumptions:


     Investment Outlay.......................>>> $   185000

     Cash Flows and/or Sales Proceeds (Reversion):


                                              CF                    SP
                                           _____             _____

         Year  One.....................>>> $   10000    >>> $   _____
         Year  Two.....................>>> $   20000    >>> $   _____
         Year  Three...................>>> $   30000    >>> $   _____
         Year  Four....................>>> $   40000    >>> $   _____
         Year  Five....................>>> $   50000    >>> $   300000

         Year  Six.....................>>> $   _____    >>> $   _____
         Year  Seven...................>>> $   _____    >>> $   _____
         Year  Eight...................>>> $   _____    >>> $   _____
         Year  Nine....................>>> $   _____    >>> $   _____
         Year  Ten.....................>>> $   _____    >>> $   _____

         Year  Eleven..................>>> $   _____    >>> $   _____
         Year  Twelve..................>>> $   _____    >>> $   _____
         Year  Thirteen................>>> $   _____    >>> $   _____
         Year  Fourteen................>>> $   _____    >>> $   _____
         Year  Fifteen.................>>> $   _____    >>> $   _____

         Year  Sixteen.................>>> $   _____    >>> $   _____
         Year  Seventeen...............>>> $   _____    >>> $   _____
         Year  Eighteen................>>> $   _____    >>> $   _____
         Year  Nineteen................>>> $   _____    >>> $   _____
         Year  Twenty..................>>> $   _____    >>> $   _____


     Discount Rate Range [k(1)...k(m)]


         From k(1).........................>>>    5.00   %
           To k(m).........................>>>   25.00   %

     IRR Estimate............................>>>   20.00   %


Press  [Alt] M  for MENU        Press  [Ctrl] [Break]  for READY
```

~~~~~~

```
        II. OUTPUT TABLE OF INTERNAL RATE OF RETURN
        ===============================================

              For any real estate investment,

    if the investment outlay is:    $    185000   , and

  if the sum of the cash flows and the sales proceeds is:


                $     10000    in Year        1
                $     20000    in Year        2
                $     30000    in Year        3
                $     40000    in Year        4
                $    350000    in Year        5

                $         0    in Year       NA
                $         0    in Year       NA
                $         0    in Year       NA
                $         0    in Year       NA
                $         0    in Year       NA

                $         0    in Year       NA
                $         0    in Year       NA
                $         0    in Year       NA
                $         0    in Year       NA
                $         0    in Year       NA

                $         0    in Year       NA
                $         0    in Year       NA
                $         0    in Year       NA
                $         0    in Year       NA
                $         0    in Year       NA


        the Internal Rate of Return is provided as follows:

$$$$$$$$$$$$$$$$$$$$$$$$$$$$$$$$$$$$$$$$$$$$$$$$$$$$$$$$$$$$$$$$$$$$$$$

   Discount         Net Present           Internal
     Rate              Value          Rate of Return
   --------------------------------------------------------
     (%)               ($)                 (%)

     5.00             175722    ...is >    5.00         1  !
     7.50             139505    ...is >    7.50         1  !
    10.00             107802    ...is >   10.00         1  !
    12.50              79958    ...is >   12.50         1  !
    15.00              55426    ...is >   15.00         1  !

    17.50              33746    ...is >   17.50         1  !
    20.00              14531    ...is >   20.00         1  !
    22.50              -2548    ...is >   22.50         0  !
    25.00             -17768    ...is >   25.00         0  !
      NA                 NA    ...is >      NA         NA  !

     -----(Computer returns 0 if FALSE, 1 if TRUE)-----
```

```
===================================================================
    Specifically, the internal rate of return for this investment is:

        >>>>>>>>>        22.1081%         <<<<<<<<

===================================================================

    Note that if "ERR" is returned, Lotus 1-2-3 cannot find the IRR
    solution since more than 20 iterations are required for this
    approximation.

    Therefore, this function cannot be used with projects where the
    investor expects cash flows or the reversion to occur later than
    five years into the holding period.  (See the Lotus 1-2-3 manual
    for more information about this function.)


    $$$$$$$$$$$$$$$$$$$$$$$$$$$$$$$$$$$$$$$$$$$$$$$$$$$$$$$$$$$$$$$$$$$$
```

Press [Alt] M for MENU   Press [Ctrl] [Break] for READY

~~~~~~

```
                III. SUMMARY OF INTERNAL RATE OF RETURN
                =======================================

    Therefore, the investor can use the following decision rules:

    $$$$$$$$$$$$$$$$$$$$$$$$$$$$$$$$$$$$$$$$$$$$$$$$$$$$$$$$$$$$$$$$$$$$


        At    5.00  percent, the investor should invest      1  !
        At    7.50  percent, the investor should invest      1  !
        At   10.00  percent, the investor should invest      1  !
        At   12.50  percent, the investor should invest      1  !
        At   15.00  percent, the investor should invest      1  !

        At   17.50  percent, the investor should invest      1  !
        At   20.00  percent, the investor should invest      1  !
        At   22.50  percent, the investor should invest      0  !
        At   25.00  percent, the investor should invest      0  !
        At     NA   percent, the investor should invest     NA  !


        The IRR is equal to approximately   22.11 percent.


    $$$$$$$$$$$$$$$$$$$$$$$$$$$$$$$$$$$$$$$$$$$$$$$$$$$$$$$$$$$$$$$$$$$$
```

Press [Alt] M for MENU   Press [Ctrl] [Break] for READY

~~~~~~

PROFITABILITY INDEX (PI)
(Template: lot1103)

The next two templates are variations on the NPV calculation. The first is called the *profitability index (PI)* or sometimes, the *benefit-cost ratio*. Instead of taking the *difference* between the present value of the benefits and costs, the investor using PI is required to take the *ratio* of benefits to costs.

Principles.   Adapted from governmental and public sector evaluation of project development, the PI is an alternative specification of discounted cash flow models. The PI is defined as the ratio of the present value of benefits (typically, after-tax cash flows and reversion) to the present value of costs (typically, the equity contribution). The same discount rate estimation process used to calculate NPV is used with the calculation of PI.

The decision rules for the use of PI are different than NPVs decision rules. If the PI is greater than (or equal to) 1.00, the present value of the benefits are expected to exceed (or equal) the present value of the costs. If so, a wise investor would want to acquire such investments. On the other hand, if PI is estimated to be less than 1.00, the reverse is true and the investor would not want to purchase the property.

A quick comparison between the methods shows that if NPV is greater than zero, IRR will be greater than the discount rate used in the NPV calculation and PI will be greater than 1.00. Thus, all of the methods provide the same choices regarding which investments should be chosen and which should be rejected. However, sometimes, NPV might prefer Investment A, IRR might prefer Investment B, and PI might prefer Investment C. If only one can be chosen, it is difficult (without some additional background) to decide which project should be chosen.

Using the Template.   The PI template uses the same format as the NPV template developed earlier in this chapter. All of the inputs are identical; even the output is very similar. However, in this case, the table shows a range of PIs associated with each discount rate. The summary applies the decision rule of the PI greater than (or equal to) or less than 1.00 for acceptance or rejection, respectively.

An Example.   In the example, note that if the discount rate chosen by the investor is equal to or less than 20.00 percent, the PI is greater than 1.00 and the investment should be accepted. If the discount rate is greater than 22.50 percent, the value of the PI is less than 1.00 and the investment should be rejected.

Actually, the cut-off rate is 22.1081 percent. Can you prove why?

Graphics. The Profitability Index function is graphed by the template. It shows the relationship between various discount rates and the profitability of the project. At rates higher than 22.1 percent, the PI is below one. This means the benefits are no longer greater than the costs and the project should be rejected.

Possible Modifications. As in all of these discounted cash flow templates, the investor may wish to narrow the range of discount rates to suit specific purposes. This can easily be done using the Lotus "Combine" option. In addition, the PI (or NPV or IRR) templates may be merged into other templates where it would be useful to do so. Be warned, however, that the merging of two or more Lotus 1-2-3 templates is for experienced users only and should be done only after backup copies of the original templates have been made. New menus will also have to be made.

EXAMPLE TEMPLATE 11.3
Profitability index (PI).

```
lot1103x                              Real Estate Diskette #4
============================================================
PROFITABILITY INDEX (PI)        Copyright (C) Reston Pub. Co., 1985
============================================================
~~~~~~~~~~~~~~~~~~~~~~~~~~~~~~~~~~~~~~~~~~~~~~~~~~~~~~~~~~~~~~~~

                 ***  TABLE OF CONTENTS  ***
                      =================
            Table                              Page
            -----                              ----

     I.   INPUTS FOR PROFITABILITY INDEX
          CALCULATIONS                           1

     II.  OUTPUT TABLE OF PROFITABILITY INDICES   2

     III. SUMMARY OF PROFITABILITY INDICES        3


~~~~~~~~~~~~~~~~~~~~~~~~~~~~~~~~~~~~~~~~~~~~~~~~~~~~~~~~~~~~~~~~
```

```
          I. INPUTS FOR PROFITABILITY INDEX CALCULATIONS
          =================================================

     Enter the following assumptions:


        Investment Outlay......................>>> $   185000

        Cash Flows and/or Sales Proceeds (Reversion):


                                                  CF                SP
                                              _____          _____

           Year One.....................>>> $   10000      >>> $   _____
           Year Two.....................>>> $   20000      >>> $   _____
           Year Three...................>>> $   30000      >>> $   _____
           Year Four....................>>> $   40000      >>> $   _____
           Year Five....................>>> $   50000      >>> $  300000

           Year Six.....................>>> $   _____      >>> $   _____
           Year Seven...................>>> $   _____      >>> $   _____
           Year Eight...................>>> $   _____      >>> $   _____
           Year Nine....................>>> $   _____      >>> $   _____
           Year Ten.....................>>> $   _____      >>> $   _____

           Year Eleven..................>>> $   _____      >>> $   _____
           Year Twelve..................>>> $   _____      >>> $   _____
           Year Thirteen................>>> $   _____      >>> $   _____
           Year Fourteen................>>> $   _____      >>> $   _____
           Year Fifteen.................>>> $   _____      >>> $   _____

           Year Sixteen.................>>> $   _____      >>> $   _____
           Year Seventeen...............>>> $   _____      >>> $   _____
           Year Eighteen................>>> $   _____      >>> $   _____
           Year Nineteen................>>> $   _____      >>> $   _____
           Year Twenty..................>>> $   _____      >>> $   _____


        Discount Rate Range [k(1)...k(m)]

           From k(1).........................>>>      5.00   %
           To k(m)...........................>>>     25.00   %


   Press  [Alt] M  for MENU          Press  [Ctrl] [Break]  for READY


~~~~~~~~~~~~~~~~~~~~~~~~~~~~~~~~~~~~~~~~~~~~~~~~~~~~~~~~~~~~~~~~~~~~~~~~~~
```

II. OUTPUT TABLE OF PROFITABILITY INDICES

For any real estate investment,

if the investment outlay is: $ 185000   , and

if the sum of the cash flows and the sales proceeds is:

$	10000	in Year	1
$	20000	in Year	2
$	30000	in Year	3
$	40000	in Year	4
$	350000	in Year	5
$	0	in Year	NA
$	0	in Year	NA
$	0	in Year	NA
$	0	in Year	NA
$	0	in Year	NA
$	0	in Year	NA
$	0	in Year	NA
$	0	in Year	NA
$	0	in Year	NA
$	0	in Year	NA
$	0	in Year	NA
$	0	in Year	NA
$	0	in Year	NA
$	0	in Year	NA
$	0	in Year	NA

the Profitability Index Table is provided as follows:

$$

Discount Rate	Profitability Index
(%)	
5.00	1.95
7.50	1.75
10.00	1.58
12.50	1.43
15.00	1.30
17.50	1.18
20.00	1.08
22.50	0.99
25.00	0.90
NA	NA

$$$

~~~~~~

III. SUMMARY OF PROFITABILITY INDICES
    =====================================

Therefore, the investor can use the following decision rules:

$$

    At   5.00   percent, the investor should invest   1 !
    At   7.50   percent, the investor should invest   1 !
    At   10.00   percent, the investor should invest   1 !
    At   12.50   percent, the investor should invest   1 !
    At   15.00   percent, the investor should invest   1 !

    At   17.50   percent, the investor should invest   1 !
    At   20.00   percent, the investor should invest   1 !
    At   22.50   percent, the investor should invest   0 !
    At   25.00   percent, the investor should invest   0 !
    At   NA   percent, the investor should invest   NA !

        -----(Computer returns 0 if FALSE, 1 if TRUE)-----

    $$$

~~~~~~

NET TERMINAL VALUE (NTV)
(Template: lot1104)

The final discounted cash flow model in this system of templates is called the *net terminal value (NTV)*. This is the least known of the set and probably the least relied upon in actual real estate investment practice.

Principles. The NTV is defined as the difference between the sum of the future values of the benefits (typically, after-tax cash flows and reversion) and the future value of the equity contribution. The date of the future values is the end of the planned holding period. The rate at which the benefits and costs are compounded is called the *reinvestment rate*.

If the NTV is greater than (or equal to) zero, the project should be accepted since the future value of the benefits would then exceed (or equal) the future value of the costs. If the NTV is less than zero, the project should be rejected. As before, this approach is consistent with the other approaches in terms of accepting or rejecting the same projects every time. However, differences can occur resulting from the choice of the reinvestment rate used to compound the flows and equity contribution to the future.

The proponents of this approach argue that it is superior to the NPV or PI approaches, since the reinvestment rate is likely to be lower than the discount rate. Therefore, applying the discount rate to obtain present values will introduce a bias which is likely to make the results of the analysis unrealistic. Everyone acknowledges that if the reinvestment rate is equal to the discount rate, there will be virtually no difference between NPV and NTV, except the date at which the cash flows and costs are valued.

Using the Template. The format of this template is the same as the other discounted cash flow formats, with the exception of the required reinvestment rate instead of the range of discount rates. The NTV output table shows the cash flows, the compounding factors and their future values. The sum of all of the future values is defined as the NTV. The summary provides the analyst with the operation of the decision rule as well as a review of the results.

An Example. In this case, a reinvestment rate of 7.00 percent was used. This resulted in the future value of the $185,000 reinvestment outlay at the end of five years being $259,472. Note that it is entered as a negative number since it represents an outlay to the investor. The sum of the future values of the cash flows and reversion is $464,756. The difference of $205,284 is the NTV at the end of year five. Therefore, using a reinvestment rate of 7.00 percent, the investor should purchase this investment according to the NTV approach.

Graphics. The NTV graph is a bar graph illustrating the difference between estimated cash flows and terminal values of each flow. Since when the cash flows occur will affect the terminal values of each flow, it is important to recognize that timing of the cash flows may alter the investment decision.

Possible Modifications. If additional reinvestment rates would be useful for comparison purposes, the investor could modify the template to include other rates. It might also be interesting to examine the potential conflicts between NPV, IRR, PI, and NTV, especially when the selected reinvestment rate is substantially different than the discount rate used in the previous methods. Indeed, it might be useful to develop a large template with all of the discounted cash flow models. This is left for ambitious readers and hardworking souls!!

EXAMPLE TEMPLATE 11.4
Net terminal value (NTV).

```
lot1104x                                    Real Estate Diskette #4
====================================================================
NET TERMINAL VALUE (NTV)          Copyright (C) Reston Pub. Co., 1985
====================================================================

~~~~~~~~~~~~~~~~~~~~~~~~~~~~~~~~~~~~~~~~~~~~~~~~~~~~~~~~~~~~~~~~~~~~~~~~~


                    ***   TABLE OF CONTENTS   ***
                          =================
                Table                              Page
                -----                              ----


     I.   INPUTS FOR NET TERMINAL VALUE
          CALCULATIONS                               1

    II.   OUTPUT TABLE OF NET TERMINAL VALUES         2

   III.   SUMMARY OF NET TERMINAL VALUE               3


~~~~~~~~~~~~~~~~~~~~~~~~~~~~~~~~~~~~~~~~~~~~~~~~~~~~~~~~~~~~~~~~~~~~~~~~~
```

```
            I. INPUTS FOR NET TERMINAL VALUE CALCULATIONS
            ================================================

      Enter the following assumptions:


          Investment Outlay......................>>> $   185000

          Cash Flows and/or Sales Proceeds (Reversion):


                                                  CF                    SP
                                              _____            _____

             Year  One....................>>> $   10000     >>> $  _____
             Year  Two....................>>> $   20000     >>> $  _____
             Year  Three..................>>> $   30000     >>> $  _____
             Year  Four...................>>> $   40000     >>> $  _____
             Year  Five...................>>> $   50000     >>> $  300000

             Year  Six....................>>> $   _____     >>> $  _____
             Year  Seven..................>>> $   _____     >>> $  _____
             Year  Eight..................>>> $   _____     >>> $  _____
             Year  Nine...................>>> $   _____     >>> $  _____
             Year  Ten....................>>> $   _____     >>> $  _____

             Year  Eleven.................>>> $   _____     >>> $  _____
             Year  Twelve.................>>> $   _____     >>> $  _____
             Year  Thirteen...............>>> $   _____     >>> $  _____
             Year  Fourteen...............>>> $   _____     >>> $  _____
             Year  Fifteen................>>> $   _____     >>> $  _____

             Year  Sixteen................>>> $   _____     >>> $  _____
             Year  Seventeen..............>>> $   _____     >>> $  _____
             Year  Eighteen...............>>> $   _____     >>> $  _____
             Year  Nineteen...............>>> $   _____     >>> $  _____
             Year  Twenty.................>>> $   _____     >>> $  _____


          Reinvestment Rate .....................>>>     7.00   %

          Expected Holding Period................>>>        5   years


  Press  [Alt] M  for MENU        Press   [Ctrl] [Break]  for READY
```

II. OUTPUT TABLE OF NET TERMINAL VALUES
===

For any real estate investment,

if the investment outlay is: $ 185000   , and

if the sum of the cash flows and the sales proceeds is:

$	10000	in Year	1
$	20000	in Year	2
$	30000	in Year	3
$	40000	in Year	4
$	350000	in Year	5
$	0	in Year	NA
$	0	in Year	NA
$	0	in Year	NA
$	0	in Year	NA
$	0	in Year	NA
$	0	in Year	NA
$	0	in Year	NA
$	0	in Year	NA
$	0	in Year	NA
$	0	in Year	NA
$	0	in Year	NA
$	0	in Year	NA
$	0	in Year	NA
$	0	in Year	NA
$	0	in Year	NA

and the reinvestment rate is: 7.00   percent,

the Net Terminal Value Table is provided as follows:

$$$

Year	Cash Flows/ Sales Proceeds	Compounding Factor	Terminal Values
	($)	(@ 7.00 %)	($)
0	-185000	1.40	-259472
1	10000	1.31	13108
2	20000	1.23	24501
3	30000	1.14	34347
4	40000	1.07	42800
5	350000	1.00	350000
6	0	NA	0
7	0	NA	0
8	0	NA	0
9	0	NA	0
10	0	NA	0
11	0	NA	0
12	0	NA	0
13	0	NA	0
14	0	NA	0
15	0	NA	0
16	0	NA	0
17	0	NA	0
18	0	NA	0
19	0	NA	0
20	0	NA	0

Net Cash Flow $ 265000   Net Terminal Value $ 205284

$$$

Press [Alt] M for MENU   Press [Ctrl] [Break] for READY

~~~~~~

```
            III. SUMMARY OF NET TERMINAL VALUE
            ===================================

    For any real estate investment project,

        if the investment outlay is:     $          185000  ,

        if the reinvestment rate is:     $            7.00  percent,

        and if the expected holding period is:        5    years,


    $$$$$$$$$$$$$$$$$$$$$$$$$$$$$$$$$$$$$$$$$$$$$$$$$$$$$$$$$


        the Net Terminal Value is:          $    205284

        Therefore, the investor should invest          1    !
        -----(Computer returns 0 if FALSE, 1 if TRUE)-----


    $$$$$$$$$$$$$$$$$$$$$$$$$$$$$$$$$$$$$$$$$$$$$$$$$$$$$$$$$$$


  Press  [Alt] M  for MENU            Press  [Ctrl] [Break]  for READY


~~~~~~~~~~~~~~~~~~~~~~~~~~~~~~~~~~~~~~~~~~~~~~~~~~~~~~~~~~~~~~~~~~~~~~~
```

VARIANCE AND STANDARD DEVIATION
(Template: lot1105)

The final template in this chapter deals with the measurement of risk. As such, it is a very important addition to the extensive list of templates in the area of real estate investment analysis.

The template deals with two very well-known measures of risk: *variance* and *standard deviation*. Both are discussed, demonstrated, and applied to real estate practice.

Principles.   These statistics are used to measure risk in real estate projects. Thus, *risk* can be defined as the probability of deviating from the expected return. In this sense, both the variance and the standard deviation are measures of dispersion around the expected value.

The *variance* is defined as the sum of the squared deviations of the observed outcomes to the expected outcome times the probability of occurrence. The *standard deviation* is the square root of the variance.

It is difficult to understand the meaning of these definitions; luckily we can look at the design of the template and the example provided in the text.

Using the Template.   Imagine that the investor forecasts a number of possible outcomes (cash flows) for each year. What determines the different outcomes are different "states of the world." For example, if there is a rent control ordinance passed, the cash flow would be one level compared to another if the rent control ordinance were not passed. Or, the level of the cash flow might vary depending upon how many new structures are put up during the next year. In effect, the identification of important states of the world is the first step toward developing a distribution of possible outcomes, in this case, cash flows.

The second step is to identify and estimate the likelihood of the states occurring. If the likelihood of rent controls is high, the investor would want to use this information and act differently than if the passage of a rent control ordinance did not have a chance. Or if it was "certain" that several new apartment complexes were going to be finished during the next year, this might alter the expected rent roll of the investor's property. The important point at this step is to identify the probability of these events occurring or not occurring.

The final step is to multiply the outcome for each state of the world by the probability of the state occurring. When this is done for each state of the world such that the sum of the probabilities are equal to 100 percent, the answer is called the "expected value."

Deviations from the expected value occur whenever the probability of a certain state of the world is greater than zero *and* the outcome is different than the expected outcome for the specific state of the world. If so, the "variance" of the outcome will be positive. If the variance is positive, the square root of the variance will also be positive. The square root of the variance is defined as the "standard deviation."

By examining the template, it is difficult to see what is going on since most of the calculations are done internally on the computer. However, it is possible to see how the template is designed before reviewing an example to show how the calculations of the variance and standard deviation are done.

Note that the user can input up to eight-year distributions (i.e., cash flows for each of five states of the world per year and their respective probabilities of occurrence). For each year, a probability distribution is thus created. This provides the entire data set for the calculations needed to perform traditional risk analysis using variances and standard deviations as measures of risk.

An Example.   Consider the inputs for year one. The user believes that one of five states will occur. The probabilities of those states vary from 5 percent to 35 percent. (Note that the sum of the probabilities must equal one; if not, then some other state(s) are possible and should be included in the analysis.)

For each state, a cash flow estimate is assigned to the state. For example, in the first case, the cash flow of $1,000 is expected if this state occurs; the analyst believes this state has a 15 percent probability of occurring. If the second state occurs (the analyst estimates that a 25 percent probability exists for this state to occur), the cash flow will be $2,000. And so on until all states have been described by the resulting cash flows.

This procedure is done for each year cash flows are estimated. Then, Lotus 1-2-3 does the calculations.

To complete the example, the expected cash flow, [E(CF)] for year one is thus calculated as [(.15*$1,000) + (.25*$2,000) + (.35*$3,500) + (.20*$4,500) + (.05*$7,600)] or $3,155. The number is a better measure of the "most likely" world (in this case, $3,500), since it also includes the other states of the world. The variance for year one is computed as follows: [$1,000 − $3,155)^2*.15 + ($2,000 − $3,155)^2*.25 + ($3,500 − $3,155)^2 *.35 + ($4,500 − $3,155)^2*.20 + ($7,600 − $3,155)^2*.05] or 2,421,475 "dollars squared." The standard deviation is equal to (2,421,475)$^{.5}$ or $1,556.

In this way, the template takes all of the inputs and calculates the outputs shown in Table II. Thus, the investor can see the expected cash flow and the measures of risk. The higher the expected cash flow the better; the lower the risk the better.

If two investments have the same expected cash flows but one has lower risk than the other, the one with the lower risk will be preferred. If two investments have the same level of risk but one has higher expected cash flows, the one with the higher expected cash flows will be preferred. Thus, both risk and return are taken into account.

The summary provides some additional information. As indicated, if the assumption can be made that the cash flows are "normally distributed," a range of values called "confidence intervals" can be developed around the expected

values using the standard deviation as a measure. The interpretation of the table in the summary is that the investor can be "95 percent confident that the first year's cash flow lies between $-\$43$ and \$6,267," given the inputs and the assumption about the normality of the distribution of cash flows. This can be very useful, especially when a lot of data is available about the distributions.

Graphics.   There are two types of output in many financial analyses of risky projects: the expected value and the variance or standard deviation. This graph illustrates both the mean value and the standard deviation around the value. The investor must consider not only the expected cash flow and thus the expected return, but also the likelihood of achieving the expected value. Thus, the standard deviation as a measure of risk is useful and essential for modern real estate investment analysis.

Possible Modifications.   The measurement of risk and the entire area of risk analysis is an important aspect of real estate investment analysis. This template has only touched the surface. The reader is referred to other more extensive treatments of the topic in several real estate investment and valuation texts and books. Users without any background in risk analysis are encouraged to refer to these sources so as to increase your understanding and maximize the use of this template.

EXAMPLE TEMPLATE 11.5
Variance and standard deviation.

```
lot1105x                                     Real Estate Diskette #4
=====================================================================
VARIANCE AND STANDARD DEVIATION      Copyright (C) Reston Pub. Co., 1985
=====================================================================

~~~~~~~~~~~~~~~~~~~~~~~~~~~~~~~~~~~~~~~~~~~~~~~~~~~~~~~~~~~~~~~~~~~~~~~

                    ***   TABLE OF CONTENTS   ***
                        =================
            Table                                      Page
            -----                                      ----

      I.    INPUTS FOR VARIANCE AND STANDARD
            DEVIATION CALCULATIONS                        1

     II.    OUTPUT TABLE OF VARIANCE AND
            STANDARD DEVIATION                            2

    III.    SUMMARY OF VARIANCE AND STANDARD
            DEVIATION                                     3


~~~~~~~~~~~~~~~~~~~~~~~~~~~~~~~~~~~~~~~~~~~~~~~~~~~~~~~~~~~~~~~~~~~~~~~




      I. INPUTS FOR VARIANCE AND STANDARD DEVIATION CALCULATIONS
      ===========================================================

  Enter the following assumptions:


      Expected Annual Cash Flows with Various Probabilities:

      Year One:
      --------
          Prob:......>>>    15.00   %      Cash Flow:...>>> $    1000
          Prob:......>>>    25.00   %      Cash Flow:...>>> $    2000
          Prob:......>>>    35.00   %      Cash Flow:...>>> $    3500
          Prob:......>>>    20.00   %      Cash Flow:...>>> $    4500
          Prob:......>>>     5.00   %      Cash Flow:...>>> $    7600

      Year Two:
      --------
          Prob:......>>>    10.00   %      Cash Flow:...>>> $    1000
          Prob:......>>>    20.00   %      Cash Flow:...>>> $    2500
          Prob:......>>>    50.00   %      Cash Flow:...>>> $    3500
          Prob:......>>>    30.00   %      Cash Flow:...>>> $    5000
          Prob:......>>>   _____    %      Cash Flow:...>>> $   _____
```

```
       Year Three:
       ----------
          Prob:......>>>      5.00    %      Cash Flow:...>>> $      800
          Prob:......>>>     20.00    %      Cash Flow:...>>> $     1200
          Prob:......>>>     50.00    %      Cash Flow:...>>> $     5000
          Prob:......>>>     20.00    %      Cash Flow:. .>>> $     5500
          Prob:......>>>      5.00    %      Cash Flow:. .>>> $    10000

       Year Four:
       ---------
          Prob:......>>>     25.00    %      Cash Flow:...>>> $     2000
          Prob:......>>>     50.00    %      Cash Flow:...>>> $     4000
          Prob:......>>>     25.00    %      Cash Flow:...>>> $     6000
          Prob:......>>>     _____    %      Cash Flow:...>>> $    _____
          Prob:......>>>     _____    %      Cash Flow:...>>> $    _____

       Year Five:
       ---------
          Prob:......>>>     _____    %      Cash Flow:...>>> $    _____
          Prob:......>>>     _____    %      Cash Flow:...>>> $    _____
          Prob:......>>>     _____    %      Cash Flow:...>>> $    _____
          Prob:......>>>     _____    %      Cash Flow:...>>> $    _____
          Prob:......>>>     _____    %      Cash Flow:...>>> $    _____

       Year Six:
       --------
          Prob:......>>>     _____    %      Cash Flow:...>>> $    _____
          Prob:......>>>     _____    %      Cash Flow:...>>> $    _____
          Prob:......>>>     _____    %      Cash Flow:...>>> $    _____
          Prob:......>>>     _____    %      Cash Flow:...>>> $    _____
          Prob:......>>>     _____    %      Cash Flow:...>>> $    _____

       Year Seven:
       ----------
          Prob:......>>>     _____    %      Cash Flow:...>>> $    _____
          Prob:......>>>     _____    %      Cash Flow:...>>> $    _____
          Prob:......>>>     _____    %      Cash Flow:...>>> $    _____
          Prob:......>>>     _____    %      Cash Flow:...>>> $    _____
          Prob:......>>>     _____    %      Cash Flow:...>>> $    _____

       Year Eight:
       ----------
          Prob:......>>>     _____    %      Cash Flow:...>>> $    _____
          Prob:......>>>     _____    %      Cash Flow:...>>> $    _____
          Prob:......>>>     _____    %      Cash Flow:...>>> $    _____
          Prob:......>>>     _____    %      Cash Flow:...>>> $    _____
          Prob:......>>>     _____    %      Cash Flow:...>>> $    _____

Press   [Alt] M  for MENU          Press   [Ctrl] [Break]  for READY

~~~~~~~~~~~~~~~~~~~~~~~~~~~~~~~~~~~~~~~~~~~~~~~~~~~~~~~~~~~~~~~~~~~~~~~~~~~~~~
```

II. OUTPUT TABLE OF VARIANCE AND STANDARD DEVIATION
==

For any real estate investment,

Year	E(CF)	Var(CF)	StdDev(CF)
	($)		($)
1	3155	2421475	1556
2	3850	1634750	1279
3	4380	4685600	2165
4	4000	2000000	1414
5	0	0	0
6	0	0	0
7	0	0	0
8	0	0	0

Press [Alt] M for MENU   Press [Ctrl] [Break] for READY

~~~~~~

III. SUMMARY OF VARIANCE AND STANDARD DEVIATION
==

For any real estate investment with normally distributed cash flows,
the investor can be 95 percent confident that the "true" cash flows
lie between the following upper and lower boundaries:

$$

Year	Mean Estimate	Confidence Interval (Lower)	---	(Upper)
	($)	($)		($)
1	3155	-43	to	6267
2	3850	-1293	to	6407
3	4380	-51	to	8709
4	4000	-1172	to	6828
5	0	0	to	0
6	0	0	to	0
7	0	0	to	0
8	0	0	to	0

$$

Press [Alt] M for MENU   Press [Ctrl] [Break] for READY

~~~~~~

12 Statistical Applications in Appraising

Overview

This is the final chapter in this book and completes the series of templates in the system. These templates are devoted to the most well known statistical applications in real estate appraisal. The templates enable the user to concentrate on obtaining the best data about property characteristics and economic, spatial relationships and leaves the number crunching to Lotus.

The first of the three templates in this chapter is the sales comparison adjustment grid, a major tool used in the practice of real estate appraising. Now it can be completed in conjunction with the computer for the first time. The second template calculates some basic descriptive statistics. This may be useful in other types of real estate analysis besides real estate appraising. Finally, the last template calculates the solution to a simple linear regression problem and provides some statistics to aid in interpretation. This is very valuable for real estate appraisers; this type of statistical analysis, while requiring careful monitoring, can enable the analyst to discover relationships which cannot be found by simply "eye balling" the data.

SALES COMPARISON ADJUSTMENT GRID
(Template: lot1201)

Traditional real estate appraisal theory and practice teaches that there are three approaches to value. The first is called the cost approach and the appraiser seeks to estimate the cost of reproducing (or replacing) the improvements, deducting for depreciation, and estimating the value of the land in order to arrive at an estimate of value using the cost approach. The second method is called the income approach. It seeks an estimate of the value of the property based upon what the typical purchaser would pay, given the expected current and future income of the project. The third and final approach is termed the sales comparison approach. Under this method, the analyst seeks to make adjustments to the values of actual sales that have recently taken place which are comparable to the property being appraised. In this manner, the appraiser can measure the local market's preferences and dislikes.

The cost approach requires the use of construction cost data and relies heavily upon construction estimates, usually derived from cost manuals and from the advice of local builders and contractors. As such, it is not readily suited to a Lotus 1-2-3 template. The income approach is a variant of some of the income capitalization methods developed in earlier chapters. Several of the income templates which were designed for investment analysis purposes could be used for appraisal purposes; the difference is that the required data, rather than the approach itself, would differ under each approach. Finally, we come to the sales comparison approach. As a result of the extensive data requirements and numerical comparisons, this approach is well-suited to adaptation to Lotus. Thus, this template is devoted to this approach in real estate appraisal: the sales comparison approach and specifically, the sales comparison adjustment grid.

Principles. The *sales comparison adjustment grid* is a device which enables the analyst to input relevant sales data about a number of comparable properties that have recently been sold and compare these properties by attribute to the property being appraised. Thus, if a neighboring house has recently sold and it contains four bedrooms while the house under appraisal has only three, most appraisers would want to make an adjustment for the difference in bedrooms. (This would be done because the theory is that buyers and sellers in the market for housing will pay a premium for extra bedrooms. If so, the extra bedroom will be "priced" in the market.)

The method requires that the adjustment be made to the comparable so that with each comparison, the comparables become increasingly similar to the subject property (the property being appraised). In addition, the analyst must decide how much each unit of comparison is worth in the market (for market value appraisals). In effect, this means the analyst must decide how much the market values the extra bedroom and this becomes the amount which is *sub-*

tracted from the sale price of the comparable. For a comparable which has fewer bedrooms than the subject property (for example, a two-bedroom house), the analyst would *add* the value of a bedroom to the sale price of the comparable so as to offset the differential attribute of extra or missing bedrooms. (Note that this discussion has implied that there is a constant difference between the second and third bedroom or between the sixth or seventh bedroom. This is unlikely at best, but remains one of the assumptions in many appraisal reports. It is also a constraint in this template.)

Using the Template.   This is a large template because so much data must be entered in order to perform an effective analysis of comparable sales. In this template, the user must enter two types of data. First, the standard unit values are entered in Table I. These indicate the presumed market values of each attribute (for example, how much an additional square foot of land is worth in the market, or how much does each year of building age reduce the value of the property in the eyes of the market) and which from among several of the attributes apply to this particular property. Note that the analyst can choose from among nearly 20 characteristics in the development of the sales comparison adjustment grid. Most appraisals in practice have fewer than 20 variables. The standard values are entered in Table I only for those which apply to the subject property.

The second type of data must be entered into Table II. Note that up to six comparable properties may be used as well as the subject property. While this is not very many by statistical standards, six comparables are generally as many or more than are typically used by many real estate appraisers. In Table II, the first set of characteristics is for the subject property; after that, the comparable data may be stored.

One of the special features of this template is that not only can ordinary variables be used, but indexed variables may also be implemented. This means that variables where the observation is not easily measurable must be assigned numerical values in order to be included into an empirical study. In this case, (for example, see the location variable) values may be included ranging from +2 (excellent) to 0 (average) to −2 (poor). In this way, difficult to quantify considerations may also be included.

An Example.   Examine the example shown in this chapter. Note that each of the variables have been included into the analysis except the number of bedrooms. (It was felt that building size and number of bedrooms measured the similar attribute and therefore, only one should be included.) Note how in each case, a single value is provided to be used for each unit of adjustment. Finally, note that the final two attributes (special features and other) allow for unique dollar adjustments per property. This provides even greater flexibility.

The data is entered for each of six comparable properties as well as the subject property. The analyst can easily see what the attributes are for any of the comparables at any time.

Finally, the adjustment grid is presented in Table III. For each property, the sales price is produced. Next, the financing characteristics are included. Finally, the physical characteristics are reported. At the bottom of the adjustment grid, a row of "total adjustments" is reported with an estimate of the market value using this approach. As suggested by modern real estate appraisal practice, the adjusted values are rounded as well. Note how the values in the adjustment grid are positive and negative. This is because some of the comparable sales are "inferior" and must be added to when making them similar to the subject property; others are "superior" and must be subtracted from for the same purpose.

In the end, the judicious use of the adjustment grid should provide estimates which all converge around a central figure. This would be the estimate of the market value of the subject property. It is sometimes difficult to get such a convergence so appraisers are urged to use care and good sense when making the adjustments.

Graphics. Graphically, the adjustments are summarized by type of adjustment. For each property, the financial adjustments, the physical adjustments, and other adjustments are shown. Note that in this case, property 5 contains several physical adjustments which are negative; property 4 has several physical adjustments which are added to the sale price. In this manner, the analyst may learn more about the comparables under consideration.

Possible Modifications. One modification would be to permit standard units of comparison to vary within each characteristic. Nearly everyone would agree that a fifth bathroom is unlikely to be valued as highly by the market as the first bathroom in a house. Yet in this grid (and much of traditional practice), all bathrooms are valued identically. Also, other indices may be developed. This would especially be useful if highly predictive indices are shown to be useful in estimating value in certain markets. Finally, other attributes for adjustment might be included. In this way, the template may be hand tailored to suit an individual appraiser's needs.

EXAMPLE TEMPLATE 12.1
Sales comparison adjustment grid.

```
lot1201x                                      Real Estate Diskette #4
=====================================================================
SALES COMPARISON ADJUSTMENT GRID      Copyright (C) Reston Pub. Co., 1985
=====================================================================

~~~~~~~~~~~~~~~~~~~~~~~~~~~~~~~~~~~~~~~~~~~~~~~~~~~~~~~~~~~~~~~~~~~~~~~~~

                    ***   TABLE OF CONTENTS   ***
                    ==================
              Table                                    Page
              -----                                    ----

     I.   STANDARD INPUTS FOR SALES COMPARISON
          ADJUSTMENT GRID                               1

    II.   COMPARABLE SALES DATA INPUTS                  2

   III.   OUTPUT FOR SALES COMPARISON ADJUSTMENT
          GRID                                          3

    IV.   SUMMARY OF RESULTS                            4


~~~~~~~~~~~~~~~~~~~~~~~~~~~~~~~~~~~~~~~~~~~~~~~~~~~~~~~~~~~~~~~~~~~~~~~~~
```

I. STANDARD INPUTS FOR SALES COMPARISON ADJUSTMENT GRID
==

This table provides information and the format for the standard adjustments to be used by the appraiser. For each characteristic, indicate whether it applies ("Yes") or does not apply ("No") by placing the number "1" under the proper column. In addition, indicate the appropriate standard adjustment for each item in the last column. For characteristics with indices, these adjustments will be modified by the relevant values. Experienced users may change the indices.

Char #	Name	Yes	No	Index	Std Adjust
					($)
201	Financing Terms:	1	_____		1500
	Excellent = +2			2	
	Good = +1			1	
	Average = 0			0	
	Fair = −1			−1	
	Poor = −2			−2	
202	Cond of Sale:	1	_____		5000
	Arms Length = 0			0	
	<Arms Length = −1			−1	
203	Date of Sale:	1	_____		7.00
	Prop Value Growth Rate (%)				
204	Location:	1	_____		2500
	Excellent = +2			2	
	Good = +1			1	
	Average = 0			0	
	Fair = −1			−1	
	Poor = −2			−2	
301	Age of Building:	1	_____		500
	Number of Years				
302	Phys Condition:	1	_____		2500
	Excellent = +2			2	
	Good = +1			1	
	Average = 0			0	
	Fair = −1			−1	
	Poor = −2			−2	
303	Bldg Size:	1	_____		30.00
	Number of Square Feet				
304	Lot Size:	1	_____		5.75
	Number of Square Feet				
305	# of Rooms:	1	_____		1000
	Number of Rooms				
306	# of Bedrooms:	_____	1		_____
	Number of Bedrooms				

```
   307     # of Baths:                 1     _____                    1500
           Number of Baths

   308     Garage:                     1     _____                    2300
           Size of Garage in Cars

   309     Fin Basement:               1     _____                    1750
           Completely Finished = +1              1
           Partially Finished = 0               0
           Unfinished = −1                     −1

   310     Fireplaces:                 1     _____                    1400
           Number of Fireplaces

   311     Landscaping:                1     _____                     300
           Excellent = +2                       2
           Good = +1                            1
           Average = 0                          0
           Fair =  −1                          −1
           Poor =  −2                          −2

   312     Arch Design:                1     _____                     200
           Excellent = +2                       2
           Good = +1                            1
           Average = 0                          0
           Fair =  −1                          −1
           Poor =  −2                          −2

   313     Air Conditioning:           1     _____                     500
           Central A/C = +2                     2
           Unit A/C = +1                        1
           Partial A/C = 0                      0
           No A/C = −1                         −1

   314     Special Feat:          _____     _____                  Various

   315     Other:                 _____     _____                  Various


Press  [Alt] M  for MENU              Press  [Ctrl] [Break]  for READY
```

~~~~~~

```
                II. COMPARABLE SALES DATA INPUTS
                =================================

        Subject Property
        ----------------
        100 Sales Price:   ??    (THIS IS THE PURPOSE OF THIS ANALYSIS!)

        201 Financing Terms:  Use Code from G42-G46: =>          0
        202 Cond of Sale:     Use Code from G49-G50: =>          0
        203 Date of Sale:     -----                            --
        204 Location:         Use Code from G56-G60: =>          1

        301 Age of Building:  Enter the Age of Bldg: =>         25
        302 Phys Condition:   Use Code from G66-G70: =>          0
        303 Bldg Size:        Enter the Square Feet: =>       1800
        304 Lot Size:         Enter the Square Feet: =>       9500
        305 # of Rooms:       Enter the Rooms:       =>          9
        306 # of Bedrooms:    Enter the Bedrooms:    =>          4
        307 # of Baths:       Enter the Baths:       =>          2
        308 Garage:           Enter the Car Size:    =>        1.5
        309 Fin Basement:     Use Code from G91-G93: =>          1
        310 Fireplaces:       Enter the Number:      =>          1
        311 Landscaping:      Use Code from G99 -103:=>          1
        312 Arch Design:      Use Code from G106-110:=>          1
        313 Air Conditioning: Use Code from G113-116:=>          0
        314 Special Feat:     Enter amount:          =>        500
        315 Other:            Enter amount:          =>      _____

**  **   **  **    **  **    **  **    **  **    **  **    **  **    **  **

        Comparable Property No       1
        ----------------------------------
        100 Sales Price:                           => $    68500

        201 Financing Terms:  Use Code from G42-G46: =>          1
        202 Cond of Sale:     Use Code from G49-G50: =>          0
        203 Date of Sale:     Enter No. of Mons Ago: =>         12
        204 Location:         Use Code from G56-G60: =>          2

        301 Age of Building:  Enter the Age of Bldg: =>         12
        302 Phys Condition:   Use Code from G66-G70: =>          1
        303 Bldg Size:        Enter the Square Feet: =>       1975
        304 Lot Size:         Enter the Square Feet: =>      10200
        305 # of Rooms:       Enter the Rooms:       =>          9
        306 # of Bedrooms:    Enter the Bedrooms:    =>          4
        307 # of Baths:       Enter the Baths:       =>        2.5
        308 Garage:           Enter the Car Size:    =>          1
        309 Fin Basement:     Use Code from G91-G93: =>          0
        310 Fireplaces:       Enter the Number:      =>          1
        311 Landscaping:      Use Code from G99 -103:=>          2
        312 Arch Design:      Use Code from G106-110:=>          2
        313 Air Conditioning: Use Code from G113-116:=>          2
        314 Special Feat:     Enter amount:          =>        100
        315 Other:            Enter amount:          =>      _____

**  **   **  **    **  **    **  **    **  **    **  **    **  **    **  **
```

```
Comparable Property No        2
------------------------------------
100 Sales Price:                            => $    75000

    201 Financing Terms:  Use Code from G42-G46: =>          0
    202 Cond of Sale:     Use Code from G49-G50: =>         -1
    203 Date of Sale:     Enter No. of Mons Ago: =>          6
    204 Location:         Use Code from G56-G60: =>          2

    301 Age of Building:  Enter the Age of Bldg: =>          6
    302 Phys Condition:   Use Code from G66-G70: =>         -1
    303 Bldg Size:        Enter the Square Feet: =>       1589
    304 Lot Size:         Enter the Square Feet: =>       8758
    305 # of Rooms:       Enter the Rooms:       =>          8
    306 # of Bedrooms:    Enter the Bedrooms:    =>          5
    307 # of Baths:       Enter the Baths:       =>        2.5
    308 Garage:           Enter the Car Size:    =>        1.5
    309 Fin Basement:     Use Code from G91-G93: =>         -1
    310 Fireplaces:       Enter the Number:      =>          1
    311 Landscaping:      Use Code from G99 -103:=>          0
    312 Arch Design:      Use Code from G106-110:=>         -1
    313 Air Conditioning: Use Code from G113-116:=>          0
    314 Special Feat:     Enter amount:          =>      _____
    315 Other:            Enter amount:          =>      _____

**   **   **  **   **   **   **  **   **   **   **   **   **  **   **  **

Comparable Property No        3
------------------------------------
100 Sales Price:                            => $    72750

    201 Financing Terms:  Use Code from G42-G46: =>          1
    202 Cond of Sale:     Use Code from G49-G50: =>          0
    203 Date of Sale:     Enter No. of Mons Ago: =>         15
    204 Location:         Use Code from G56-G60: =>          1

    301 Age of Building:  Enter the Age of Bldg: =>          8
    302 Phys Condition:   Use Code from G66-G70: =>          1
    303 Bldg Size:        Enter the Square Feet: =>       1725
    304 Lot Size:         Enter the Square Feet: =>       8500
    305 # of Rooms:       Enter the Rooms:       =>          7
    306 # of Bedrooms:    Enter the Bedrooms:    =>          3
    307 # of Baths:       Enter the Baths:       =>          1
    308 Garage:           Enter the Car Size:    =>          2
    309 Fin Basement:     Use Code from G91-G93: =>          1
    310 Fireplaces:       Enter the Number:      =>          2
    311 Landscaping:      Use Code from G99 -103:=>          1
    312 Arch Design:      Use Code from G106-110:=>          0
    313 Air Conditioning: Use Code from G113-116:=>          1
    314 Special Feat:     Enter amount:          =>      _____
    315 Other:            Enter amount:          =>      _____

**   **   **  **   **   **   **  **   **   **   **   **   **  **   **  **
```

```
Comparable Property No        4
----------------------------------
100 Sales Price:                               => $    63800

201 Financing Terms:  Use Code from G42-G46: =>        0
202 Cond of Sale:     Use Code from G49-G50: =>        0
203 Date of Sale:     Enter No. of Mons Ago: =>       10
204 Location:         Use Code from G56-G60: =>       -2

301 Age of Building:  Enter the Age of Bldg: =>       23
302 Phys Condition:   Use Code from G66-G70: =>       -1
303 Bldg Size:        Enter the Square Feet: =>     1350
304 Lot Size:         Enter the Square Feet: =>     7950
305 # of Rooms:       Enter the Rooms:       =>        7
306 # of Bedrooms:    Enter the Bedrooms:    =>        3
307 # of Baths:       Enter the Baths:       =>        1
308 Garage:           Enter the Car Size:    =>        1
309 Fin Basement:     Use Code from G91-G93: =>       -1
310 Fireplaces:       Enter the Number:      =>        0
311 Landscaping:      Use Code from G99 -103:=>        0
312 Arch Design:      Use Code from G106-110:=>        0
313 Air Conditioning: Use Code from G113-116:=>       -1
314 Special Feat:     Enter amount:          =>     _____
315 Other:            Enter amount:          =>     _____

** ** ** ** ** ** ** ** ** ** ** ** ** ** ** **

Comparable Property No        5
----------------------------------
100 Sales Price:                               => $    75000

201 Financing Terms:  Use Code from G42-G46: =>        2
202 Cond of Sale:     Use Code from G49-G50: =>        0
203 Date of Sale:     Enter No. of Mons Ago: =>        3
204 Location:         Use Code from G56-G60: =>        2

301 Age of Building:  Enter the Age of Bldg: =>        4
302 Phys Condition:   Use Code from G66-G70: =>        1
303 Bldg Size:        Enter the Square Feet: =>     2200
304 Lot Size:         Enter the Square Feet: =>    11000
305 # of Rooms:       Enter the Rooms:       =>       10
306 # of Bedrooms:    Enter the Bedrooms:    =>        5
307 # of Baths:       Enter the Baths:       =>        2
308 Garage:           Enter the Car Size:    =>        2
309 Fin Basement:     Use Code from G91-G93: =>        1
310 Fireplaces:       Enter the Number:      =>        2
311 Landscaping:      Use Code from G99 -103:=>        2
312 Arch Design:      Use Code from G106-110:=>        1
313 Air Conditioning: Use Code from G113-116:=>        2
314 Special Feat:     Enter amount:          =>      200
315 Other:            Enter amount:          =>     _____

** ** ** ** ** ** ** ** ** ** ** ** ** ** ** **
```

```
Comparable Property No        6
--------------------------------
100 Sales Price:                              => $    65750

201 Financing Terms:  Use Code from G42-G46: =>        0
202 Cond of Sale:     Use Code from G49-G50: =>       -1
203 Date of Sale:     Enter No. of Mons Ago: =>       14
204 Location:         Use Code from G56-G60: =>        0

301 Age of Building:  Enter the Age of Bldg: =>      27.5
302 Phys Condition:   Use Code from G66-G70: =>        1
303 Bldg Size:        Enter the Square Feet: =>     1505
304 Lot Size:         Enter the Square Feet: =>     8679
305 # of Rooms:       Enter the Rooms:       =>        9
306 # of Bedrooms:    Enter the Bedrooms:    =>        3
307 # of Baths:       Enter the Baths:       =>        1
308 Garage:           Enter the Car Size:    =>        0
309 Fin Basement:     Use Code from G91-G93: =>       -1
310 Fireplaces:       Enter the Number:      =>        0
311 Landscaping:      Use Code from G99 -103:=>       -1
312 Arch Design:      Use Code from G106-110:=>        0
313 Air Conditioning: Use Code from G113-116:=>        0
314 Special Feat:     Enter amount:          =>     _____
315 Other:            Enter amount:          =>     _____

**  **  **  **  **  **   **  **   **  **   **  **   **  **   **  **

Press  [Alt] M  for MENU        Press  [Ctrl] [Break]  for READY
```

```
          III. OUTPUT FOR SALES COMPARISON ADJUSTMENT GRID
          =================================================

                                     PROPERTIES
                  ----------------------------------------------------
  Characteristics    1       2       3       4       5       6
  ----------------------------------------------------------------------
  Sales Price      68500   75000   72750   63800   75000   65750

  Financing Terms  -1500       0   -1500       0   -3000       0
  Cond of Sale         0    5000       0       0       0    5000
  Date of Sale      4795    2625    6366    3722    1313    5370
  Location         -2500   -2500       0    7500   -2500    2500

  Age of Building  -6500   -9500   -8500   -1000  -10500    1250
  Phys Condition   -2500    2500   -2500    2500   -2500   -2500
  Bldg Size        -5250    6330    2250   13500  -12000    8850
  Lot Size         -4025    4267    5750    8913   -8625    4721
  # of Rooms           0    1000    2000    2000   -1000       0
  # of Bedrooms        0       0       0       0       0       0
  # of Baths        -750    -750    1500    1500       0    1500
  Garage            1150       0   -1150    1150   -1150    3450
  Fin Basement      1750    3500       0    3500       0    3500
  Fireplaces           0       0   -1400    1400   -1400    1400
  Landscaping       -300     300       0     300    -300     600
  Arch Design       -200     400     200     200       0     200
  Air Conditioning -1000       0    -500     500   -1000       0
  Special Feat       400     500     500     500     300     500
  Other                0       0       0       0       0       0
                   ------  ------  ------  ------  ------  ------
  Total Adjust $  -16430   13672    3016   46184  -42363   36340
  EST. MKT VAL $   52070   88672   75766  109984   32638  102090

  (Rounded)   $    52100   88700   75800  110000   32600  102100


  Press  [Alt] M  for MENU         Press  [Ctrl] [Break]  for READY
```

```
                       IV.  SUMMARY OF RESULTS
                       ========================

            A sales comparison was made of the following     6 sales:

    Comp     Sales Financing Physical   Other     Total     EST.    % Adjust
  Property   Price   Adjust   Adjust   Adjust    Adjust   MKT VAL  of Price

              ($)     ($)      ($)      ($)        ($)       ($)       (%)

       1     68500  (1,500) (17,625)   2,695   (16,430)    52070    (0.24)

       2     75000      0    8,047     5,625    13,672     88672     0.18

       3     72750  (1,500)  (2,350)   6,866     3,016     75766     0.04

       4     63800      0   34,463    11,722    46,184    109984     0.72

       5     75000  (3,000) (38,475)    (888)  (42,363)    32638    (0.56)

       6     65750      0   22,971    13,370    36,340    102090     0.55
             ------  ------  ------    ------    ------    ------    ------
  AVE   $    70133  (1,000)  1,172     6,565     6,737     76870     0.12


Press   [Alt] M  for MENU          Press   [Ctrl] [Break]  for READY

~~~~~~~~~~~~~~~~~~~~~~~~~~~~~~~~~~~~~~~~~~~~~~~~~~~~~~~~~~~~~~~~~~~~~~~~~~~~
```

STATISTICAL ANALYSIS
(Template: lot1202)

As in the template above, the analysis of real estate appraisal problems is essentially an analysis of market data. Statistical analysis can be very useful, if used properly, to analyze market data. (In addition, the use of Lotus reduces the probability of calculation errors to practically zero!) The next two templates provide statistical tools for appraisers to use.

Principles. It is sometimes difficult, if not impossible, to accurately estimate an average value for a long set of numbers. In addition, with several numbers in a list, it is difficult to ensure that all of the observations have been included. Finally, it may be useful to calculate more than just the average value. This template solves all of these problems.

Using the Template. This template produces a small output (only one small table) but is a relatively large model since it permits the inclusion of a large amount of data. The analyst can enter up to 50 observations for up to six series of data. The model will accept any type of numerical data, in any acceptable form to Lotus 1-2-3 and will store the values as entered.

The output of this template consists of several well-known descriptive statistics. These include the number of observations by series, the sum of the values of the data by series, and the maximum value in each series. Also calculated are the mean (or average), the variance, and standard deviation. (The reader is referred to the discussion of Template lot1105 for definitions and illustrations of the calculations of the variance and standard deviation in another context.)

An Example. In this example, data has been collected for four cities. Each has a different number of observations and each series has been entered in thousands of dollars. Note that each series reports its own statistics. This is particularly useful for comparative purposes.

Graphics. The bar graph shows four sets of data for each data series: the maximum value in the series, the mean, the variance, and the standard deviation. The graphs are merely illustrative representations of the descriptive statistics.

Possible Modifications. For many purposes, fifty observations is more than sufficient. However, for many others, it is not nearly enough. It is quite easy to increase the number of observations available to be used in this template. In addition, other statistics may be useful for one or more of several purposes. Some of these are shown in the following template.

EXAMPLE TEMPLATE 12.2
Statistical analysis.

```
lot1202x                                  Real Estate Diskette #4
================================================================
STATISTICAL ANALYSIS            Copyright (C) Reston Pub. Co., 1985
================================================================

~~~~~~~~~~~~~~~~~~~~~~~~~~~~~~~~~~~~~~~~~~~~~~~~~~~~~~~~~~~~~~~~~~

               ***   TABLE OF CONTENTS   ***
                     ==================
            Table                                  Page
            -----                                  ----

      I.   INPUTS FOR STATISTICAL ANALYSIS           1

     II.   OUTPUT OF DESCRIPTIVE STATISTICS           2


~~~~~~~~~~~~~~~~~~~~~~~~~~~~~~~~~~~~~~~~~~~~~~~~~~~~~~~~~~~~~~~~~~
```

I. INPUTS FOR STATISTICAL ANALYSIS
==

Enter the names and data in the following columns:

#	x(1)	x(2)	x(3)	x(4)	x(5)	x(6)
Example	15.75	3.5	1000	394.8	_____	_____
Data Series	City 1	City 2	City 3	City 4	_____	_____
# of Obs.	21	16	19	15	_____	_____
1	125	72.4	73	82.9	_____	_____
2	147	56	76.1	75.3	_____	_____
3	67	75	65.2	56	_____	_____
4	120	106.5	64.1	62.5	_____	_____
5	110	92	54	65.5	_____	_____
6	89	71	68	73.8	_____	_____
7	54.6	60.5	148	69.9	_____	_____
8	130.5	61	65	70	_____	_____
9	87	76	49	75.2	_____	_____
10	67.4	56	56.8	87	_____	_____
11	39.9	51.7	64	55	_____	_____
12	45	89	78	49.7	_____	_____
13	76.2	57	52	63	_____	_____
14	110	75.1	98.3	72.3	_____	_____
15	55.9	58	78	78	_____	_____
16	48.2	69	59	_____	_____	_____
17	56	_____	59.3	_____	_____	_____
18	74	_____	46	_____	_____	_____
19	50.9	_____	49.5	_____	_____	_____
20	115	_____	_____	_____	_____	_____
21	82	_____	_____	_____	_____	_____
22	_____	_____	_____	_____	_____	_____
23	_____	_____	_____	_____	_____	_____
24	_____	_____	_____	_____	_____	_____
25	_____	_____	_____	_____	_____	_____
26	_____	_____	_____	_____	_____	_____
27	_____	_____	_____	_____	_____	_____
28	_____	_____	_____	_____	_____	_____
29	_____	_____	_____	_____	_____	_____
30	_____	_____	_____	_____	_____	_____
31	_____	_____	_____	_____	_____	_____
32	_____	_____	_____	_____	_____	_____
33	_____	_____	_____	_____	_____	_____
34	_____	_____	_____	_____	_____	_____
35	_____	_____	_____	_____	_____	_____
36	_____	_____	_____	_____	_____	_____
37	_____	_____	_____	_____	_____	_____
38	_____	_____	_____	_____	_____	_____
39	_____	_____	_____	_____	_____	_____
40	_____	_____	_____	_____	_____	_____

```
41      -----    -----    -----    -----    -----    -----
42      -----    -----    -----    -----    -----    -----
43      -----    -----    -----    -----    -----    -----
44      -----    -----    -----    -----    -----    -----
45      -----    -----    -----    -----    -----    -----
46      -----    -----    -----    -----    -----    -----
47      -----    -----    -----    -----    -----    -----
48      -----    -----    -----    -----    -----    -----
49      -----    -----    -----    -----    -----    -----
50      -----    -----    -----    -----    -----    -----
```

Press [Alt] M for MENU   Press [Ctrl] [Break] for READY

~~~~~~

II. OUTPUT OF DESCRIPTIVE STATISTICS
=====================================

Using the data above, the following statistics are found:

	x(1)	x(2)	x(3)	x(4)	x(5)	x(6)
# of Obs.	21	16	19	15	0	0
Total	1750.60	1126.20	1303.30	1036.10	0.00	0.00
Max Value	147	106.5	148	87	0	0
Mean	83.36	70.39	68.59	69.07	0.00	0.00
Variance	974.15	217.55	503.76	102.67	ERR	ERR
Std Dev	31.21	14.75	22.44	10.13	ERR	ERR

Press [Alt] M for MENU   Press [Ctrl] [Break] for READY

~~~~~~

SIMPLE LINEAR REGRESSION
(Template: lot1203)

The final template in this chapter (and in this system) is a particularly useful one as well as an exciting addition to the others. It is called *simple linear regression* although relative to many of the others in this book, it is hardly simple. This may prove to be one of the most useful templates, especially for appraisers and other data analysts.

Principles.   It is unlikely, if not impossible, to explain the theory and practice of regression analysis in this space. Entire volumes have been written on this subject alone and it is generally regarded as one of the more advanced topics in statistics. However, this discussion will attempt to provide some introductory comments to provide a first step at using regression analysis for some real estate decisions.

Simple linear regression analysis fits a line between two sets of data when the data are graphed on the same xy axis. Note that we have said "simple linear regression." Simple regression refers to analysis using only two variables: x (called the *independent* variable) and y (called the *dependent* variable). If more than two variables are used, the analysis is called "multiple regression analysis." The analysis is called linear regression because in the case of simple regression, a straight line is the output. In some methods, other figures can be estimated.

The typical procedure fits the line through the points on the axis between x and y. The criterion used to "guide" the line is to locate the line so that the sum of the differences from the points to the line is minimized. This criterion is called *ordinary least squares* or "OLS." The solution to the problem is then solved by finding the Y-intercept and the slope of the line which meets the OLS criterion. This is the basic procedure used in simple linear regression analysis!

Using the Template.   First, you should be aware of the fact that in this template, there are several calculations which must be done before the correct output is provided and most of the calculations are done "off screen." Note that the user can input up to 50 observations for each series. The method requires that an equal number of observations of each series be included since without an x or y value, it is impossible to plot the point on an xy grid.

Note also that the output is relatively small. It reports the number of observations, the means and other statistics useful for calculating the real output of the model: the estimates. These include an estimate of the "constant" or a (the y-intercept), an estimate of the *coefficient of X* or b (the *slope* of the regression line), the *standard error of the estimate* or S, the *standard error of the coefficient* or $S(b)$, the *t-statistic for the Null Hypothesis:* $\beta = 0$, the *correlation coefficient* or r, and the *coefficient of determination* or R^2 (read "R-squared"). The estimated equation of the regression line is also shown. These statistics will not be examined in detail, but the reader unfamiliar with regression analysis should still be able to get an idea about the use of this template after examining the discussion of the example below.

An Example.   In this example, the analyst is seeking to identify (1) the relationship between two variables: sales prices of homes and their respective building sizes, (2) a predictive model of this relationship, (3) evidence regarding the numerical direction (called *sign*) and magnitude (called *size*) of the relationship, and (4) evidence about the likelihood of the validity and reliability of this relationship. All of this can be done using simple regression.

In this case, data on 20 properties which have sold have been collected along with their respective building sizes. Note that the sales prices are entered as dollars and the sizes of the buildings are entered as square feet. This is not a problem with this type of analysis.

The underlying model which the subject is testing is that the sales price is a positive function of building size. In other words, the analyst expects that the larger the size of the building, the higher the sales price. In addition, the analyst believes that the relationship is an important one since there are numerous other variables that probably also affect sales prices, but the analyst, in this case chose this one.

The output presents the results of this test. In addition to the respective means of the two variables ($66,831.50 and 1,767.20 square feet), the estimates of the equation are provided. (Remember, the equation tested here is that sales price is a positive function of building size.) The estimate of the constant, a, is $4,889.97 and the estimate of the coefficient of x, b, is $35.05. The interpretation is that the estimate of sales prices in this market is that the land is worth about $4,900 and each square foot of building space adds about $35.00 per square foot.

The application of this result is straightforward: plug the building size of the subject property into the equation and get an estimate of the sales price of the subject property! It is important to note that it is only by coincidence that the estimate of the sales price of the subject property is equal to the average sales price in the market.

Finally, the other statistics provide measures to test the validity and reliability of the results. Of principal importance is the *t-statistic*. Without getting involved in the development of this measure, the rule of thumb for interpretation is that if the *t-statistic* is greater than about 2.5, the relationship is a strong one between the independent and dependent variable. (Users with statistical background can supplement this rule of thumb by testing the null hypothesis, given the number of degrees of freedom for each equation.) In this case, note that the *t-statistic* is 8.13, a very high value.

Therefore, one can conclude that there is a very strong (positive, in this case) relationship between sales price and building size in this market. Finally, the *correlation coefficient* and the *coefficient of determination* measure relationships between the variables. The interpretation of the correlation coefficient is that the closer the measure is to 1.00 (-1.00), the stronger (weaker) the relationship between the variables. At .89, it is very strong. (Note if r is negative, the variables exhibit an inverse relationship to each other.) The interpretation of the coefficient of determination is that the closer it is to 1.00, the more of the relationship between the two variables has been "explained" by the model. At .79, this too, is very strong. (Note that failure to explain the relationship may be due to the selection of an insignificant independent variable, the misspecification of the model, errors in entering the data, other variables which affect the dependent variable but have not been included in the analysis, or any combination of these results.)

Once again, the reader is encouraged to consult a statistical textbook if some actual statistical analysis will be done. Hopefully, as shown in this template, statistical analysis such as linear regression can be a powerful tool for real estate analysis in several areas.

Graphics.   The final graph of the set presents what is known as a scattergram. It is through these points that the OLS line is fit. By casually looking at the relationship between sales price and building size, one can see that it is positive. Our statistical tests confirm this observation and also provide some measure of the strength of the relationship.

Possible Modifications.   Fifty observations is far too few for some statistical analysis. This may be changed with relatively little difficulty. In addition, some other statistics may be useful for some studies. However, the real constraint is not the limited number of statistics shown for simple regression, but rather the limit on only one independent variable. Multiple regression analysis is a much more powerful tool. However, before even an experienced Lotus user attempts to develop a template for multiple regression, the user should make sure he/she knows how to build it. It can be done, but it requires a very large amount of space and is very complicated to construct. Serious users interested in multiple regression analysis are probably better advised to seek one of several statistical software packages currently on the market.

EXAMPLE TEMPLATE 12.3
Simple linear regression.

```
lot1203x                                    Real Estate Diskette #4
==================================================================
SIMPLE LINEAR REGRESSION           Copyright (C) Reston Pub. Co., 1985
==================================================================

~~~~~~~~~~~~~~~~~~~~~~~~~~~~~~~~~~~~~~~~~~~~~~~~~~~~~~~~~~~~~~~~~~~~~

                    ***   TABLE OF CONTENTS   ***
                          =================
              Table                                  Page
              -----                                  ----

      I.   INPUTS FOR LINEAR REGRESSION                1

      II.  OUTPUT OF LINEAR REGRESSION                 2


~~~~~~~~~~~~~~~~~~~~~~~~~~~~~~~~~~~~~~~~~~~~~~~~~~~~~~~~~~~~~~~~~~~~~
```

```
           I. INPUTS FOR LINEAR REGRESSION
           ==================================

    Enter the names and data in the following columns:

        #                    Y                 X
-------------------------------------------------------------------
    Variable            Dependent         Independent

    Data Series         Sales Price       Bldg Size

    # of Obs.               20                20

        1                 45000              1300
        2                 65000              1950
        3                 72500              2000
        4                 70000              1675
        5                 82000              1975
        6                 56500              1400
        7                 67500              1689
        8                 71750              2000
        9                 69500              1800
       10                 80500              2155

       11                 56780              1835
       12                 75000              1900
       13                 46750              1275
       14                 75500              1800
       15                 66000              1665
       16                 58500              1450
       17                 60000              1500
       18                 87500              2300
       19                 75250              2100
       20                 55100              1575

       21                 -----             -----
       22                 -----             -----
       23                 -----             -----
       24                 -----             -----
       25                 -----             -----
       26                 -----             -----
       27                 -----             -----
       28                 -----             -----
       29                 -----             -----
       30                 -----             -----

       31                 -----             -----
       32                 -----             -----
       33                 -----             -----
       34                 -----             -----
       35                 -----             -----
       36                 -----             -----
       37                 -----             -----
       38                 -----             -----
       39                 -----             -----
       40                 -----             -----
```

```
41                    -----              -----
42                    -----              -----
43                    -----              -----
44                    -----              -----
45                    -----              -----
46                    -----              -----
47                    -----              -----
48                    -----              -----
49                    -----              -----
50                    -----              -----


Press  [Alt] M  for MENU        Press  [Ctrl] [Break]  for READY


~~~~~~~~~~~~~~~~~~~~~~~~~~~~~~~~~~~~~~~~~~~~~~~~~~~~~~~~~~~~~~~~~~~~~
```

```
            II. OUTPUT OF LINEAR REGRESSION
            =================================

       Using the data above, the following results are found:

 ----------------------------------------------------------------------

      # of X Obs.           20        Sum of X Values       35344
      # of Y Obs.           20        Sum of X^2 Values  64043696

      Mean of X        1767.20        Sum of Y Values     1336630
      Mean of Y       66831.50        Sum of Y^2 Values   9.2E+10

                                      Sum of Products      2.4E+09
                                      Error Sum of Sq      5.3E+08

      Estimates:
      ---------
           Constant: a                4889.97

           Coefficient of X: b          35.05

           The estimated equation is:

               Y  = 4889.97      +       35.05      X

           Standard Error of Est.: S    5428.46
           Standard Error of Coef.: S(b)   4.31
           t-Statistic for Null Hyp: B=0:  8.13

           Correlation Coef.: r          0.89
           Coef. of Determination: R^2   0.79

 ----------------------------------------------------------------------


 Press  [Alt] M  for MENU          Press  [Ctrl] [Break]  for READY

 ~~~~~~~~~~~~~~~~~~~~~~~~~~~~~~~~~~~~~~~~~~~~~~~~~~~~~~~~~~~~~~~~~~~~~~~~
```

Appendices

A Table of LOTUS 1-2-3 Conventions and Functions

The following table is provided as a summary of the Lotus 1-2-3 Conventions and Functions. Additional information can be obtained in the Lotus 1-2-3 manual.

Lotus 1-2-3 Conventions

Key	Meaning
	SPECIAL KEYS
Carriage Return	(Large Arrow)
Cursors	(Up, Down, Left, Right)
Home	Return to A1
PgUp	Moves cursor up 1 screen (20 rows)
PgDn	Moves cursor down 1 screen (20 rows)
Esc	Cancel command or last key
Del	Delete entry left of cursor
Ins	Insert entry right of cursor
/	Command is expected
@	Function is expected
' (or letter)	Label is expected
(number)	Number is expected
+ − * / ∧	Addition, Subtraction, Multiplication, Division, Exponentiation
< > =	Less Than, Greater Than, Equals
<= >= <>	Less Than or Equal To, Greater Than or Equal To, Not Equal To

Key	Meaning

FUNCTION KEYS

There are ten function keys located on the lefthand side of the keyboard. The following description provides an overview of their usage.

F1	The **HELP** key. Used to display 200 help screens in the Lotus program.
F2	The **EDIT** key. Used when editing formulas or labels in any cell.
F3	The **NAME** key. Used to call named ranges on a spreadsheet.
F4	The **ABSOLUTE** key. Used when programming the spreadsheet to change the cell address from relative to mixed or absolute.
F5	The **GOTO** key. Used to go to any cell location in the spreadsheet.
F6	The **WINDOW** key. Used to move control between the windows.
F7	The **QUERY** key. Used to repeat most recent data query question.
F8	The **TABLE** key. Used to repeat most recent data table operation.
F9	The **CALC** key. Used to recalculate the spreadsheet.
F10	The **GRAPH** key. Used to display current graph of the template.

Command Paths

BASIC LOTUS 1-2-3 MENU STRUCTURE

Worksheet Range Copy Move File Print Graph Data Quit

<u>Worksheet</u> Range Copy Move File Print Graph Data Quit
Global Insert Delete Column-Width Erase Titles Window Status

<u>Global</u> Insert Delete Column-Width Erase Titles Window Status
Formal Label-Prefix Column-Width Recalculation Protection Default

Global <u>Insert</u> Delete Column-Width Erase Titles Window Status
Column . . . Row . . .

Global Insert <u>Delete</u> Column-Width Erase Titles Window Status
Column . . . Row . . .

Global Insert Delete <u>Column-Width</u> Erase Titles Window Status
Set . . . Reset . . .

Global Insert Delete Column-Width <u>Erase</u> Titles Window Status
[Erase whole worksheet] No . . . Yes . . .

Global Insert Delete Column-Width Erase <u>Titles</u> Window Status
Both Horizontal Vertical Clear

Global Insert Delete Column-Width Erase Titles <u>Window</u> Status
Horizontal Vertical Synchronized Unsynchronized Clear

Global Insert Delete Column-Width Erase Titles Window <u>Status</u>
[View worksheet default values]

Worksheet <u>Range</u> Copy Move File Print Graph Data Quit
Format Label-Prefix Erase Name Justify Protect Unprotect Input

<u>Format</u> Label-Prefix Erase Name Justify Protect Unprotect Input
Format Scientific Currency , General +/− Percent Date Text Reset

Format <u>Label-Prefix</u> Erase Name Justify Protect Unprotect Input
Left Right Center

Format Label-Prefix <u>Erase</u> Name Justify Protect Unprotect Input
[Range]

Format Label-Prefix Erase <u>Name</u> Justify Protect Unprotect Input
Create Delete Labels Reset

Format Label-Prefix Erase Name <u>Justify</u> Protect Unprotect Input
[Range]

Format Label-Prefix Erase Name Justify <u>Protect</u> Unprotect Input
[Range]

Format Label-Prefix Erase Name Justify Protect <u>Unprotect</u> Input
[Range]

Format Label-Prefix Erase Name Justify Protect Unprotect <u>Input</u>
[Range]

Worksheet   Range   <u>Copy</u>   Move   File   Print   Graph   Data   Quit
From . . . To . . .

Worksheet   Range   Copy   <u>Move</u>   File   Print   Graph   Data   Quit
From . . . To . . .

Worksheet   Range   Copy   Move   <u>File</u>   Print   Graph   Data   Quit
Retrieve   Save   Combine   Xtract   Erase   List   Import   Directory

<u>Retrieve</u> Save Combine Xtract Erase List Import Directory
[File]

Retrieve <u>Save</u> Combine Xtract Erase List Import Directory
[File]

Retrieve Save <u>Combine</u> Xtract Erase List Import Directory
Copy Add Subtract

Retrieve Save Combine <u>Xtract</u> Erase List Import Directory
Formulas Values

Retrieve Save Combine Xtract <u>Erase</u> List Import Directory
Worksheet Print Graph

Retrieve Save Combine Xtract Erase <u>List</u> Import Directory
Worksheet Print Graph

Retrieve Save Combine Xtract Erase List <u>Import</u> Directory
Text Numbers

Retrieve Save Combine Xtract Erase List Import <u>Directory</u>
[Dir]

Worksheet   Range   Copy   Move   File   <u>Print</u>   Graph   Data   Quit
Printer   File

<u>Printer</u> <u>File</u>
Range Line Page Options Clear Align Go Quit

Worksheet   Range   Copy   Move   File   Print   <u>Graph</u>   Data   Quit
Type   X   ABCDEF   Reset   View   Save   Options   Name   Quit

Type <u>Type</u> X ABCDEF Reset View Save Options Name Quit
Line Bar XY Stacked Bar Pie

Type <u>X</u> <u>ABCDEF</u> Reset View Save Options Name Quit
X A B C D E F [Data Ranges]

Type X ABCDEF <u>Reset</u> View Save Options Name Quit
[Reset graph settings]

Type X ABCDEF Reset <u>View</u> Save Options Name Quit
[View graph]

Type X ABCDEF Reset View <u>Save</u> Options Name Quit
[Save file]

Type X ABCDEF Reset View Save <u>Options</u> Name Quit
Legend Format Titles Grid Scale Color B&W Data-Labels Quit

Type X ABCDEF Reset View Save Options <u>Name</u> Quit
Use Create Delete Reset

Type X ABCDEF Reset View Save Options Name <u>Quit</u>
[Return to DOS]

| Worksheet | Range | Copy | Move | File | Print | Graph | <u>Data</u> | Quit |
| Fill | Table | | Sort | | Query | | Distribution | |

<u>Fill</u> Table Sort Query Distribution
[Range]

Fill <u>Table</u> Sort Query Distribution
1 2 Reset

Fill Table <u>Sort</u> Query Distribution
Data-Range Primary Key Secondary Key Reset Go Quit

Fill Table Sort <u>Query</u> Distribution
Input Criterion Output Find Extract Unique Delete Reset Quit

Fill Table Sort Query <u>Distribution</u>
[Ranges]

| Worksheet | Range | Copy | Move | File | Print | Graph | Data | <u>Quit</u> |
| | | | [Exit to DOS] | | | | | |

Title Input(s) Output(s) Solutions Summary User Options Quit

Title   Input(s)   Output(s)   Solutions   Summary   User   Options   Quit

Title Input(s) Output(s) Solutions Summary User Options Quit
Return to table of contents for template

Title Input(s) Output(s) Solutions Summary User Options Quit
Enter input assumptions . . .

Title Input(s) Output(s) Solutions Summary User Options Quit
Evaluate output table . . .

Title Input(s) Output(s) Solutions Summary User Options Quit
Calculate solutions . . .

Title Input(s) Output(s) Solutions Summary User Options Quit
Evaluate summary . . .

Title Input(s) Output(s) Solutions Summary User Options Quit
Display special user options

Title Input(s) Output(s) Solutions Summary User Options Quit
Return to Lotus Access System

Title   Input(s)   Output(s)   Solutions   Summary   User   Options   Quit
Display   special   user   options

Display special user options
Print Graph Save Retrieve Menu Index Quit

Functions

Mathematical Functions

@**ABS**(value)	Absolute value
@**ACOS**(value)	Arccosine
@**ASIN**(value)	Arcsin
@**ATAN**(value)	Arctangent
@**ATANX**(value)	Arctangent x/y
@**COS**(value)	Cosine
@**EXP**(value)	Exponential function: *e* to a power
@**INT**(value)	Integer
@**LN**(value)	Natural logarithum
@**LOG**(value)	Base 10 logarithum
@**MOD**(value)	Remainder x/y
@**PI**	3.1415926536
@**RAND**	Random number generator
@**ROUND**(values)	Round x to n places
@**SIN**(value)	Sine
@**SQRT**(value)	Square root
@**TAN**(value)	Tangent

Financial and Statistical Functions

@**AVG**(list)	Computes average in list
@**COUNT**(list)	Counts the number of non-blank spaces
@**FV**(values)	Computes future value of an annuity
@**IRR**(values)	Computes internal rate of return
@**MAX**(list)	Chooses maximum value in list
@**MIN**(list)	Chooses minimum value in list
@**NPV**(values)	Computes net present value
@**PMT**(values)	Computes ordinary annuity payment
@**PV**(values)	Computes present value of an annuity
@**STD**(list)	Computes standard deviation in list
@**SUM**(list)	Computes sum in list
@**VAR**(list)	Computes variance in list

#AND#	Logical AND
@CHOOSE(values)	Selects value in list
@FALSE	Shows (**0**) FALSE
@HLOOKUP(values)	Lookup in row
@IF(logical value, value, value)	Shows second value if first value is true; shows third value if first value is false
@ISERR(value)	Shows (**1**) TRUE if value is error; otherwise, (**0**) FALSE
@ISNA(value)	Shows (**1**) TRUE if value is not available; otherwise, (**0**) FALSE
@NA	Shows **NA** (Not Available)
#NOT#	Logical NOT
#OR#	Logical OR
@TRUE	Shows (**1**) TRUE
VLOOKUP(values)	Lookup in column

B Graphs of LOTUS 1-2-3 Template Examples

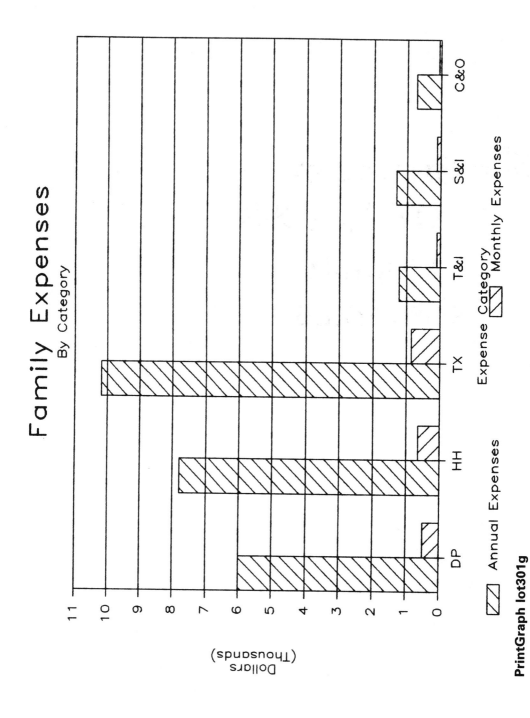

PrintGraph lot301g

316

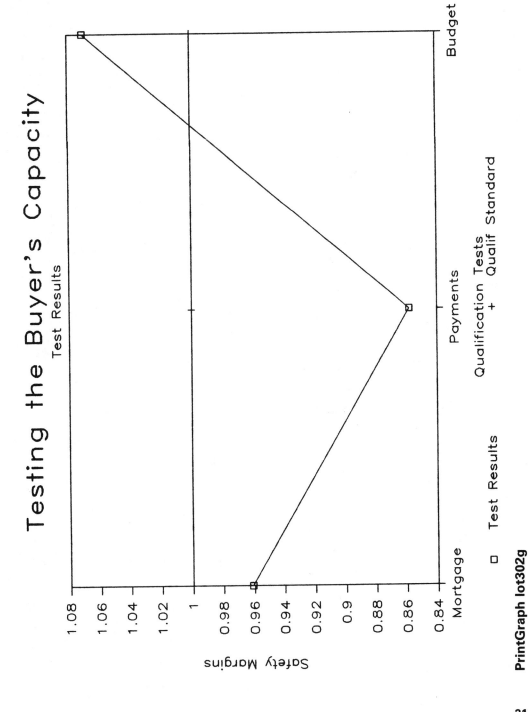

Testing the Buyer's Capacity

Test Results

Safety Margins

Mortgage
Payments
Budget

Qualification Tests
+ Qualif Standard

□ Test Results

PrintGraph lot302g

317

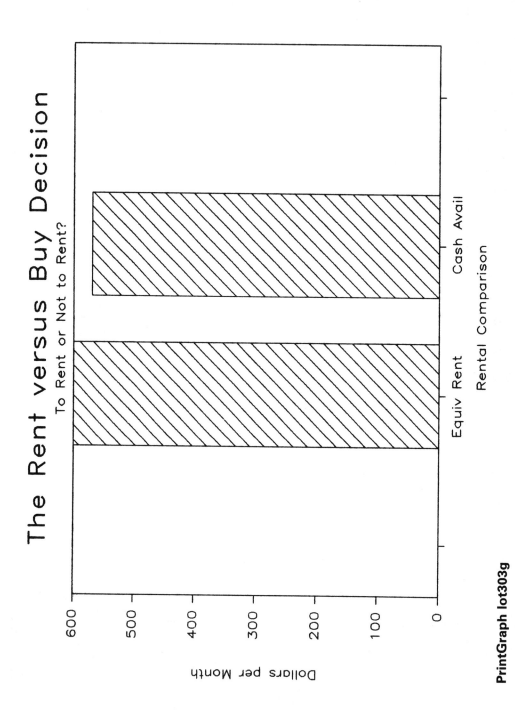

PrintGraph lot303g

318

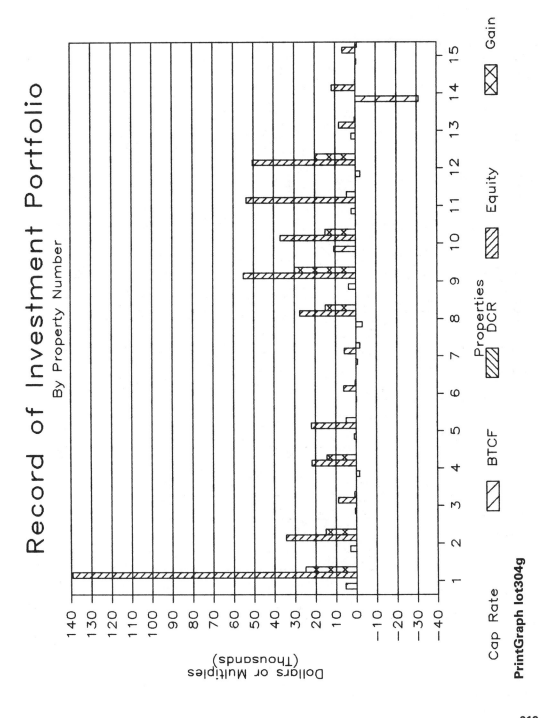

Record of Investment Portfolio
By Property Number

Dollars or Multiples (Thousands)

Properties

BTCF   Cap Rate   DCR   Equity   Gain

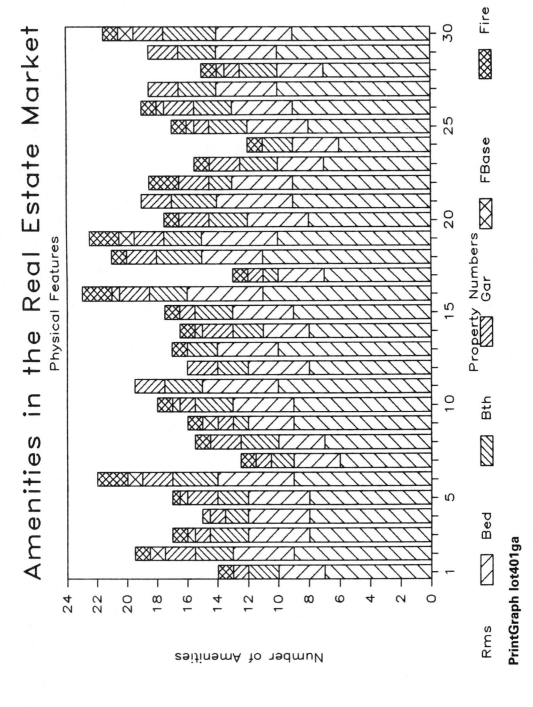

Amenities in the Real Estate Market

Physical Features

Number of Amenities

Property Numbers

Rms   Bed   Bth   Gar   FBase   Fire

PrintGraph lot401ga

320

The Relationship Between Size and Price

By Total Feet

Size (Thousands)

Lot Size

(Thousands)
Listing Prices

+ Building Size

□ Building Size

Breakdown of Debt Financing Expenses
By Percentage of Total Payments

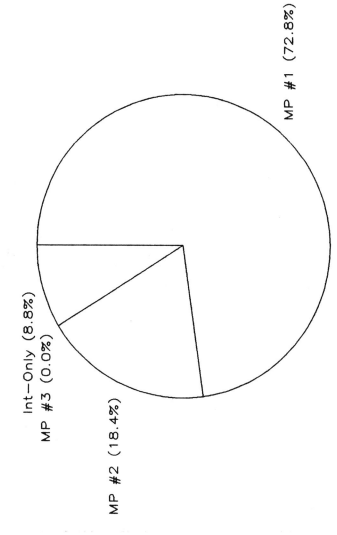

MP #1 (72.8%)

Int-Only (8.8%)
MP #3 (0.0%)

MP #2 (18.4%)

PrintGraph lot402g

322

Gross Amounts Due at Closing
By Category

Dollars
(Thousands)

60
50
40
30
20
10
0

REst Persl SetCh MunTx CtyTx Assess

Market Participant

Borrower Seller

PrintGraph lot403g

323

Future Value Table I

By Interest Rate Level

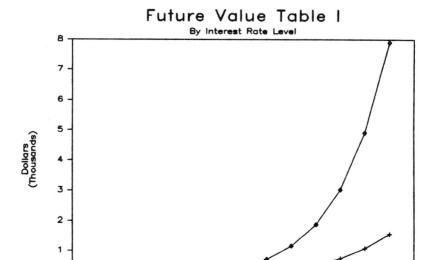

PrintGraph lot501ga

Future Value Table II

By Interest Rate Level

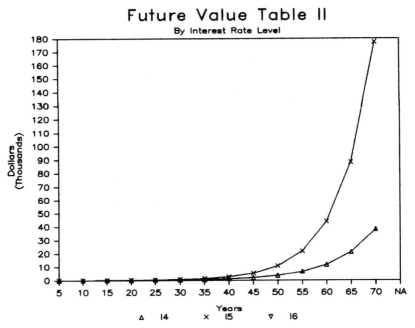

PrintGraph lot501gb

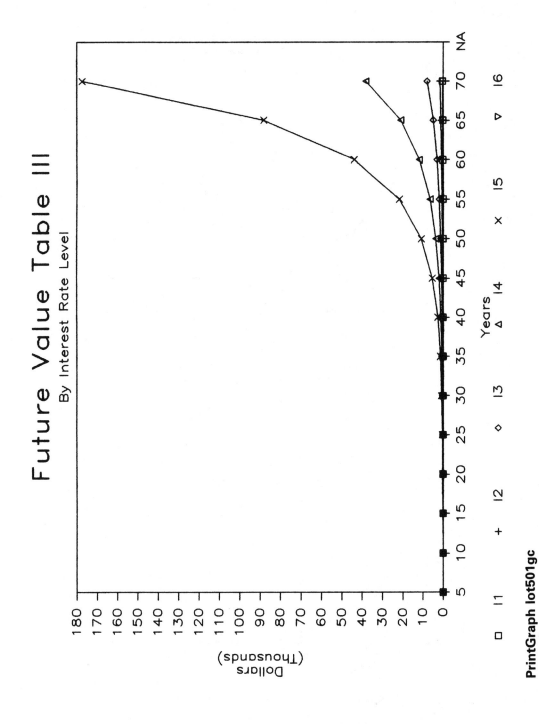

Future Value Table III

By Interest Rate Level

PrintGraph lot501gc

Present Value Table I

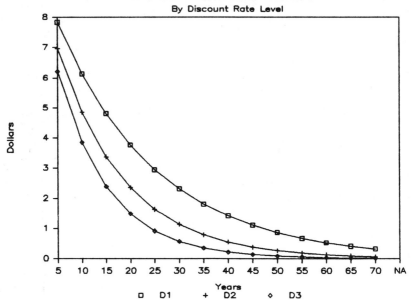

PrintGraph lot502ga

Present Value Table II

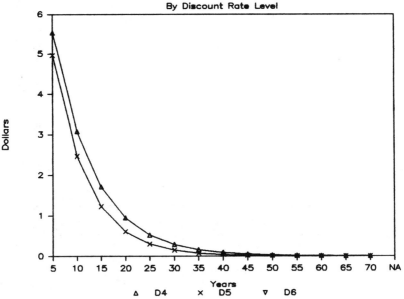

PrintGraph lot502gb

Present Value Table III

By Discount Rate Level

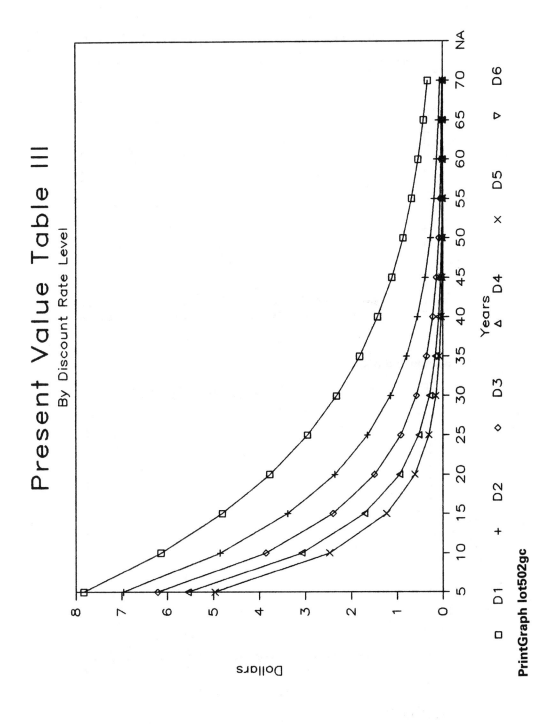

PrintGraph lot502gc

327

Future Value of an Annuity Table I

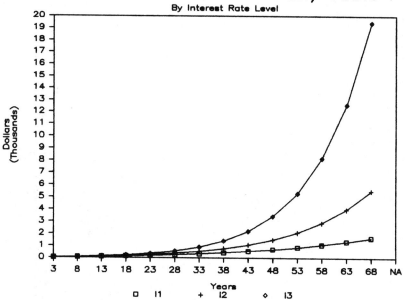

By Interest Rate Level

PrintGraph lot503ga

Future Value of an Annuity Table II

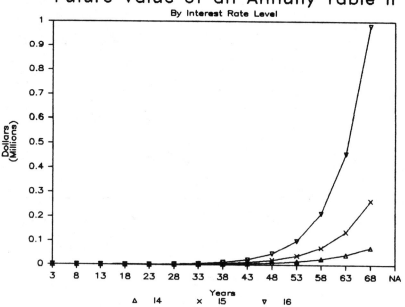

By Interest Rate Level

PrintGraph lot503gb

Future Value of an Annuity Table III

By Interest Rate Level

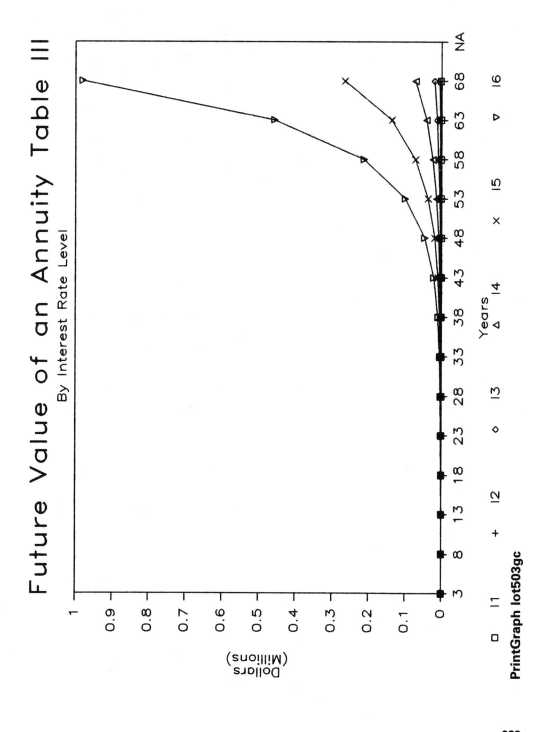

Dollars
(Millions)

329

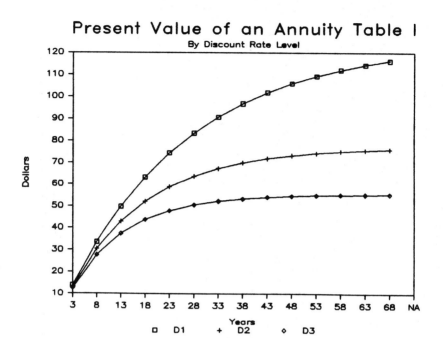

PrintGraph lot504ga

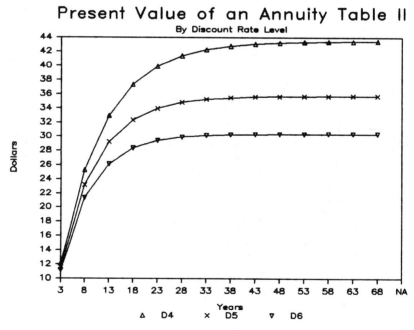

PrintGraph lot504gb

Present Value of an Annuity Table III
By Discount Rate Level

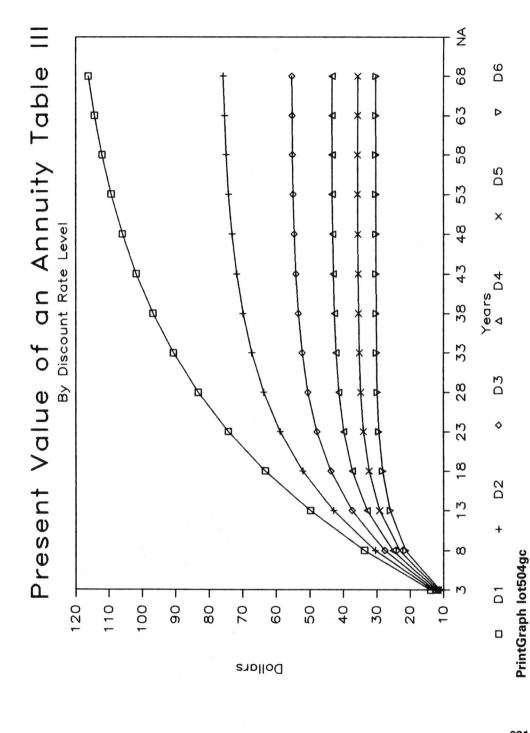

Dollars

Years

□ D1   + D2   ◇ D3   △ D4   × D5   ▽ D6

PrintGraph lot504gc

331

Sinking Fund Table I

By Interest Rate Level

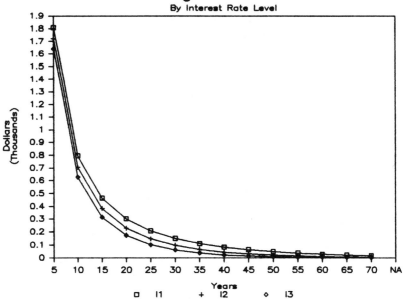

PrintGraph lot505ga

Sinking Fund Table II

By Interest Rate Level

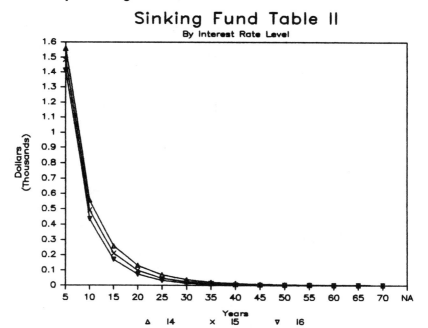

PrintGraph lot505gb

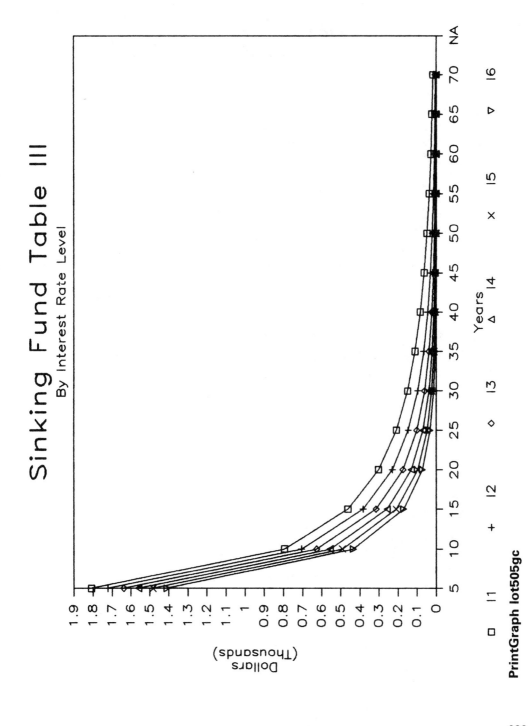

Sinking Fund Table III

By Interest Rate Level

Dollars (Thousands)

Years

Mortgage Constant Table I

By Discount Rate Level

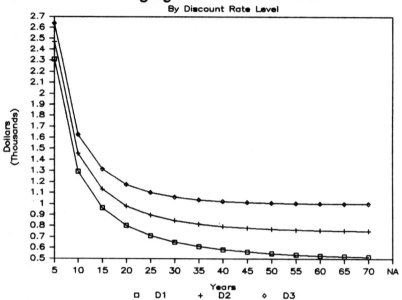

PrintGraph lot506ga

Mortgage Constant Table II

By Discount Rate Level

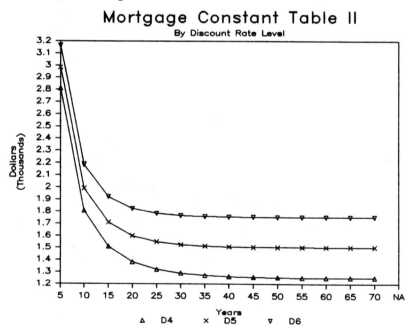

PrintGraph lot506gb

334

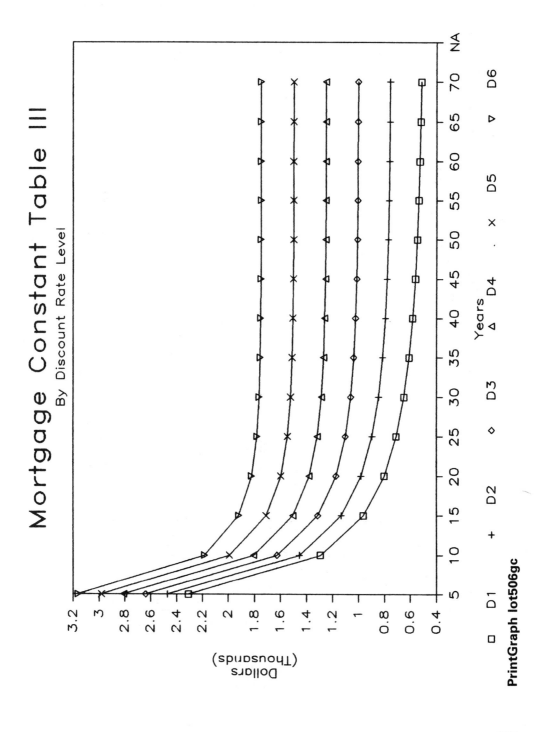

Mortgage Constant Table III
By Discount Rate Level

Dollars (Thousands)

Years

□ D1   + D2   ◇ D3   △ D4   × D5   ▽ D6

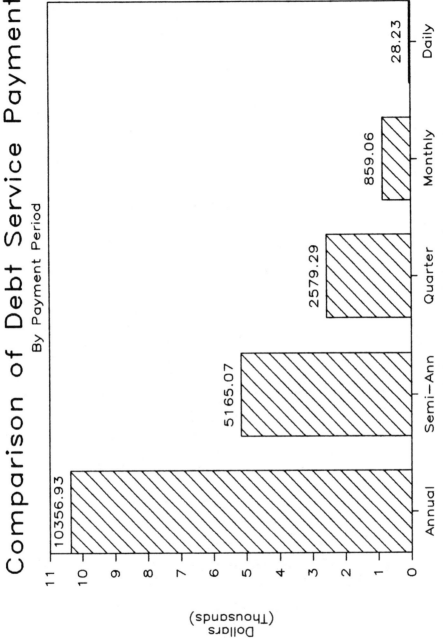

Comparison of Debt Service Payments

By Payment Period

10356.93

5165.07

2579.29

859.06

28.23

Annual   Semi-Ann   Quarter   Monthly   Daily

Debt Service Payments

Dollars (Thousands)

PrintGraph lot601g

The Amortization of Mortgages:

The Slow Process of Equity Build-Up

Debt Service in $ (Thousands)

Loan Repayment Period

Amortization   Interest

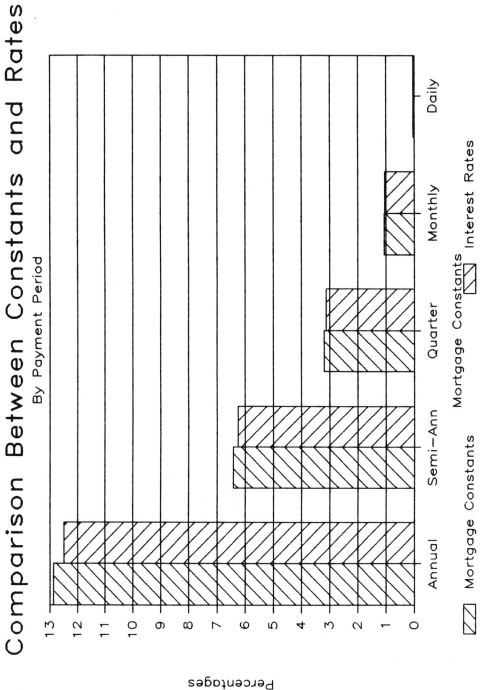

Comparison Between Constants and Rates

By Payment Period

Percentages

13 12 11 10 9 8 7 6 5 4 3 2 1 0

Annual   Semi-Ann   Quarter   Monthly   Daily

Mortgage Constants   Mortgage Constants   Interest Rates

PrintGraph lot603g

338

Breakdown of Special Loan Provisions
By Item Percentage

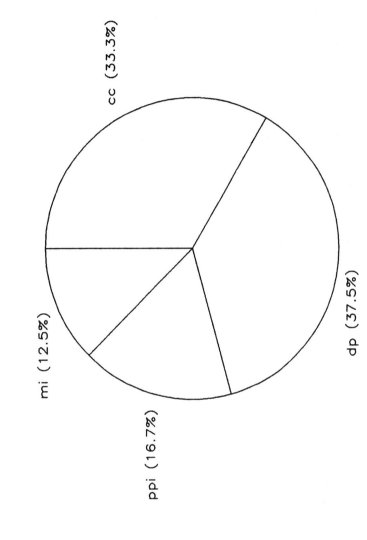

cc (33.3%)

dp (37.5%)

ppi (16.7%)

mi (12.5%)

PrintGraph lot604g

339

Breakdown of Special Lender Features
By Item Percentage

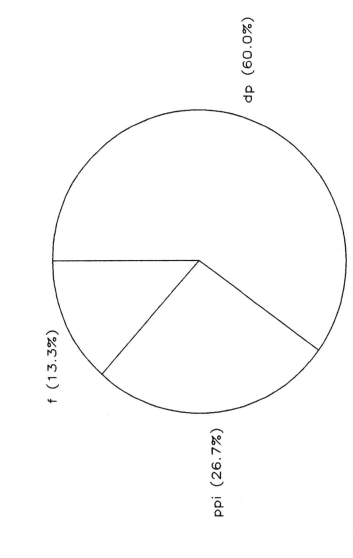

f (13.3%)

ppi (26.7%)

dp (60.0%)

PrintGraph lot605g

340

Testing for Favorable Leverage

Comparison Between ROI and After-Tax K

Percentages

18
17
16
15
14
13
12
11
10
9
8
7
6
5
4
3
2
1
0

ROI

K(1−t)

Measures

PrintGraph lot701g

341

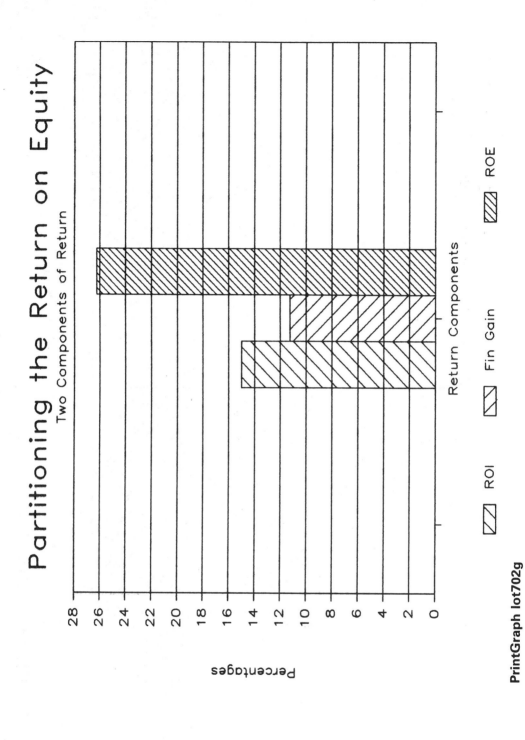

Partitioning the Return on Equity

Two Components of Return

Percentages

28
26
24
22
20
18
16
14
12
10
8
6
4
2
0

Return Components

ROI   Fin Gain   ROE

PrintGraph Iot702g

342

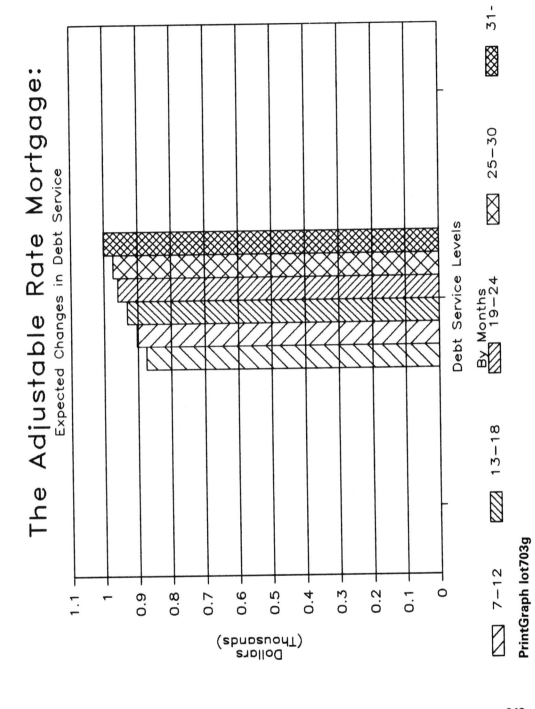

The Adjustable Rate Mortgage:
Expected Changes in Debt Service

Dollars (Thousands)

1.1
1
0.9
0.8
0.7
0.6
0.5
0.4
0.3
0.2
0.1
0

Debt Service Levels
By Months

7-12   13-18   19-24   25-30   31-

PrintGraph lot703g

343

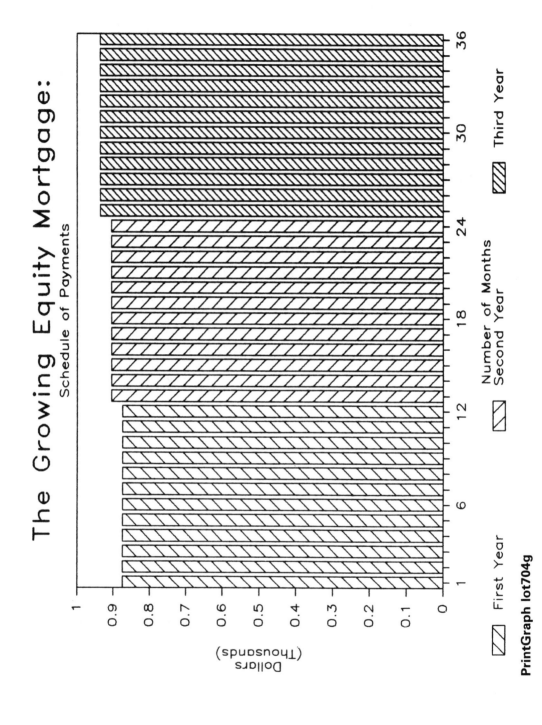

The Growing Equity Mortgage:
Schedule of Payments

Dollars (Thousands)

Number of Months

First Year

Second Year

Third Year

PrintGraph lot704g

344

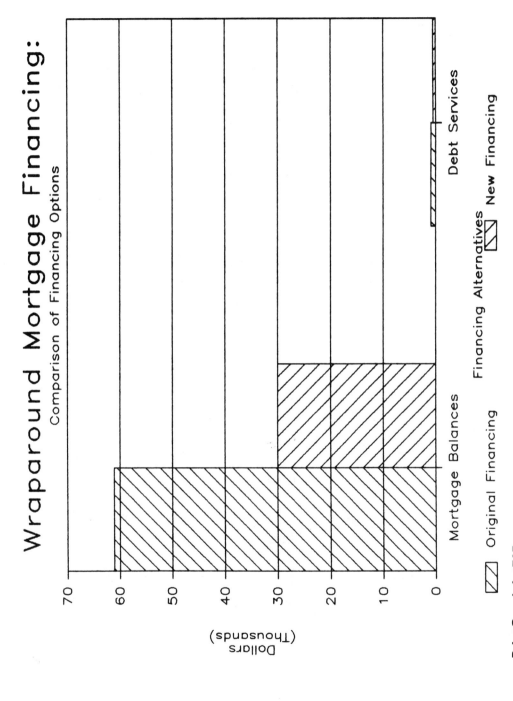

Wraparound Mortgage Financing:
Comparison of Financing Options

Dollars (Thousands)

70
60
50
40
30
20
10
0

Mortgage Balances

Debt Services

Financing Alternatives

Original Financing

New Financing

PrintGraph lot705g

345

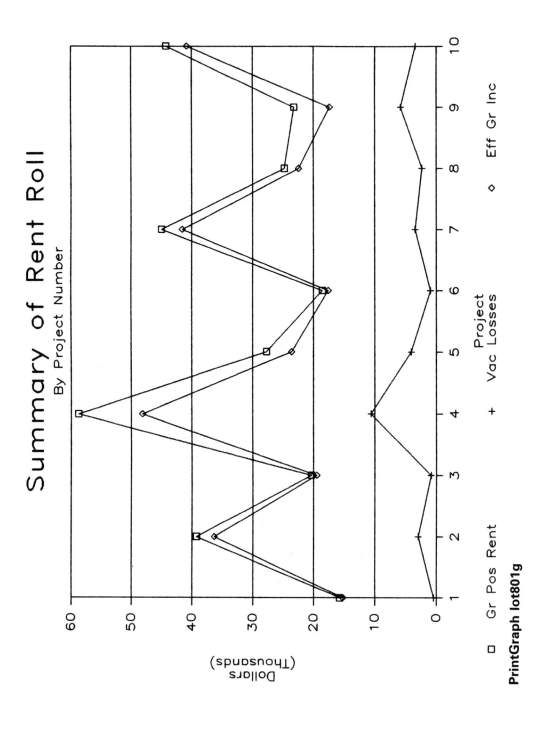

Summary of Rent Roll
By Project Number

Dollars (Thousands)

Project

□ Gr Pos Rent   + Vac Losses   ◇ Eff Gr Inc

PrintGraph lot801g

346

Summary of Operating Expense Analysis
By Expense Category

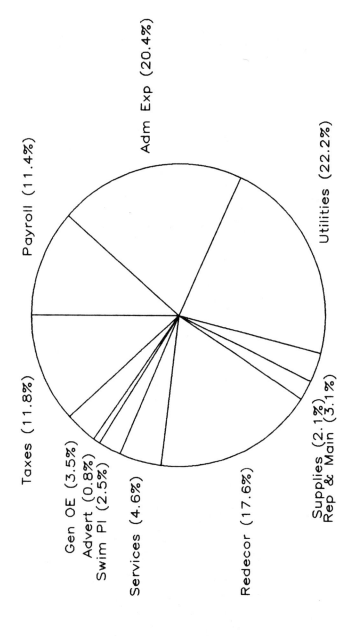

Payroll (11.4%)

Adm Exp (20.4%)

Utilities (22.2%)

Taxes (11.8%)

Gen OE (3.5%)
Advert (0.8%)
Swim Pl (2.5%)

Services (4.6%)

Redecor (17.6%)

Supplies (2.1%)
Rep & Main (3.1%)

PrintGraph lot802g

Comparison Between NOI and BTCF
By Year

Dollars (Thousands)

Year

+ NOI   ◇ BTCF

PrintGraph lot803g

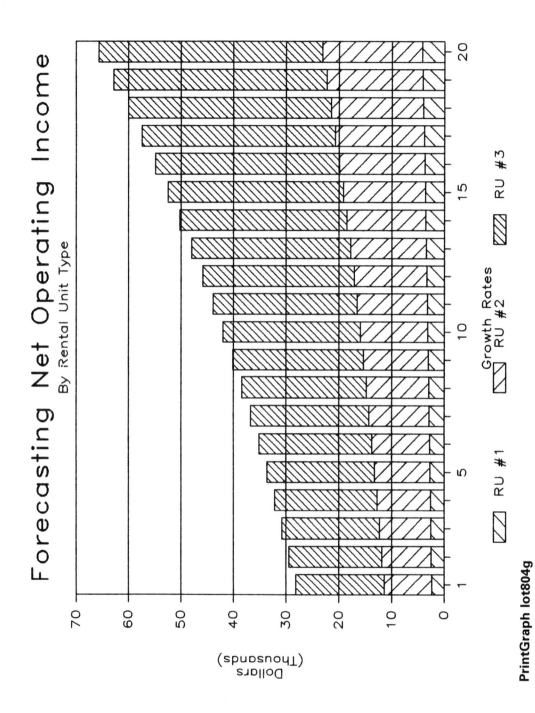

Forecasting Net Operating Income
By Rental Unit Type

Dollars (Thousands)

Growth Rates

RU #1   RU #2   RU #3

PrintGraph lot804g

349

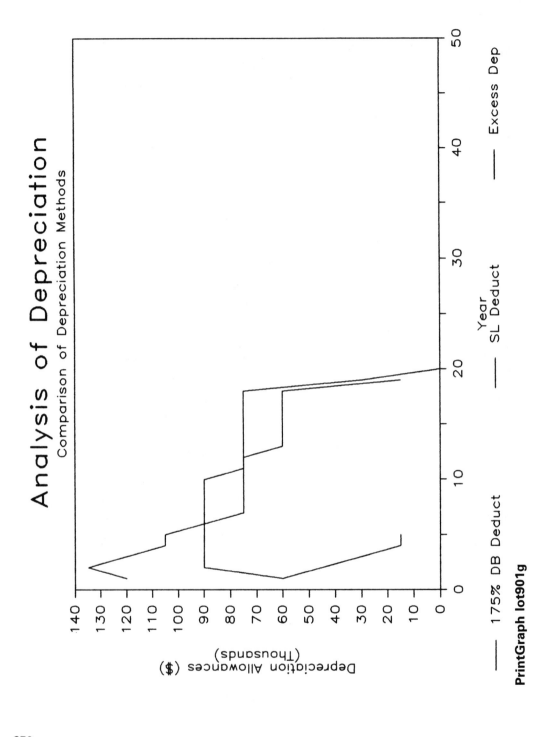

Analysis of Depreciation

Comparison of Depreciation Methods

Depreciation Allowances ($) (Thousands)

Year

—— 175% DB Deduct   —— SL Deduct   —— Excess Dep

PrintGraph lot901g

350

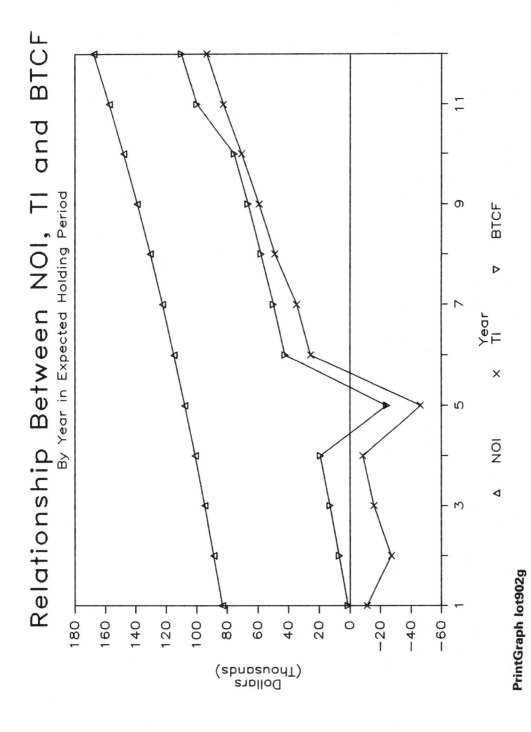

Relationship Between NOI, TI and BTCF

By Year in Expected Holding Period

Dollars (Thousands)

Year

NOI △   TI ×   BTCF ▽

PrintGraph lot902g

351

Relationship Between NOI, BTCF and ATCF
By Year in Expected Holding Period

352

PrintGraph lot903g

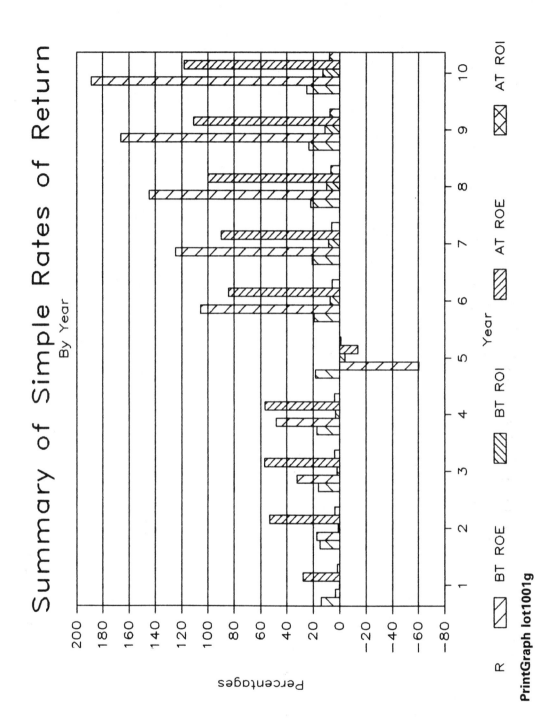

Summary of Simple Rates of Return

By Year

Percentages

Year

R □ BT ROE   ■ BT ROI   □ AT ROE   ■ AT ROI

PrintGraph lot1001g

353

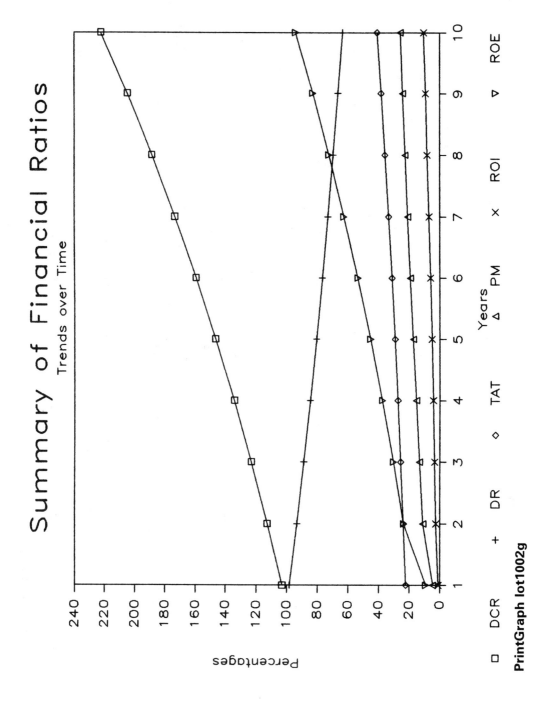

Summary of Financial Ratios

Trends over Time

Percentages

Years

□ DCR   + DR   ◇ TAT   △ PM   × ROI   ▽ ROE

PrintGraph lot1002g

354

The Effective Rate of Interest
By Year

Percentages

Years

Net Present Value

As a Function of the Discount Rate

Dollars (Thousands)

Discount Rates (%)

PrintGraph lot1101g

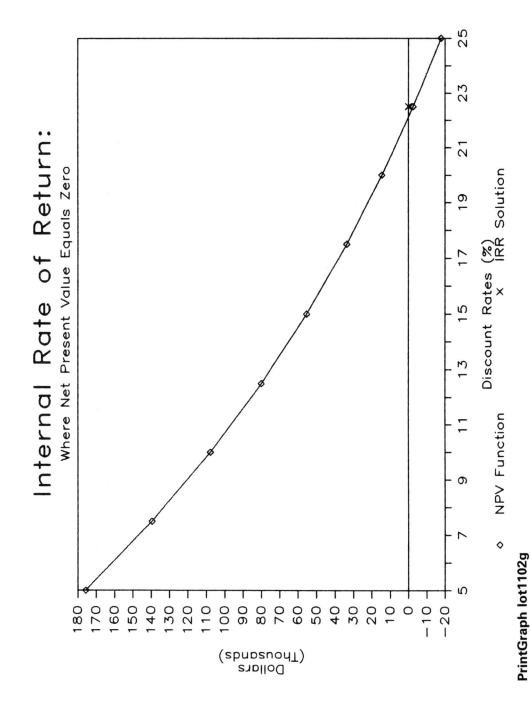

Internal Rate of Return:
Where Net Present Value Equals Zero

Dollars
(Thousands)

180
170
160
150
140
130
120
110
100
90
80
70
60
50
40
30
20
10
0
−10
−20

5   7   9   11   13   15   17   19   21   23   25

Discount Rates (%)
◇ NPV Function   × IRR Solution

PrintGraph lot1102g

357

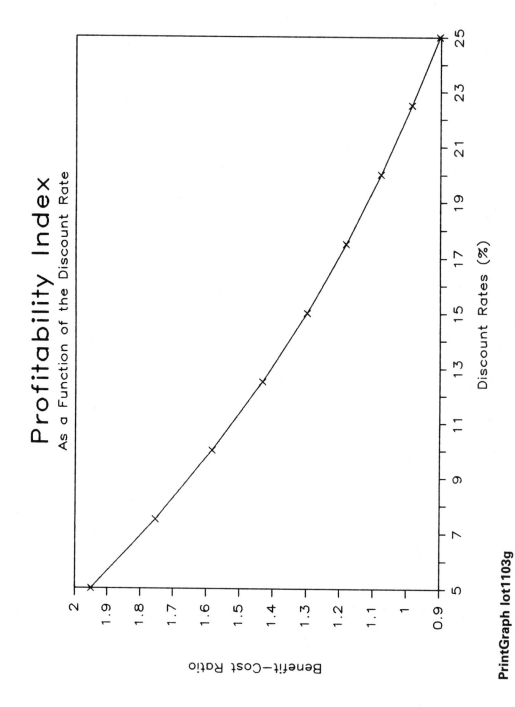

Profitability Index
As a Function of the Discount Rate

Benefit−Cost Ratio

Discount Rates (%)

PrintGraph lot1103g

358

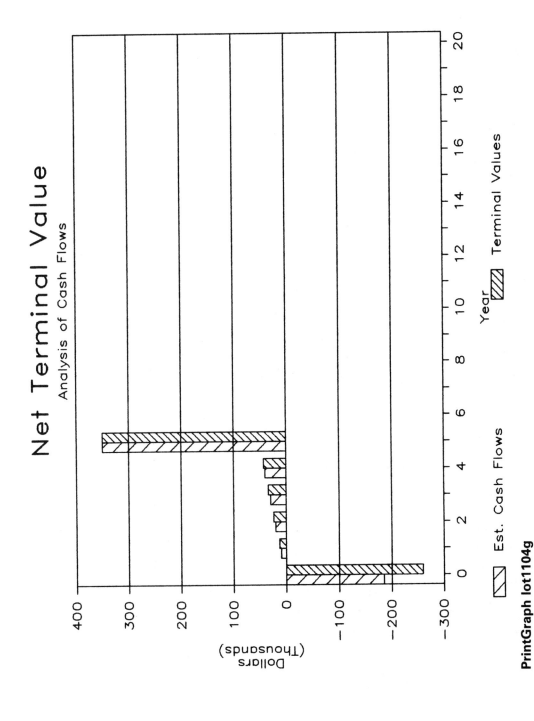

Net Terminal Value

Analysis of Cash Flows

Year

Est. Cash Flows

Terminal Values

Dollars (Thousands)

400 300 200 100 0 -100 -200 -300

0 2 4 6 8 10 12 14 16 18 20

PrintGraph lot1104g

359

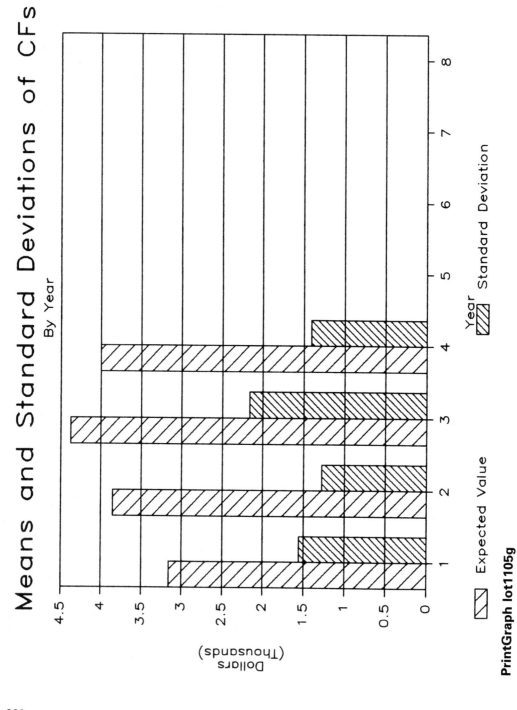

Means and Standard Deviations of CFs

By Year

Year

Expected Value

Standard Deviation

Dollars (Thousands)

PrintGraph lot1105g

360

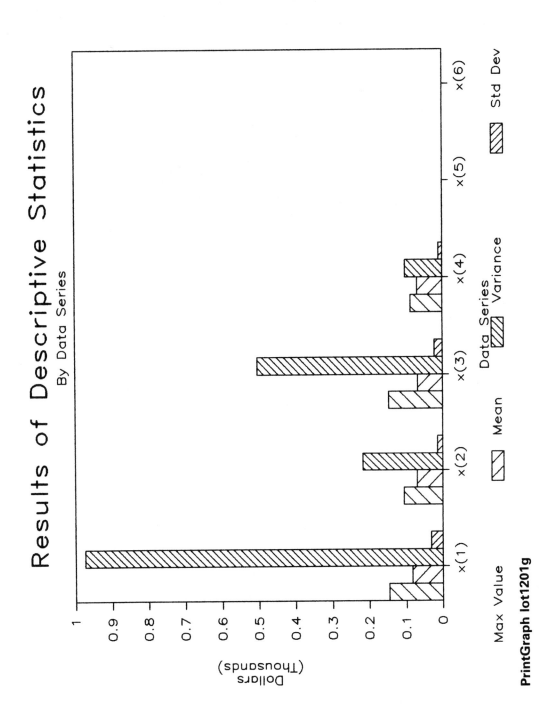

Results of Descriptive Statistics

By Data Series

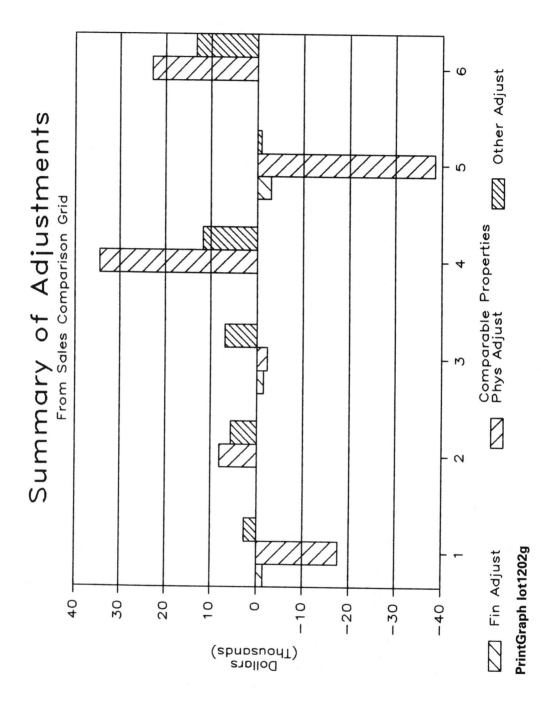

Summary of Adjustments

From Sales Comparison Grid

Comparable Properties

Fin Adjust   Phys Adjust   Other Adjust

PrintGraph lot1202g

362

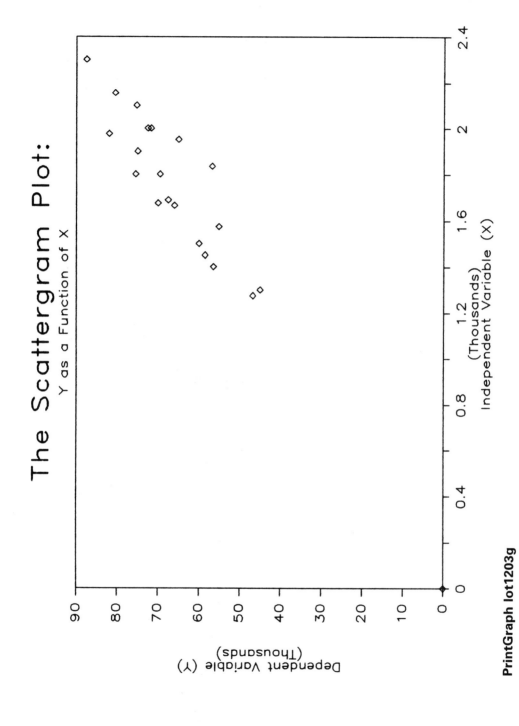

The Scattergram Plot:
Y as a Function of X

Dependent Variable (Y) (Thousands)

Independent Variable (X) (Thousands)

PrintGraph lot1203g

363

Index